C000007913

# Africa by Road

## 4WD • Motorbike • Bicycle • Truck

## THE BRADT TRAVEL GUIDE

### Third Edition

## Charlie Shackell & Illya Bracht

Bradt Travel Guides, UK
The Globe Pequot Press Inc, USA

First published in 1991 by Bradt Publications.
This third edition published in 2001 by Bradt Travel Guides,
19 High Street, Chalfont St Peter, Bucks SL9 9QE, England
web: www.bradt-travelguides.com
Published in the USA by The Globe Pequot Press Inc, 246 Goose Lane,
PO Box 480, Guilford, Connecticut 06475-0480

Text copyright © 2001 Charlie Shackell & Illya Bracht
Maps copyright © 2001 Bradt Travel Guides

The author and publishers have made every effort to ensure the accuracy of the
information in this book at the time of going to press. However, they cannot accept
any responsibility for any loss, injury or inconvenience resulting from the use of
information contained in this guide.

All rights reserved. No part of this publication may be reproduced, stored in a
retrieval system, or transmitted in any form or by any means, electronic, mechanical,
photocopying, recording or otherwise without the prior consent of the publishers.
Requests for permission should be addressed to Bradt Travel Guides,
19 High Street, Chalfont St Peter, Bucks SL9 9QE in the UK;
or to The Globe Pequot Press Inc,
246 Goose Lane, PO Box 480, Guilford, Connecticut 06475-0480
in North and South America.

**British Library Cataloguing in Publication Data**
A catalogue record for this book is available from the British Library
ISBN 1 84162 017 3

**Library of Congress Cataloging-in-Publication Data**
Shackell, Charlie
    Africa by road : 4WD, motorbike, bicylce, truck / Charlie Shackell
& Illya Bracht — 3rd ed.
    p. cm.
    Rev. ed. of: Africa by road / Bob Swain and Paula Snyder. 2nd ed.
1995.
    Includes bibliographical references and index.
    ISBN 1-84162-017-3
DT2.S53 2001
916.04'33—dc21
                                                          00-057850

**Photographs** Ariadne Van Zandbergen
**Illustrations** Illya Bracht, Sarah Elder, Jo Stearn
**Maps** Steve Munns, Alan Whitaker

Typeset from the author's disc by Wakewing
Printed and bound in Italy by Legoprint SpA, Trento

# Authors

Charlie (Shackell) was born in the UK but has travelled extensively since the age of 18, including various trips to Africa where he made Ghana his home for a while. Illya (Bracht) was born in South Africa but is of German origin. She has travelled extensively in Europe with intermittent trips in southern Africa and Tanzania.

'Taking a car and driving through Africa' was a dream that was set in motion late one drunken evening whilst discussing the future. Three months later they had the 'car' and three years later they waved goodbye to family and friends, heading towards Komatiepoort and the first of many border crossings.

It took three years to save the money and research the trip as well as plan and prepare the vehicle – a 1981 45-series diesel Landcruiser, nicknamed Daisy because of her bright yellow colour. During that time they tested the vehicle on trips in Botswana and Namibia.

Charlie and Illya left South Africa on August 16 1998. The first stop was Mozambique, then up the east coast via Zimbabwe, Malawi, Tanzania, Kenya, Uganda and Ethiopia. In Kenya, the continuing tribal warfare in the Democratic Republic of Congo effectively blocked their planned route across Africa. However, a fellow traveller, Nick, had just crossed the Sudan from west to east, which opened up another possibility; with sheer persistence they eventually got their Sudanese visa with the help of a friend, Vim, in Ethiopia. Their new route took them along the edge of the Sahara through Sudan, Chad and Nigeria. From Nigeria they headed along the west coast, then up into the Sahara through Mali, along the coast of Mauritania, across Western Sahara and into Morocco, finally reaching West Sussex, UK, on Tuesday, August 8 1999.

The year has left them with an array of stories, many adventures, and countless memories of people and places never to be forgotten. And Daisy performed like a star, proving the saying, 'You can't kill a Landcruiser'.

# Contents

## LIST OF MAPS

# Acknowledgements

Thanks to all at Bradt Travel Guides for always being one step ahead. Special thanks to Warren Burton and Kath Larsen at Encounter Overland Ltd, David Mozer at Bicycle Africa Tours, Philip Briggs and Ariadne Van Zandbergen, Alex Marr and Tim Larby. Thanks also to Lonely Planet for permission to use some of the information from *Africa on a Shoestring*.

To the previous authors of *Africa by Road*, first and second editions, Bob Swain and Paula Snyder, thank you for allowing us to utilise your existing material. Thank you also to all travellers worldwide who wrote their stories enabling us to report the latest news on Africa. To our families and friends for keeping our heads above water and, lastly, to the land and people of Africa for making our trip such a very special one.

## MEASUREMENTS AND CONVERSIONS

| To convert | Multiply by |
|---|---|
| Inches to centimetres | 2.54 |
| Centimetres to inches | 0.3937 |
| Feet to metres | 0.3048 |
| Metres to feet | 3.281 |
| Yards to metres | 0.9144 |
| Metres to yards | 1.094 |
| Miles to kilometres | 1.609 |
| Kilometres to miles | 0.6214 |
| Acres to hectares | 0.4047 |
| Hectares to acres | 2.471 |
| Imperial gallons to litres | 4.546 |
| Litres to imperial gallons | 0.22 |
| US gallons to litres | 3.785 |
| Litres to US gallons | 0.264 |
| Ounces to grams | 28.35 |
| Grams to ounces | 0.03527 |
| Pounds to grams | 453.6 |
| Grams to pounds | 0.002205 |
| Pounds to kilograms | 0.4536 |
| Kilograms to pounds | 2.205 |
| British tons to kilograms | 1016.0 |
| Kilograms to British tons | 0.0009812 |
| US tons to kilograms | 907.0 |
| Kilograms to US tons | 0.000907 |

5 imperial gallons are equal to 6 US gallons
A British ton is 2,240 lbs. A US ton is 2,000 lbs.

### Temperature conversion table

The bold figures in the central columns can be read as either centigrade or fahrenheit.

| °C | | °F | °C | | °F |
|---|---|---|---|---|---|
| −18 | **0** | 32 | 10 | **50** | 122 |
| −15 | **5** | 41 | 13 | **55** | 131 |
| −12 | **10** | 50 | 16 | **60** | 140 |
| −9 | **15** | 59 | 18 | **65** | 149 |
| −7 | **20** | 68 | 21 | **70** | 158 |
| −4 | **25** | 77 | 24 | **75** | 167 |
| −1 | **30** | 86 | 27 | **80** | 176 |
| 2 | **35** | 95 | 32 | **90** | 194 |
| 4 | **40** | 104 | 38 | **100** | 212 |
| 7 | **45** | 113 | 40 | **104** | 219 |

# Introduction

As you sit there contemplating this once-in-a-lifetime trip, discarding or packing up all that was once dear to you, the one question you will ask over and over again is 'Why? I must be mad to contemplate such an expedition!' Reactions from others will vary from disbelief to awe, envy and apprehension. You will often be asked, 'Why not fly? It's a lot quicker!' Our prompt response to this was, 'It's not the destination but the adventure along the way.' So, we are here to tell you not the why but the how.

Driving, cycling or motorbiking the African continent is nothing new: explorations have been evident for centuries. Although others have been there before you, you will still have your own wonderful experiences. Nothing is ever certain in Africa and it is never really knowing what is ahead of you that makes overlanding in Africa so special.

This third edition of *Africa by Road* outlines the funds you will need for your period of travel, possible routes through Africa, planning and preparation before and during your trip, and on the road issues. It also includes a summary of each African country, highlighting the pros and cons. With the ever-changing political climate in Africa, you will find that a lot of your planning will change once you are on the road. Your best sources of information with regard to possible routes, what to see and where to avoid are other travellers. This does not mean that gathering relevant information while on the road takes preference over planning your trip before departure. Rushing off without careful planning is the biggest mistake you can make. Allow plenty of time. A well-spent period of preparation means you will be more likely to avoid potential disaster.

If that does not sound like your kind of trip, then an organised expedition may be the answer. The tour companies will do most of the planning for you, just leaving you to find the price of your ticket and set off to enjoy yourself – although you should still be prepared for your share of hard work while on the road.

Everyone else, however, will be in for a great deal of planning and preparation – on a sliding scale depending on what kind of vehicle you intend to take. If you take your own vehicle you will be in for the works; if you are brave enough to cycle you will avoid much of the paperwork and mechanical preparation. Motorbikes probably fall somewhere between the two.

We have tailored this edition more towards planning and preparation and details specific to overland travel in Africa, rather than information about particular countries. This book does not aim to replace country guides and we strongly recommend you take along relevant guides such as the Bradt series for the areas you wish to visit.

*Carpe diem* – seize the day!

## Note on place names

Confusion inevitably arises between the Democratic Republic of the Congo (DRC) – formerly Zaire – and the People's Republic of the Congo. For the purposes of this book we have used Democratic Republic of the Congo or DRC for the former and Congo for the latter.

*Africa – Environment & Wildlife*
and
*Africa – Birds & Birding*

Award-winning magazines
about a continent
worth saving

**For subscription details contact:**
*Africa – Environment & Wildlife/*
*Africa – Birds & Birding*
P O Box 44223, Claremont 7735, Cape Town, South Africa
Tel: (+27-21) 686 9001  Fax: (+27-21) 686 4500
E-mail: wildmags@iafrica.com  Website:

# Part One

# Before You Leave

# The Basics

There are certain priorities to be considered before departure and one of these will be your budget. Like it or not, money, or the lack of it, are likely to dominate most plans for travel in Africa. The budget you have available will determine what kind of trip you can choose, the route you take and the duration of your trip.

Travelling under your own steam can be relatively economical if you cycle or take a motorbike. Tour buses are one of the cheapest options – but you may want more independence than they can offer. Your costs will mount once you've made the decision to take your own vehicle. But even if your aims are relatively modest, you will undoubtedly be shocked as the expenses add up – most of them before you even set off. You should take all these costs into account from the start for a realistic assessment of what you can afford. Look in detail at some of the costs involved in your trip (see below). Decide what is essential, what is merely desirable and what is plain luxury. Then think again about how you aim to tackle the whole thing on the basis of how much money you are going to be able to raise. Only after all this can you start really planning your trip.

The possibilities of routes are limitless. With the political unrest and violence in the Democratic Republic of the Congo and Central African Republic, crossing central Africa has been abandoned by all but the most hardened travellers. The classic trans-Saharan route via Tamanrassat was abandoned in the early 1990s but is slowly opening its doors again to overland travel. For the time being Angola, Burundi, Sierra Leone and Liberia are effectively off-limits, although the situation in Burundi is improving.

The necessity to ship your vehicle around 'hot spots' has become more of an issue and should be carefully considered and investigated during your planning.

## THE BUDGET

Trying to work out what you might need regarding cash is always a mystery to any traveller attempting an overland expedition. Each person has different needs, and while some could survive on only US$10 a day, others could not survive on less than US$60 a day. We have tried to find a balance between the two, initially listing costs incurred before you leave, and then costs incurred while on the road.

We spent an average of US$38 per day which included fuel, visas, accommodation, living expenses and attractions for two people. This was for a one-year trip from Johannesburg to London from August 1998 to August 1999, driving over 40,000km with a total on-road expenditure of US$13,870. You will find as you travel that some countries, like Kenya, are a lot more expensive due to the activities you undertake, like climbing Mount Kenya or visiting the various national parks, while in other countries, like the Sudan, your expenses will be minimal as fuel only costs US$0.21 per litre and there isn't much else to spend money on. We found that at times we would spend as much as US$50 one day, and the next only US$12 – it usually balances itself out.

Realistically you will need to budget for as much as US$20,000 in total before you leave, plus US$7,000 per head for a one-year trip in your own four-wheel-drive vehicle. Even with a bicycle the total initial investment will be over US$2,000. Planning a trip with a motorbike will fall somewhere between the two.

Your preparation costs can quickly add up with the purchase of a vehicle, equipping it appropriately, getting full medical cover, a medical kit, a carnet and many more hidden costs that you might not have considered. It is possible to do it on the cheap – but the less you invest, the tougher your trip is likely to be. At the other extreme you could buy a fully converted six-wheel drive and be kissing goodbye to something like US$100,000 before you even start. If it all sounds ridiculously expensive, then you are beginning to get the right idea!

The following are some of the major costs you will have to meet. The figures quoted are a rough guide. Ideally, you should look at your own requirements under each of the headings listed in *Chapter 2* and check out what these are likely to cost.

## Sponsorship

You may be thinking that sponsorship will fall into your lap as soon as you announce to the world that you are off to explore Africa. Be under no illusions; sponsorship is a tough nut to crack. Companies have been approached so many times in the past that they will want you to demonstrate exactly how they are going to get a return on their investment. Local firms are more likely to be sympathetic than nationally known names – but they are also unlikely to have as much to offer. You must ask yourself whether the massive investment of time you will need to find any sort of sponsorship is worth it.

## ROUTE PLANNING

Planning your route is loads of fun and brings you that much closer to your destination. Start out by poring over maps and setting down a list of places you would like to visit. But beware – nothing is quite what it seems in Africa. That wonderful red highway cutting through the jungle may not even exist, and many excellent roads are not even marked on the most recent maps, such as the latest Michelin series, which are undoubtedly the best general maps of the continent. You will also have to confront the reality of Africa, fitting your desires in with the political and climatic factors that will do so much to shape your ultimate route. The bottom line is have a good idea of what you want to

## ESTIMATED BUDGET COSTS

The costs listed below are based on taking your own vehicle. Information on taking your own motorbike or bicycle is discussed further in this chapter and Chapter 2.

### Before you leave
*Vehicle*
Based on an early 1980s Toyota Landcruiser or a series III Land Rover
Fully equipped, ie: overland ready      US$6,000–10,000
Vehicle only      US$2,000–6,000

*Vehicle preparation*
If you were lucky enough to find a fully equipped vehicle you may only need to check everything works and fine tune the vehicle for your trip. If you are starting from scratch you may be up for this full amount.
     US$3,000–5,000

*Equipment*      US$1,500–3,000

*Spares and tools*      US$2,000–5,000

*Medical insurance*
Based on each person for one year full cover      US$300–800

*Medical kit*      US$400

### On the road
Per person, per day, based on two people in one vehicle travelling for one year      US$38–60

see and where you want to go, but keep up to date with changes while on the road by asking locals or other travellers, and be prepared to alter your route accordingly.

It is important to have an idea of what type of trip you wish to undertake. For example, you may wish to leave from Europe and spend time in the Sahara and West Africa, then return to Europe, or you may wish to do a full trans-African trip. The following route planning map and route description indicates the more conventional routes across the remoter areas, ie: the Sahara crossing and east to west (or vice versa) Africa routes. We have also included all the major routes, but have not taken into account the political viability of undertaking the various journeys. We have found from experience that borders, routes and countries open and close regularly, and what may not have been possible or sensible when you left home is no problem at all when you arrive in the area. Therefore, the routes covered should give an overall idea of what you want to achieve and also provide alternatives once you are on the road.

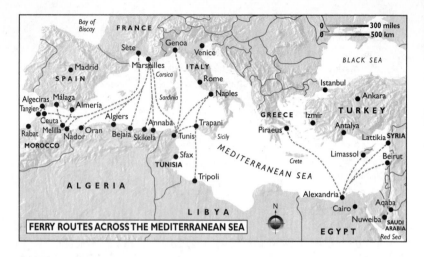

**FERRY ROUTES ACROSS THE MEDITERRANEAN SEA**

## Ferry routes

At the beginning or end of your trip, you will need to consider the ferry routes from Europe into Africa or vice versa; most of us are looking for the cheapest and shortest route across.

The most popular route is Spain to Morocco from either Algeciras, Málaga or Gibraltar to Ceuta or Tangier. Those with a vehicle or motorbike will probably opt to go via Ceuta because the city forms part of Spanish Morocco and its tax-free status means that fuel is cheap. It's always a good idea to fill up those jerry cans.

Other popular routes include France to Morocco, Algeria or Tunisia; Italy to Tunisia, and Greece, Turkey or the Middle East to Egypt. Further routes include Gibraltar to Morocco, Malta to Libya and Jordan to Egypt.

A route that needs some thought is Egypt to Saudi Arabia. Do not attempt this during *hajj*, the pilgrimage to Mecca. *Hajj* is the fifth pillar of Islam and it is a sacred duty for Muslims to make a pilgrimage to Mecca. It should be accomplished in Zuul-Hijja, the twelfth month of the Muslim year – which basically means between March and July, depending on when the new moon is sighted. Check with the local Muslim community or your nearest embassy for exact dates.

### Prices

Shop around when getting into the ports: it isn't difficult. At most ports, there are sales people representing the major ferry companies who can sell you a ticket there and then. Most ferries running the Spain to Morocco route run regular services every 15–20 minutes both ways. A standard ferry crossing from Algeciras to Ceuta usually takes up to 45 minutes.

The average price for the short ferry crossings – ie: Spain to Morocco or Trapani (Sicily) to Tunis – is US$30–60 per person and US$52–60 for a standard four-wheel drive. If you are going by motorbike expect to pay US$15–20; a bicycle is seen as extra luggage costing US$3–12 per item. For the longer ferry routes – ie: France to Morocco or Greece to Egypt – expect to pay US$250–300 per person and US$300–350 per vehicle one way, since the crossing takes up to 38 hours.

Note when asking about ferry prices that harbour tax, embarkation fees and GST (VAT) are not always included in the quote. It is safest to add on another 25% to the original quote to get a correct pricing on a route.

A lot of the ferry companies offer concessions, depending on the seasons. Plan ahead during the European summer months and school holidays, particularly if you are in a vehicle or on a bike, as there is a flood of people crossing the Mediterranean at those times.

## Ferry companies
Below is a list of ferry companies with international representation:

### Spain to Morocco
**Compañia Trasmediterránea** Head office: 61 C/Alcalá, CP Madrid, 28014; tel: +34 91 423 8500; fax: +34 91 423 8555; Information and booking: +34 902454645; email: correom@trasmediterranea.es; web: www.trasmediterranea.es. Offices and agents: *Algeciras* (Cádiz) Recinto del Puerto, s/n, CP 11201; tel: +34 95 6656244; *Ceuta* Muelle Canonero Dato 6, CP 51001; tel: +35 95 6509381; *Málaga* Estación Maritima, Recinto del Puerto, Local E1, CP 29016; tel: +34 95 2224391; *Morocco* Limadet; 3 Rue Ibn Roch, Tangier; tel: +212 9 933633; *UK* Southern Ferries; 1st Floor, 179 Piccadilly, London, W1V 9DB; tel: +44 207 4914968.

**Ferrimaroc SA** web: www.ferrimaroc.com; *UK* Tel: +44 71 8285949; fax: +44 71 6307628; email: helpdesk@ferrimaroc.com; *Morocco* Voyage Wasteels SA, Port of Beni Enzar, 62050 Post du Beni Enzar, Nador; tel: +212 6 348786; fax: +212 6 348781; *Spain* Ferrimaroc Agencias SL, Muelle Ribera s/n, 04002 Almería; tel: +34 9 50 274800; fax: +34 9 50 276366; email: mmarin@ferrimaroc.com

### Spain to Morocco and Italy to Tunis
**Viamare UK Ltd** Graphic House, 2 Sumatra Rd, London NW6 1PU; tel: +44 20 7431 4560; fax: +44 207 431 5456; email: ferries@viamare.com; web: www.viamare.com

### France to Morocco or Algeria
**SNCM Ferryterranee**; 61 Bd des Dames, 13226 Marseilles, France; tel: +33 4 91 563200; fax: +33 4 91 563636; email: info@sncm.fr; web: www.sncm.fr

### Greece, Turkey, Middle East to Egypt
**Poseidon Lines** c/o Paleologos Shipping & Travel Agency; 5, 25th August Street, 71202 Heraklion, Crete, Greece; tel: +30 81 346185 – 330598; fax: +30 81 346208; email: info@greekislands.gr; web: www.greekislands.gr Currently Poseidon Lines carry only freight, not passengers, to Egypt

### International companies:
**MBendi Information Services** PO Box 23498, Claremont, 7735, South Africa; tel: +27 21 6719889; fax: +27 21 6716361, email: MBendi@MBendi.co.za; web: www.mbendi.co.za

## Websites
Two general websites have information on international ferry companies:

www.routesinternational.com

www.ferrycenter.se

# Overland routes
## North Africa and the Sahara
North Africa and the Sahara include the following countries: Morocco, Tunisia, Algeria, Libya, Mali, Niger, Mauritania, Chad, Egypt and the Sudan.

Try to cross the Sahara between October and March, when there is less danger from the heat.

### Route S1 – Morocco to Mauritania
This is probably the most popular trans-Saharan route at the moment. The road all the way through Morocco and the Western Sahara is tarmac. Going south you must clear Moroccan immigration and customs in Dakhla and then wait for the convoy south that leaves from Dakhla to Nouâdhibou every Tuesday and Friday at 09.00. The border area is mined but the border guards clearly indicate the safe track to the Mauritania border post. Once in Mauritania it is easy to pick up a guide to take you across the desert from Nouâdhibou to Nouakchott, or you can put your vehicle on the longest train in the world to Atâr, from where you can take the tarmac road to Nouakchott.

On the direct route across the desert there are three main areas of dunes to cross and a 150km (90-mile) drive down the beach. Check with locals when high and low tides take place as the area is not drivable at high tide. The drive along the beach can easily be done during one low tide. Plan to do this stretch in one go as there are very few places that allow you to drive off the beach, and high dunes hug most of the coastline. Carry enough fuel for approximately 1,000km (620 miles). This route can easily be done in reverse but it is advisable to take a guide as you will have to negotiate the minefields at the border.

At the time of writing the Mauritanian government did not allow overland travel into Morocco. (In 1975 the area was evacuated by the Spanish and both countries raised claims to the territory because of phosphate in the area. The two countries fought over the occupied territory of Western Sahara until 1996, when a ceasefire was reached. Since then, the Moroccans have occupied the region and have been allowing convoys through.) A good guide will have no problem avoiding the military posts and delivering you safely to the Moroccan border. Guides that will take you to the Moroccan border post can be found in Nouakchott. Heading north you will need to carry enough fuel for 1,300km (800 miles) as you don't want to stop in Nouâdhibou since you may have problems with the officials if you are heading towards Morocco. Finally, heading to and from Mauritania via Mali, beware of occasional bandit problems on the stretch of road from Nema to Bamako.

### Route S2 – Algeria to Niger
This route used to be the main Sahara overland route until the mid 1990s when trouble with Muslim fundamentalists in the north and the Tuaregs in

the south of Algeria effectively closed the route to foreigners. By 1999 a few intrepid travellers were starting to take this route again, but the general advice is still to be very wary and to try to avoid the major coastal towns in Algeria.

The route runs from Algiers to Agadez via Tamanrasset and is sometimes referred to as the Route du Hoggar after the spectacular mountain range outside Tamanrasset. The total driving distance is approximately 3,800km (2,370 miles) and takes about ten days, but we would suggest spending at least three weeks to visit the Hoggar Mountains and enjoy the desert scenery. The road all the way from Algiers to Tamanrasset is paved but major sections south of In-Salah are reported to be in bad condition. The road from Tamanrasset to Arlit is a mixture of desert pistes and dunes: real desert driving. This section is approximately 600km (370 miles) with no fuel available, so carry enough with you, bearing in mind that your vehicle will use up to 50% more fuel in the sand than on paved roads. The road from Arlit to Agadez is known as the Uranium Highway due to the mines at Arlit; it is paved.

The more scenic route from the border at Assamaka to Agadez via Tegguida-n-Tessoum is not paved and there is no fuel available, but it does take you past an old salt-mining area where you may be lucky enough to see a salt caravan.

### Route S3 – Algeria to Mali

This route is less popular than the S2 route above, mainly because the distance between fuel stops is much larger – Adrar to Gao is approximately 1,500km (930 miles) and the unpaved section is 1,350km (840 miles). However there are less difficult areas of soft sand. There have been reports of fuel occasionally available at both Reggane and Borj-Mokhtar but I wouldn't bank on either of these. The road is paved from Adrar to Reggane, and then mainly hard-packed piste via the Algerian border post at Borj-Mokhtar all the way to Malian customs at Tessalit. The last section from Tessalit to Gao along the Vallée du Tilemsi is the hardest section, with areas of soft sand; this section is often impassable during the wet season. Once in Gao you can continue on to the Malian capital Bamako on a paved road or follow the River Niger along a scenic but difficult sandy road to Niamey, the capital of Niger. The total driving time from Adrar to Gao is approximately ten days but once again we suggest taking your time and enjoying the vastness of the Sahara. As with the S2 route there has been some political unrest in the area, particularly in northern Mali, so seek advice before you set out.

### Route S4 – Libya to Niger

The peace accord with the Tuaregs came into effect in May 1995, but northern Niger was still seen as unsafe up until 1997. Even on our visit to Agadez and the Aïr Mountains in early 1999, we needed a travel permit and guide to investigate the area. The most common route from Libya into Niger or vice versa is through the Ténéré Desert, via Sebha, Gatrun, Séguédine, Bilma and Agadez. The total distance is about 1,480km (917 miles) with fuel available at Agadez, Bilma, Dirkou and Sebha. You will need to carry fuel for approximately 1,200km (745 miles). It is easy to lose your way on this route

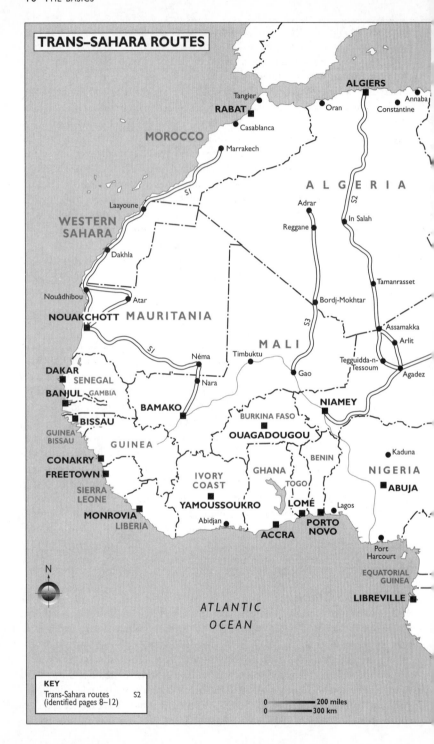

# TRANS–SAHARA ROUTES

ALGIERS

Annaba

Tangier

Oran

Constantine

**RABAT**

Casablanca

**MOROCCO**

Marrakech

A L G E R I A

Laayoune

Adrar

In Salah

S1

S2

Reggane

**WESTERN
SAHARA**

Dakhla

Tamanrasset

Nouâdhibou    Atar

Bordj-Mokhtar

**NOUAKCHOTT**    **MAURITANIA**

Assamakka

Arlit

S1

M A L I

S3

Néma    Timbuktu

Tegguidda-n-
Tessoum

**DAKAR**

Nara    Gao

Agadez

**SENEGAL**

**BANJUL** GAMBIA

**BISSAU**

**BAMAKO**

**NIAMEY**

GUINEA
BISSAU

BURKINA FASO

**CONAKRY**

G U I N E A

**OUAGADOUGOU**

BENIN

Kaduna

**FREETOWN**

N I G E R I A

SIERRA
LEONE

IVORY
COAST

GHANA

TOGO

**ABUJA**

**MONROVIA**

LIBERIA

**YAMOUSSOUKRO**

Abidjan

**LOMÉ**    Lagos

**PORTO
NOVO**

**ACCRA**

Port
Harcourt

EQUATORIAL
GUINEA

N

**LIBREVILLE**

*ATLANTIC
OCEAN*

**KEY**

Trans-Sahara routes    S2
(identified pages 8–12)

0 ———— 200 miles
0 ———— 300 km

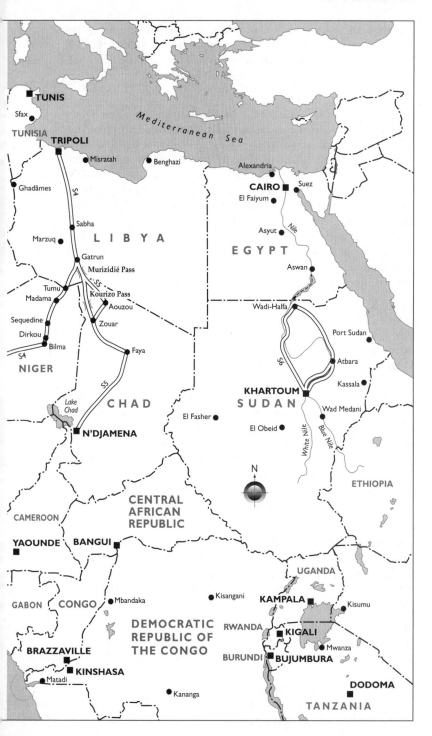

and there are some difficult sandy sections. Travelling in convoy with at least one other vehicle is essential and taking a guide from Agadez, Bilma or Gatrun would also be a good idea. Remember also, do not take alcohol into Libya and do have your passport officially translated into Arabic.

### Route S5 – Libya to Chad
The Libya to Chad routes are not for the inexperienced. The Tibesti area of northern Chad is very remote and renowned for its landmines and bandits. However, it is also reputedly one of the most spectacular areas of the Sahara with volcanoes and mountains up to 3,200m (10,500ft) high. The main routes are either Gatrun-Murizidié Pass–Aozou–Zouar or Gatrun–Murizidié Pass–Kourizo Pass–Zouar. It is possible to do these routes in either direction, but getting permission from the Chadians to head north is probably harder then heading south from Libya. The crossing is about 1,240km (770 miles) via Zouar and an extra 300km (185 miles) if you go via Aozou. Fuel should be available at Faya in Chad and Gatrun in Libya. This route is not for the faint-hearted, you must be very well equipped and research all the latest information.

### Route S6 – Egypt to Sudan
There are two options when crossing from Egypt to Sudan or vice versa. The first is via the Red Sea coast, or you could drive from Aswan to Wadi Halfa to Khartoum. The Red Sea route has been closed north of Port Sudan for many years and you are unlikely to be granted a travel permit. The most common route is south via the ferry from Aswan to Wadi Halfa and then on to Khartoum by following either the Nile or the railway line. This route is relatively straightforward and fuel is available at most of the larger river towns. Heading north, the ferry can be expensive and difficult to get on to at Wadi Halfa. It is possible to drive along the lake from Wadi Halfa and catch a pontoon ferry across to Abu Simbel, but this whole area is run by the military and is effectively off-limits, so you may need to do some sweet talking.

Bear in mind that evidence of having been in Israel renders your passport useless for travel in any other Arab countries. Most travellers that we spoke to who had crossed from Israel into Egypt and onwards carried two passports.

### East–west routes: Northern Africa or Sahel
Avoid the West African rains. If you get caught in an area with poor roads and bridges you could be stuck for quite some time. The rains tend to start around May and last through the summer months. They start slightly later the further north you go.

### Route EW1 – Chad to Sudan to Ethiopia
The most common route is from N'Djamena to Abéché (Chad border) then to El Geneina (Sudan border), Nyala, El Fasher, El Obeid, Kosti and Khartoum. From Khartoum it is possible to get to Ethiopia either via Eritrea or Gedaref (Sudan border) to the Metema border and on to Gonder in Ethiopia.

Leaving from N'Djamena and heading to Khartoum will take ten days of straight driving during the dry season. The route is uncomplicated and the tracks are mostly hard-packed sand. There are usually two tracks, one for the Bedford trucks acting as the local taxi service and another for cars. These tracks run parallel to each other and at the best of times you will lose the car tracks while trying to negotiate the vehicle in the deep ruts left behind by the Bedfords. It is hard to lose your way on the Sudan side and if in doubt, just follow the railway line or drive on it. A few police checks are evident along the way, but if your paperwork is in order it's an absolute breeze. More often than not we politely had to decline the invitation of lunch at most police checks! The hospitality in Sudan is extraordinary. Make sure you get your Sudan visa before entering (either in Ivory Coast, Chad, Ethiopia or Kenya) and get a travel permit stating your route. (See also *Red tape*, page 241.)

## East–west routes: Central Africa

Central Africa has plenty of rain and mud to slow you down; this is where four-wheel drive really comes into its own. On the standard route across the Democratic Republic of the Congo (DRC), through Mobayi, Bumba, Kisangani and Beni, the easiest time to cross is in the dry season from about December to February. There is also a 'less wet' season in June/July. In the Central African Republic (CAR) rain barriers are set up during the rainy season to stop vehicles using and damaging the roads. These could cause you considerable delays. The route between the CAR and DRC has been closed to travellers since June 1998, but with the changing political climate in Africa, this challenging route might open its doors once again to overland travel.

### Route C1 – CAR to the DRC to Uganda/Rwanda

This is the classic trans-African route, renowned for broken bridges and enormous bog holes. It may be the only time you need your winch, snatch blocks, and full capacity of fuel; not to mention your reserves of inner strength and patience.

The main crossing from Cameroon is at Béloko (although there are fewer police checks within Cameroon on the road to Gamboula). Entry from Chad at Kabo is reasonably straightforward. All routes then converge on Bangui. There are three ferry crossings over the Oubangui River into the DRC: Bangui, Mobaye and Bangassou. The Bangui crossing is hardly ever used by overland vehicles because of persistent problems over the river in Zongo – if you do choose to go this way, make sure you cross early in the day and carry on for at least 50km (30 miles) from Zongo before stopping. The previously preferred crossing at Mobaye has been out of action for the past few years – because of its proximity to the Congolese presidential palace in Gbadolite – so currently Bangassou is the best option for entry into the DRC.

Few travellers will take anything other than the main route across the north of the DRC, linking CAR and the eastern highlands.

The most common route is to go via Monga and Bondo to Buta, with a choice of the northern route through Isiro or the southern one through Kisangani. These roads converge again at Nia Nia. An alternative is to take the track from Monga using two ferries to Yakoma and then down to Bumba, where you can take the river steamer as far as Kisangani (although do check the

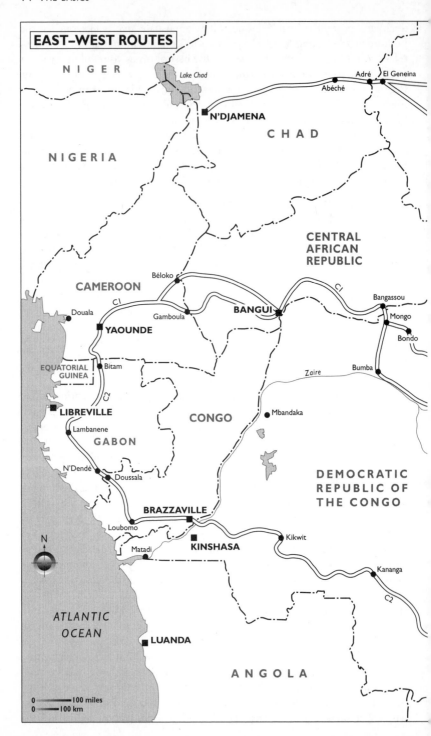

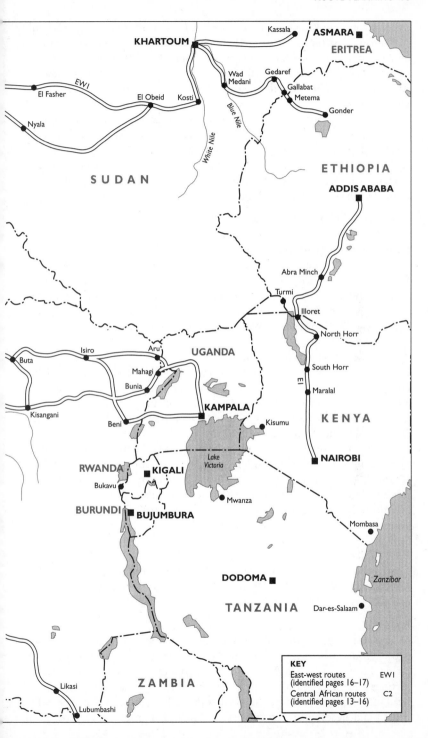

safety situation in Kisangani first). After Nia Nia, the road goes through Epulu to Komanda. At the moment the only option is then to cross into Uganda – either via Bunia and Mahagi or further south from Beni into the Queen Elizabeth National Park. A final option is to cross from Isiro to Aru, then to Arua in Uganda, but note that Ugandan rebels have been active in the border area for years.

If the political situation improves, it may once again be possible to continue down through the extremely beautiful eastern highlands of the DRC or through Rwanda and Burundi into Tanzania. The only way into Burundi without entering Rwanda is by the difficult but spectacular route via Nya-Ngezi down to Uvira; large sections of this have been compared with driving in the Hoggar Mountains in Algeria!

### Route C2 – Gabon to Congo to DRC to Zambia

The current problems in the DRC have effectively ruled out this route and it is difficult to know what permits are now required. If the situation changes it could become a viable alternative to cross from east to west, or vice versa. Until then it is strictly for the crazy. The route is fraught with gun-toting soldiers, difficult bureaucracy and bad roads – the worst countries are the two Congos. Cameroon and Gabon are fairly stable at the time of writing and thus reasonably safe. However, as with most countries in this region, many of the roads are in poor shape.

From west to east you pass through Gabon via Bitam (Cameroon border), Lambaréné, N'Dendé and into the Congo via Doussala. The roads in Gabon are generally dirt roads but reasonably well maintained. Visas are expensive and difficult to obtain and your best bet is to apply in Cameroon or Equatorial Guinea. From Doussala you carry on to Loubomo and on to Brazzaville where you can cross the Congo River into Kinshasa.

The Congolese roads are notoriously bad and there has been violent political unrest in the country recently – make sure you get up-to-date information before entering the country. From Kinshasa head southwest towards Lubumbashi via Kikwit, Kananga and Likasi. You have to obtain permits in Kinshasa to cross the mining region. It may also be possible to put your vehicle on the train at Kananga.

### East Africa

Hitting the wrong climate in eastern and southern areas is more likely to be a nuisance than a disaster, as the roads tend not to be so bad. Most rain in the east falls between March and June and October to December.

### Route E1 – Kenya to Ethiopia

Most people crossing from Kenya into Ethiopia or vice versa use the Isiolo to Moyale route, where you are required to take the armed convoy leaving daily at 15.00 from Isiolo. The Moyale road is paved but treacherous, with ruined sections and large potholes. The other option is to go via Lake Turkana and head into Ethiopia via Illoret (marked as Banya Fort on most maps), avoiding Turmi and heading up towards Arba Minch. This route is very beautiful, covering the Chalbi Desert and Omo region. However, there are no official border posts and you usually have to do a great deal of explaining when you end up in Addis Ababa or Nairobi with no official stamp in your passport.

### Route E2 – Northern Mozambique to Tanzania
At the time of writing the bridge over the Ravuma at Mtwara was currently under construction, with newly built roads as far as Pemba. But with the heavy floods so evident during March 2000, the status of roads and bridges could have changed.

## Southern Africa
With so many varied routes through southern Africa, it is impossible to list each of them. Furthermore, the standard of roads is excellent compared with the rest of Africa. Most roads in southern Africa can be compared to European ones.

There are a few routes through southern Africa that are four-wheel drive and will get you into the unknown. For further information on four-wheel drive in southern Africa read *Southern Africa 4X4 Trails* (1997–1998) by Andrew St Pierre White and Gwynn White.

## Suggested routes
We have suggested three possible routes looking at various time frames – namely six months and one year. For an overland trip from London to Cape Town or vice versa, which could be done in six to eight months, we would suggest no less than a year if you really want to make the most of it.

### Six-month route
If you only have six months available we suggest a circular route along either the north and west coasts of Africa or southern and east Africa. This of course depends on what you want to experience, see and do.

### Route NW – north and west African itinerary
Spain to Morocco–Mauritania–Senegal and the Gambia–Mali–Burkina Faso–Ghana–Togo–Benin–Nigeria–Niger–Algeria or Libya and back to Spain, France or Italy.

### Route SE – southern and east Africa
Cape Town–Namibia–Botswana–Zambia–Zimbabwe–Malawi–Mozambique–Swaziland–Cape Town.

### One-year route
The route we have suggested is completely dependant on the political situation at the time:

Morocco–Mauritania–Senegal and the Gambia–Mali–Burkina Faso–Ivory Coast–Ghana–Togo–Benin–(Niger–Nigeria–Cameroon–CAR and DRC)–or (Niger–Chad–the Sudan–Ethiopia)–Uganda–Kenya–Tanzania–Malawi–Zambia–Botswana–Zimbabwe–Mozambique–South Africa.

## Maps

When it comes to Africa, many people seem to be geographically challenged. Spinning a globe to familiarise yourself with the lay of the continent makes an excellent beginning. Often people do not have a sense of distances in Africa. Use the scale to take a couple of sample distances for points you might travel between. Make a mental note that travel times in Africa can be several times longer for a given distance than they are in areas with more developed transport infrastructures.

After you've finished with the globe, switch to flat maps of the area you plan to visit. In the early planning stage a smaller-scale map is sufficient, and it should help you avoid getting bogged down trying to make decisions on details which are better left until later. In addition to locating a few familiar cities, maps can lead to information about relative distances, general topography and the availability of roads. Michelin make the best, most easily obtainable maps of Africa. Most travel bookstores stock these. (Large-scale maps are increasingly available in travel bookstores. If you can't find the one you need in your home country, detailed maps are usually available and much less expensive in major cities in Africa.)

### Accessing preference and limitations

Some of the parameters that you need to determine are total number of days available, daily travel distance, acceptable range of climate, geography, road condition, level of accommodation, flexibility with food, availability of water and wild beasts.

Time: Because of the large number of fascinating destinations in Africa, your inclination might be to try to fit too much into too little time. Seven game parks in seven days in a four-wheel drive can be as gruelling as a European bus tour of seven countries in seven days. Experienced travellers generally recommend that quality is better than quantity. Don't be surprised if your scratch paper begins to look more like a matrix with rows of 'if, then' conditions for each separate possible itinerary.

## PLANNING A BICYCLE TRIP

### David Mozer of Bicycle Africa Tours

Those thinking of driving across Africa will be amazed to learn there is an even more adventuresome bunch planning the trip on a bicycle. If you have plenty of time and do not mind the hardship and physical effort, done intelligently cycling can be the perfect way to see the continent. It certainly brings you into closer contact with both the people and the environment than most other methods. But honour the *caveat* – this means taking in to account the geography, weather patterns, political reality, culture, and availability of food and water, being prepared and having the proper equipment.

Just as it is in Western countries, there is something nicely different, and sometimes inspirational, about arriving almost anywhere in Africa by bicycle. In the cities bicycles are efficient – even in Africa streets are congested and parking spaces few, not a problem with a bike.

In the countryside the bicycle is liberating. It reduces your dependency on mechanically questionable, over-crowded and unpredictable public transport. It expands your range over those who walk and it creates more social interaction than is possible from a tourist van or overland truck. As you cycle you are certain to meet people who you would not meet any other way, generating rich experiences. The physical activity benefits your health and fitness and the unrestricted access to the environment puts you into the middle of an exciting world that begs exploration.

Even if you don't like a lot of extreme hardship and can settle for seeing a carefully selected area of the continent, you can get the people-to-people benefits of a bike tour in Africa. Because of the flexibility of a bike and the ease with which it integrates with planes, trains, buses and boats, you can start and stop your road adventure almost anywhere you want.

If you are riding coast-to-coast it goes without saying you should not dream of such a trip unless you are in good health – cycling across the Sahara or through muddy forest trails can be extremely hard work. Some previous experience of long-distance cycling is vital before setting out. More modest cycling tours in Africa require similar preparation to that which you would need for a similar tour in Europe or north America: a basic level of physical activity in your life, and proper equipment. Of course there are no written rules and attitude can prevail over all else; Christian and Gilly Lee, who contributed to earlier editions of this book, didn't do any cycling at all before they set off on their successful trip from Victoria Station to Victoria Falls.

Bicycle Africa Tours reports that they regularly have complete bicycle touring novices and African travel novices on their programmes who do very well because they have so much enthusiasm for exploring Africa.

In most ways, the fundamentals of long-distance cycling in Africa differ very little from those of long-distance summer cycling in north America or Europe: The hills go up and down; the weather can be wet and dry; the temperature is hot and cold; the humidity varies from high to low; and it seems that regardless of which direction you are going there is a head wind. BUT, there are also major differences to keep in mind:

- Repair facilities are fewer and farther between, so that the initial quality, ongoing upkeep of your bike and your general self-sufficiency need to be more of a concern. This is covered in the sections on selecting and preparing a bike for travel in remote areas and the bike tools section of the packing list.
- Although there are tens of thousands of kilometres of paved roads in Africa, the proportion of major roads which are unpaved is much higher than in most industrialised countries – and many of the paved roads are deteriorating. The rotating joke for countries that have fallen on hard times is, 'What do you call a driver going in a straight line?' Answer: 'Drunk.' On the other hand, new stretches of roads are being paved each year and the dust is gradually disappearing.

- Cycling in Africa can easily be made more rigorous than is typical of touring in Europe and north America, especially if you are motivated to get off the highways and off the beaten track into the villages. It is there that you will find some of the most interesting scenes the continent has to offer. On any long-distance tour in Africa it is likely that you will find a mix of riding conditions. You will enjoy it a lot more if you prepare appropriately. Important points on this are covered in all the sections of this guide.
- Don't expect generic highway feeding. The food will be different. If you keep your expectations of the variety of food modest and learn to like Africa's cuisine, you will find plenty to eat in most areas. Cuisine in Africa is not homogeneous; some is more elaborate than others. If you are willing to explore, chances are that you will find some excellent hole-in-the-wall restaurants and great local cooks and dishes. Unless you have heard that a specific area is suffering from famine it probably has adequate, if not abundant food supplies.
- Quiet and personal privacy may become a luxury.
- Water acquisition may need to be carefully planned. Bottled water, carbonated drinks and beer are not always available in grocery stores, restaurants or bars. When they are, they probably won't be as cold as you would like and the choice will be limited – with a different selection than the last town. Even coffee, in countries that export tons of it each year, may not be brewed and sold outside the major cities. If you are drinking water from other sources it may need to be boiled, filtered or treated so that it is a blessing and not a curse.
- There is also an element of truth to some of the myths: toilet facilities may not meet the standards of cleanliness and freshness of the Western service station or may be absent altogether. Smells engulf markets, towns, people and all aspects of life more than in the West.
- Lastly, unless your initial cycling is in Burkina Faso, or a few other select spots where cycling is a popular mass activity, you will quickly note that cycling does not command the status in Africa that it does in China, much of the rest of Asia, or even Europe and North America. This is not a point of concern per se, but may explain some bewildering looks and questions of disbelief. Hold your ground: cyclists may be in the minority, but Africans are used to minorities and they are willing to bestow respect on deserving innovators.

The watchwords are 'be flexible, be tolerant and plan ahead'.

Bicycle touring may be one of the hardest, but it also is one of the most economic means of travel. The only costs you need incur are on your bike, visas, food and accommodation. If you eat the local cuisine and camp or stay in rock-bottom guesthouses, you can keep expenses to the absolute minimum. Even at the end of your trip, many airlines will ship your bike back free as part of your luggage (but not all of them, so shop around).

If the idea appeals to you a good first stop would be to contact the Internet Guide to Travel in Africa by Bicycle, www.ibike.org/africaguide or the

Cyclists' Touring Club (Cotterell House, 69 Meadrow, Godalming, Surrey, GU7 3HS; tel: 01483 417217; fax: 01483 426994; email: cycling@ctc.org.uk). Once you join the CTC, you get a wide range of services – insurance, technical advice, touring itineraries and travel information. Information sheets are published by the CTC on various aspects of travelling with a bicycle and on specific countries and areas in Africa – including West Africa, South Africa, Seychelles, Malawi, Gambia, Zambia, Zimbabwe, Algeria and Tunisia, Egypt and Sudan, Morocco, and the Sahara. Information is also available for trans-African journeys and those planning round-the-world trips.

No guide to overland travel in Africa would be complete without some reference to cycling – a mode of transport that is more popular than you might imagine. But there are plenty of practical questions that need to be addressed by anyone who has plans for such a trip. So that you learn a minimum of the lessons the hard way here are some general aspects that are worth considering.

Constructing an itinerary, especially for a bike tour, is a multi-faceted project: the desire to see what you want to see, the limitation of daily range, the need for food and lodging and the complications of weather and topography can make it seem like solving a Rubik's cube. Here are some of my approaches and considerations:

## Mileage

Experienced international bicycle travellers find that for a variety of reasons their daily mileage in foreign countries is less than they would typically ride at home. For starters there is a lot to see, and because everything is so different you will want to leave extra time just to look around. It also tends to be the case that everyday chores, small business matters (ie: banking, posting mail and buying supplies), transportation and unfamiliar procedures in a foreign culture generally take longer than similar tasks at home. If you are travelling in a less-developed country, you might need double, triple or quadruple the amount of time you would regularly set aside for these matters.

As a practical tip, it is more comfortable and easier on your health to plan your itinerary with conservative estimates of daily distance so that most of the bicycling can be done in the morning or late afternoon if necessary. If this is a once-in-a-lifetime opportunity you want to enjoy the places you go, not merely pass through. Don't overestimate the daily distance you will cover.

## Planning for daylight

Because Africa straddles the equator, in most of the continent the sun rises at about 06.00 and sets around 18.00 (natural time), plus or minus half an hour all year round. An excellent, practical and recommended routine on cycling days is to live by the sun: mostly pack the night before, get up at 6am, eat breakfast around 06.30 and try to be on the road by 07.00. For the next few hours bicycle, sight-see and stop as necessary to eat and drink. If you don't reach your destination before the midday heat hits, stop from 12.30 to 15.30, eat a good meal, take a siesta, read, write and/or watch the local life. When it starts cooling down, saddle-up and finish the day's ride. If you are staying in villages where there is no electricity it is easy to be in bed by 20.00. You will then get a good ten hours sleep before you have to confront the journey again.

## Route

There are now thousands of kilometres of excellent paved roads in developing countries. As modernisation continues new stretches are paved every year. Even unpaved, the laterite (clay) and black cotton soil roads, common in Africa, can be nearly as smooth to ride on as paved roads – when they are dry. When wet, laterite and black cotton soil roads are virtually impossible to ride on. Depending on the situation, they may take from a few hours to several weeks to dry out after the last rains. Washboard, rocky and rutted dirt roads create their own discomfort and fall somewhere between dry and wet laterite roads. It is on the unpaved roads that you tend to find a much more traditional and interesting side of Africa. To best enjoy these areas you need to schedule your visit to correspond with the dry season – though Nature always reserves the right to be spontaneous. Even where the roads have good, all-weather surfaces, you should take note of the prevailing winds for the time of year you plan to travel. The wind can determine the direction of travel. If the route is a loop – *c'est la vie*. If your itinerary involves large net changes in elevation, the geography may also be a major influence on your choice of starting and finishing points and your direction of travel.

## Climate

The weather can be an important determinant for the ease and enjoyment of bicycling, especially in less-developed areas. If you have a choice, schedule your travels for the cool, dry season. This varies from month to month and place to place. The cool part of the dry season is usually at the beginning of the dry season, just after the end of the rains. This period has the added advantage that the dust is relatively low, though the high-altitude *harmattan* dust affects West Africa a couple of months into the dry season. In addition to moisture and heat another important factor can be wind – try to keep it on your back.

## $Safari$ $Drive$ ◄▮▦▨◈▨▦▮►

Safari Drive operates self drive fully equipped Land Rover Defender vehicles that are ideal for exploring Africa. We can supply all lodge and national parks bookings and create flexible itineraries. Please call for a colour brochure. www.safaridrive.com  Tel:UK 01488 681611  Safari_Drive@compuserve.com

# Vehicle Selection and Preparation

You have the finances and you've decided on your route, now all you want to do is *go*! But rushing off without careful planning and preparation is the biggest mistake you can make. Planning and preparing is half the fun, and not only makes your trip that much more enjoyable, but brings you that much closer to your destination.

If you are taking your own vehicle we would recommend a planning period of about a year. You should have bought your vehicle six months before you leave at the very least. It may sound like a long time, but once you get started you will be amazed at just how much preparation is necessary and how many details you hadn't considered. Don't be put off. Planning the trip can be a really exciting time.

We have divided the planning stages into vehicle, motorbike and bicycle preparation, detailing every requirement before and during your trip.

Take this time to soak up as much information as you can about Africa, its culture and people. The more you know and respect the places you plan to visit, the less likely you are to disrupt local culture when you get there, and the more you will get out of your trip. Travelling carries responsibilities as well as bringing pleasure: not encouraging dependence by casually handing out gifts; respecting religious sites and artefacts; burning your rubbish wherever possible; and respecting people's dignity and wishes, particularly when taking photographs.

At the end of the book we have included a checklist which will help you with your planning decisions.

## WHICH VEHICLE?
The biggest decision is what sort of transport to choose. Of course all have their advantages and disadvantages.

### Four-wheel drives
This is the best option if you want the best of all worlds – and can afford it. Some people say travelling in a vehicle can distance you from the environment you are travelling through, cocooning yourself in a self-contained world. Our experience is that this is only true if you allow it to be. The major advantage is that you are free to go more or less anywhere. Add to this relative comfort and reliability and the capacity to carry a fair amount of supplies and you have a winning formula. As long as you can hold down costs and not allow yourself

to get trapped inside the comfort of the goldfish bowl, it can be a great way to see Africa.

### Petrol or diesel?

Diesel engines usually offer superior fuel consumption. Diesel is also safer to carry, unlike petrol, which is lethal once it has been shaken about in hot jerry cans. Diesel engines are also simpler in that they have no points, coils, condensers or distributors, though they do have more complex fuel systems. Diesel engines produce high torque at low revs, whereas petrol engines tend to produce maximum torque at high revs, which can be a disadvantage in difficult conditions where wheel spin is a problem.

Fuel availability (either diesel or petrol) varies from country to country. As a general rule, however, diesel is cheaper throughout Africa and more readily available than petrol.

### Short or long wheelbase?

A long wheelbase has the obvious advantage of space, but there are certain advantages in buying a short wheelbased vehicle and attaching a trailer for extra storage space.

The one major advantage with a short wheelbase and trailer is that you can unhook the trailer and push or pull it over difficult sections, leaving you free to manoeuvre a weightless vehicle. A trailer can also be left behind at a campsite (safely locked up), allowing you to use your vehicle whenever you wish without having to break camp. Just remember to take out necessary equipment, like your high-lift jack, spare tyre (if not attached to the vehicle), water, etc before departure.

The disadvantage of towing a trailer is that it can be a severe hindrance in any terrain where traction is a problem. It is also difficult to tow over loose and uneven surfaces and a badly loaded trailer can cause instability when cornering and braking. It can also cause major damage to your vehicle if it is badly loaded or driven by inexperienced drivers.

Further information on storage and driving techniques regarding a short wheelbase vehicle with trailer can be obtained from major four-wheel-drive or trailer outlets. Companies offering four-wheel-drive courses will also be able to assist. For a list of four-wheel-drive clubs, research the following website: www.fourwheeler.com/facts/clublist.html.

### Vehicle types

By far the most common four-wheel drives in Africa are the Land Rover and Toyota Landcruiser. You are more likely to find spares and experienced mechanics for these vehicles than any other.

The older models are more common, such as the III series Land Rover and 45 to 60 series of the Landcruiser, and mid-80s Hilux, and there is a thriving second-hand spares market. You will also find Land Rover and Toyota dealers in most capital and larger cities, although the stock of spares varies greatly from dealer to dealer and they will often only stock spares for the newer models.

Unless you are either a very experienced mechanic, have a very reliable vehicle or can afford to have spares sent out to you, avoid newer models and go for an older Land Rover or Landcruiser.

The following is a brief rundown of vehicles available and a few of their advantages and disadvantages.

### Land Rover

Favourites include the III series and Defender Land Rover series, which are the most suitable for African roads. Their simple and robust design makes them ideal for the wide variety of difficult conditions. They are available in a long or short wheelbase with six-cylinder petrol or four-cylinder diesel engines. The III series has leaf-spring suspension whereas the Defender's has been changed to coil springs. The III series also has part-time four-wheel drives with a two-ratio transfer gearbox while the Defender has permanent four-wheel drive. Web: www.landroverworld.com/products/defender/ and www.4wdonline.com/LandRover/Series/S3.html.

### Range Rover

This vehicle was designed to bridge the gap between off- and on-road driving. It offers greater comfort than the Land Rover and is an excellent vehicle, but for a trans-African journey it is of fairly limited use. It does not have much in the way of storage capacity and the compensating advantages of its powerful engine and comfortable interior can now be found in the newer Land Rovers. Web: www.4wdonline.com/LandRover/Intro.html.

### Toyota Landcruiser

The Landcruiser's design is rugged and very reliable, and spare parts are readily available throughout Africa. Toyota have a rather confusing numbering system for their various Landcruiser models. To put it simply, they started with the 40 series and have worked up to the 80 series in the early 1990s. The FJ prefix denotes a petrol engine and the HJ series diesel engines. Just to confuse you further, BJ refers to the short wheelbase. The engines tend to be large but very reliable and in particular the H2 engine (fitted in the HJ 40 to 60 series) which will go forever if looked after. Suspension is by solid axle and leaf springs, and the older models are all part-time four-wheel drive with a two-ratio transfer gearbox. Local mechanics tend to be familiar with the vehicles. Web: http://4wd.sofcom.com/Toyota/40.html.

### Toyota Hilux

The Hilux is available as a double or single cab and with either a 2.2 litre petrol or 2.4/2.8 litre diesel engine. It also has part-time four-wheel drive with a two-ratio transfer gearbox. They are quite a popular vehicle in Africa and nearly rate up there with Landcruiser and Land Rover. They are a little easier to roll over on to their roofs if you are not careful, so take particular care when crossing slopes and cornering at speed. Web: http://4wd.sofcom.com/Toyota/Hilux/Hilux.html.

### Mercedes Unimog

The Unimog is popular among some German travellers and it is indeed a wonderful vehicle. It's an extremely powerful four-wheel-drive truck with very high clearance. Storage space and living quarters are separate from the driving cab. Although you can buy Unimogs quite cheaply at auction in Germany, costs can really start to mount on the road -- fuel consumption can be very high indeed. You should also test drive the Unimog in various conditions as they can tip easily in soft sand. Web: http://4wd.sofcom.com/Unimog/Unimog.html.

### Bedford trucks

Four-wheel-drive Bedford trucks, especially ex-British army models, are much favoured by British-based trans-Africa overland tour companies such as Encounter Overland. It's not the most suitable vehicle to invest in unless there are quite a few of you. You will need to carry most parts, spares and tools with you, preferably taking a Bedford expert along too. Bedfords are used along the desert tracks of the Sahara as local taxis and 'souk' trucks.

### Top of the range

For a go-anywhere vehicle there is the Pinzgauer, which is available in either four- or six-wheel drive – this is a phenomenal vehicle at a phenomenal price. Others include the Land Rover Discovery, Landcruiser GX and Prado models, Isuzu Trooper and Mitsubishi Pajero. You're more likely to find these in supermarket car parks in the smart suburbs of London or Sydney than you will crossing the Sahara. That may be more to do with the price than their off-road ability, but it does mean that you will struggle to find a mechanic who can fix them or any spares outside of Europe or South Africa.

### Isuzu Trooper

One of the top-of-the-range vehicles for those who want a comfortable ride. It is reported to suffer from a very sensitive accelerator that may cause difficulty when delicate accelerator work is required. It may also cause excessive wheelspin in sandy and muddy conditions. Web: www.4wdonline.com/Isuzu/Isuzu.html.

### Mitsubishi Pajero

The Pajero is reportedly one of the better top-spec vehicles when it comes to off-road ability, but its front suspension is said to let it down (better stick to the school run).

Any of the above vehicles could be used as your overland vehicle, but you must be able to fix it yourself and carry all the spares you may need.

### Other vehicles

Here are just a few examples of other four-wheel drives available on the market – but do remember that finding spares and mechanics may be a problem:

### Ford Courier

Ford Courier is a similar type of vehicle to the Toyota Hilux and is similarly available as a single or double cab. It is a part-time four-wheel drive vehicle with high- and low-range transfer gearbox. Web: http://www.4wdonline. com/Ford/Courier/Courier.html.

### Jeeps

The Jeep Wrangler is probably a bit small for all the equipment you'll be taking and the Cherokee range tend to be gas guzzlers. Web: http://www.4wdonline. com/Jeep.

### Mitsubishi Colt

The Colt is another vehicle in the same vein as the Hilux. The Mitsubishi Colt has part-time four-wheel drive with automatic free-wheel hubs. Web: http://4wd.sofcom.com/Mitsubishi/Colt.html.

### Nissan Patrol

We met a Swiss couple in Niger with a Patrol and they swore by it. However, it did look a little low to the ground to me, which could cause trouble in rocky terrain. It has coil-spring suspension and part-time four-wheel drive. Its seems to have a very good reputation in Australia and South Africa and it is reported to be very reliable. Web: http://www.4wdonline.com/Nissan/Nissan.html.

## Two-wheel drives

Although not really suitable for more adventurous, full-blooded trans-African trips, two-wheel-drive vehicles can be used quite happily if you plan your route with care or will be travelling in areas with better roads. Some actually have definite advantages, either because of their comfort or their light weight – the lighter the vehicle the less power you need to get it through difficult conditions.

It is possible to drive across the Sahara and even right across Africa in a vehicle like a VW Combi – and they provide far more comfort than most four-wheel-drive vehicles. But you have to time the seasons precisely and be prepared to get stuck more often than with a four-wheel drive.

Some smaller two-wheel-drive cars can be surprisingly good in all but the muddier sections of central Africa. Citroen 2CVs and Renault 4s are economical on fuel and quite capable of desert crossings on main tracks, although their clearance is limited. If you don't mind the lack of space they could prove a low-cost option. We met someone who had converted his 2CV to adapt to the harsh African conditions and had travelled not only most of the Sahara, but also Zaire (as it was then known). It is advisable to go with a convoy if you are travelling in a two-wheel drive and wanting to cross the Sahara or any other difficult sections.

## Car hire

There is no need to drive all the way if you are short of time or do not complete trans-African trip. Much of southern Africa and parts of th west are perfectly accessible by two-wheel-drive vehicles that can be hired locally. If you want to get off the beaten track once you arrive, you should be able to find more substantial vehicles for hire in some of the major tourist centres. In a city like Nairobi, for example, there is no shortage of places to hire four-wheel-drive vehicles such as Suzuki, Isuzu Troopers and Land Rovers, already kitted out with camping gear, cooking equipment, water containers etc. The Africa Travel Centre in London (21 Leigh Street, London WC1H 9QX; tel: 020 7387 1211; fax: 020 7383 7512; email: chris@ africatravel.co.uk; web: www.africatravel.co.uk) or South Africa (74 New Church Street, Cape Town 8001; tel: +27 21 423 4530 or 423 5555; fax: +27 21 423 0065; email: backpack@gem.co.za; web: www.backpack.co.za) can arrange hire in advance.

## VEHICLE PREPARATION

The range of possibilities for vehicle preparation is obviously enormous – from paying someone else to do the job for you to having the fun of tackling most of it yourself.

Varying degrees of help are available. A company like Gumtree Enterprises will provide a completely customised vehicle to your own requirements. Others will give advice and help so you can prepare your own vehicle.

Whatever choice you make, it is crucial you should know your vehicle well. If you have not had a hand in getting it ready to leave, it is even more important that you should take time to become totally familiar with it before setting off. What follows is a guide to some of the more important issues to bear in mind. Everyone will have their own ideas on what are essentials and optional extras.

The first and most important part of vehicle preparation is to ensure that the basic vehicle (ie: before you add on any extras) is in sound mechanical order. If you are not a mechanic it would be advisable to take it to a garage for a major check/overhaul. This should include the engine, cooling system, fuel system, suspension, gearbox, transfer box, clutch, differentials, brakes, etc. If you do have some mechanical knowledge, take the vehicle on a few long test drives, two weeks around Europe for example, and try to identify any problems and get them fixed while you still have access to good mechanics.

Once you are satisfied that the basic vehicle is in good working order, you can start to fit it out for overland travel.

### Sleeping options

You h~ following choices: a rooftop tent, sleeping space inside the r alternative accommodation. The ultimate choice is obviously here and how long you intend to travel for.

the cheapest option, but not always the most convenient if ith a vehicle. Particularly when driving long stretches for a ching a tent daily can be a nuisance.

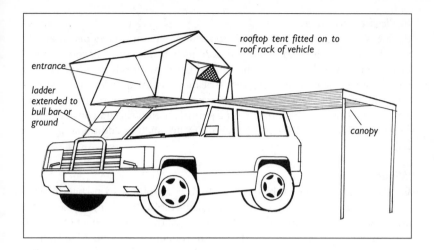

*rooftop tent fitted on to roof rack of vehicle*

*entrance*

*ladder extended to bull bar or ground*

*canopy*

### Rooftop tents

Most other overland vehicles that you see throughout Africa have rooftop tents of various designs. They are the most convenient option as they do not require much space, are quick and easy to put up, keep you away from people and large and small wildlife, and do not present any ventilation problems. There is the standard air camper, the folding roofrack tent or the pop-up variety. Any one of these can usually fit a double mattress which stays in the tent as it is folded up and can be fitted to most vehicles.

### Sleeping inside the vehicle

If you intend to sleep inside the vehicle, you will need to come up with a system which avoids the need to move everything every time you go to bed and also provides some form of ventilation. Most people build a platform that can slide in and out which lies above the equipment. Sleeping in the vehicle is clearly the most secure option for both you and your belongings.

## Roof rack

Roof racks are available in all shapes and sizes and can be used as a low-cost alternative to a rooftop tent by simply adding a sheet of plywood so you can sleep under the stars. This will be perfectly adequate in many situations but is far from offering a comprehensive solution. Most four-wheel-drive vehicles are not built to take heavy loads on the roof and if overloaded have a tendency to tip over on uneven roads. Structural parts, like windscreens, also have a habit of cracking under the strain if overloaded. Roof racks should only be used to store light equipment like sand ladders and empty jerry cans.

## Security

One hundred percent security is impossible to achieve, but every effort you make is worthwhile. The most important security system will ultimately be your own vigilance.

### Padlocks and hasps

Padlocks should be added to all doors and put on any items mounted outside the vehicle. Avoid any delicate mechanisms, such as combination locks which will very quickly become clogged by the thick dust that will cover your vehicle once it hits the African roads. Also make sure that you buy a set of padlocks with a common key or it will take forever to find the right one. Hasps can be forced with a jemmy, so you should consider some form of internal mechanism to back them up, such as additional locks or bolts.

### Windows

Windows are another problem area. Rubber surrounds in particular are a security hazard as they can easily be cut away – replace these if possible. Metal grilles on windows will help, but they also have the adverse effect of making you look like a security van – and so worth robbing. If you intend to sleep in the vehicle, metal grilles along the windows will allow you to leave the windows open while asleep. Sand ladders can also be mounted and locked over windows.

### Curtains

Curtains are worth putting up, whether or not you intend to sleep inside all the time. They provide instant shade in strong sun and dissuade prying eyes. Simple strips of fabric on curtain stretchers can fit inside the inner roof gulley of most vehicles, though some travellers are more sophisticated and fit curtain rails with proper hooks.

### Safety box

Precious commodities like your passport, documents and cash should obviously be kept in a safe place. All original documentation should be kept in a standard wall safe that can be bolted or welded into the vehicle behind the seats, for example, and should be easily accessible. It is also advisable to hide copies of documents in some other area of the vehicle, carrying one set with you at all times in a document case.

### Alarm systems

Some form of alarm system will undoubtedly help as it should deter a thief from continuing with a break-in. But do not depend on it to safeguard your gear. There is a wide selection of systems available from all accessory shops.

## Bull bars

Bull bars are not an essential piece of equipment. They are designed to protect the lights and radiator from anything you may hit. Bearing in mind the amount of cattle and general debris on the roads it may be advisable to fit one, although most manufacturers fit them as standard these days. They can also be used to mount additional driving lights, or mesh to prevent stones breaking your headlights.

## Baffle/bash plate

A baffle plate is a steel plate fitted beneath the vehicle. This helps protect its vulnerable underside from rocks. It can, however, make routine maintenance considerably more awkward. You should consider putting baffle plates under the sump and gearbox, and covering the tie rods on your vehicle.

## Suspension

The biggest enemy for vehicles in Africa is the state of the roads. That means your suspension is more at risk than anything else. There is a great deal to be said for fitting new springs and shock absorbers all round before setting off. Some people even strengthen the chassis – certainly a good idea if you are likely to be carrying heavy loads.

Opinion is divided as to which springs are the best. Mechanics in Europe will tend to recommend fitting heavy-duty springs for the additional strains of African roads, but African mechanics will often tell you lighter springs are more supple and less likely to break under the strain.

If you can afford it, Old Man Emu shock absorbers and springs still have the best reputation throughout Africa, and are an advisable investment.

## Spare battery and split-charge system

If you are intending to run other electrical items, like a refrigerator, off your battery, we would suggest a dual battery and split-charge system. This enables the second battery to run other electrical items while the vehicle's main battery stays unaffected. The second battery should be a deep-cycle type, like the Willard 722 Pleasure Master (available in South Africa), designed to cope with charge and recharge. Delco Voyager batteries, available at most vehicle battery outlets, is a good option for the main vehicle battery.

## Oil cooler

Recommended by many, ignored by others. Probably a good idea if you are likely to take full advantage of fast roads in the hottest conditions. Less useful if you are in an older vehicle.

## Raised air intake

This is standard on many African four-wheel-drive vehicles, reducing the intake of large quantities of dust and acting as a safeguard if you intend to drive through deep water. It will certainly do no harm to fit one and you could end up saving your engine from damage. The Australian Safari Snorkel is the most popular and available at most off-road outlets. You could also have loads of fun making up your own from old drain pipes!

Another tip, if you think you are likely to do some deep wading, is to extend your gearbox and axle breathers. These are small air valves mounted on the top of the axles and gearbox that allow air to be drawn in or out as the parts heat up and cool down. The problem is when you go into deep water the axles cool quickly and suck in water through the breathers. The easiest way to deal with this is to fix a length of plastic tube over the breather and thread it up into the vehicle.

## Wheel rims

Riveted steel rims should be selected for tougher terrain as they are more reliable. Magnesium alloy rims are not very convenient as the bead, the part of the rim most often damaged in tougher terrain, cannot be hammered back into place like the steel rim.

A lot of older cars are fitted with split rims which are very convenient when you are repairing your own tyre. Ensure that the tyre is properly deflated prior to splitting the rim as air pressure remaining in the tyre will cause an explosion and could cause serious injury. When fitting the tyre back on to the rim, make sure that it is fitted with a flap consisting of a ring of shaped rubber. The tube will otherwise wear and rip.

## Tyres, spare tyres and tubes

### Tyres

You really should set off with a completely new set of tyres. Aim to fit the best you can – it will be well worth the extra expense. You will be facing a wide variety of terrain – sand, mud, laterite, rocks and tarmac roads. Good quality, all-terrain tyres are the best bet. The brand you use is often a very personal choice. Many people opt for the Michelin XZY or the Continental Super All Grips. There is no way of saying which manufacturer is the better. Get as much advice from enthusiasts as you can so you make an informed decision.

### Spare tyres

If you are getting new tyres fitted, keep the two least-worn tyres from the old set as spares. Most spares are either fitted on the bonnet or the roof of the vehicle. Other options include: under the rear overhang, which reduces ground clearance; inside the vehicle, which could be difficult to get to; and on the rear door, where the hinges and clamps should be periodically tightened.

Many people take a set of sand tyres for the desert, but ask yourself if you really believe the extra weight and cost are worth it. If you are likely to spend an extended period in sandy conditions, you may decide in favour. If not, you can do a great deal to cope with sandy conditions by reducing tyre pressure until you get back on firmer roads.

### Tubed or tubeless tyres

This is a personal choice. Tubed tyres are generally easier to remove from the rim as the bead does not need to be so tight but it is possible to fix a puncture in a tubeless tyre without removing it from the rim. I used to swear that tubed tyres were the way to go but my latest vehicle came with tubeless tyres and now I'm not so sure. There are pros and cons to each type, but in the end it comes down to personal preference.

### Inner tubes

It is important to carry two or three spare inner tubes, particularly if you are visiting isolated areas where tubes can be found but not necessarily in the correct size or make. It is also important to inflate, deflate and re-inflate the tyre once the new tube has been fitted. This will remove twists in the tube which can cause splits and major blow-outs while driving.

## Valves

It is better to fit your tyre with a short-stemmed valve rather than the longer one. Longer valves are more susceptible to breakage, particularly in tough terrain. Always carry some extra valves with you.

## Extra fuel and water tanks
### Fuel

If you want to avoid filling your vehicle with jerry cans, consider fitting extra tanks – particularly for older models with higher fuel consumption. Land Rovers are particularly easy to modify.

You can supplement the standard long wheelbase, 15-gallon, rear-mounted fuel tank with short wheelbase 10-gallon tanks – one under each front seat. That's a total of 35 gallons. Customised tanks with even larger capacities for both fuel and water are also available and can be fitted to most vehicles. Plan to carry as much fuel as possible – always bearing in mind weight restrictions. Fuel and water are the two most important items you need – but they are also incredibly heavy. There is little point in being well prepared if you destroy your suspension or even break your chassis in the process.

Fuel is actually more readily available than you might think in most parts of Africa. Unless you really do aim to get right away from the normal routes you should not experience any problems. There are not many places where you will need to go more than 600km (370 miles) without supplies. On the other hand, you cannot always guarantee getting fuel when you expect to – and you may want to take full advantage of cheaper supplies when you can get them. The final judgement on how much you should carry is always likely to be something of a balancing act. We would recommend a 1,000km (620-mile) capacity.

## Water

Much the same applies to water as to fuel. Make sure you carry enough – but beware of overloading. The greater your carrying capacity, the more tempting it becomes to load your vehicle up to the gills. A built-in water tank can be far more convenient than a vehicle full of leaking jerry cans. The fewer items that can move around the better as far as loading is concerned. If you can do away with the need for loose fuel and water containers, so much the better.

If you do use jerry cans, however, you can get them out of the way when empty by putting them on the roof (do not do so if they are full – never overload your roof rack with heavy items). If you have petrol in jerry cans on the roof it spells double trouble as the sun will soon make it hot and very dangerous.

## Storage

Careful planning of your storage facilities can make all the difference between comfort and a nightmare. Try to achieve a closely packed but accessible arrangement. At all costs avoid having anything loose that can be thrown about in

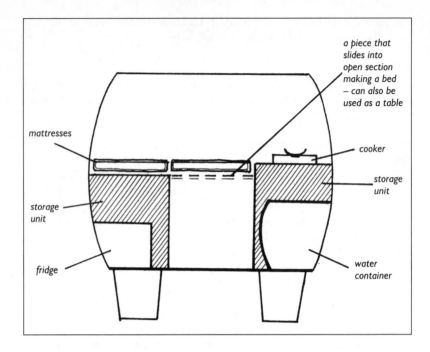

*a piece that slides into open section making a bed – can also be used as a table*

mattresses

cooker

storage unit

storage unit

fridge

water container

the back. Fitted cupboards and storage space can be built by customising companies, or, if you feel confident, you can do the job yourself. Remember the whole thing can easily get shaken to bits unless it has been well made.

Some kind of modular system is probably the best approach to storage. You need to be able to pull things out quickly, find what you are looking for and repack into the same space you started with. This process is generally a lot harder than it sounds. It can be very useful to split your storage space into compartments and within this into a series of rigid sections or boxes.

Rigid plastic storage boxes are good, or even metal flight cases if you can afford them. Elastic bungee cords and canvas or webbing belts are useful for lashing things down. Anything removable on your roof rack should be secured with padlocks.

## Comfort
### Seat covers
The choice of seat covers depends on the seats in the vehicle. If they are plastic, they will be very uncomfortable in the hot sun if they are not covered. Towelling is ideal to cover these. With removable covers you have the added advantage of being able to wash out the grime that will inevitably build up. Even if you have fabric-covered seats already you will appreciate washable covers – you will pick up more dust and grime than you could believe possible!

A set of seat covers, beaded are a good option, helps in extreme heat when long hours behind the wheel cause sweat and sores. They also ease your back over long distances.

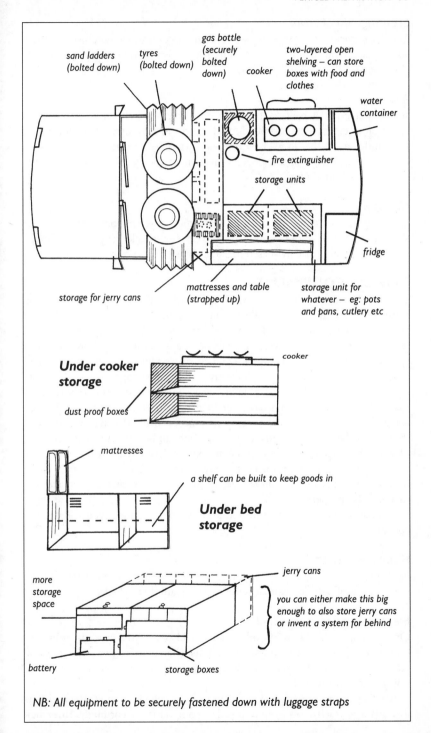

NB: All equipment to be securely fastened down with luggage straps

### Steering-wheel cover

Standard black plastic steering wheels can become extremely hot in direct sunlight and your hands can easily slip. It is advisable to fit some type of non-slip cover on them before you leave.

### Music

Install a standard tapedeck and radio, mounted securely, and bring a good selection of tapes. When driving long distances in a country where you might not understand the local language, a variety of music is irreplaceable. Mounting the stereo in the glove compartment and keeping tapes in a dust-proof box is a good idea.

### Canopy

Not only will a canopy keep you dry during the wet season, but it will also offer shade and a certain amount of privacy. You can either make up your own canopy with strong canvas or vinyl-based material, or have one fitted to your vehicle.

## VEHICLE EQUIPMENT

Everyone has their own set of priorities, but when deciding what to take, you must ask yourself very carefully if you really need it – overloading is your vehicle's worst enemy. With four wheels you will be nothing like as restricted as with a motorbike or bicycle in terms of what you can carry, but when your springs start to go you will bitterly regret every extra kilo of unnecessary weight.

Ensure that all equipment is correctly stored and strapped down. If you are carrying a cooker with a gas cylinder, always ensure that it is tightly secured, that both are locked into a base, and that both have been turned off when leaving the vehicle for long periods of time or while driving. Refrigerators should also be secured tightly with straps but can be kept switched on while driving. We would highly recommend taking a **fire extinguisher** with you, which is not only compulsory in many countries, but might very well be needed at some point. If your vehicle already has a fire extinguisher make sure that it works properly.

Here are a few of the most important items of equipment you will need to consider:

### Recovery gear

Recovery gear is defined as anything you might need when trying to get yourself out of a difficult situation or rescuing another vehicle.

### Electronic or manual winches

Opinions vary as to how useful a winch will be. If you have an unlimited budget, it will do no harm, but the situations when it is likely to come in useful are normally fairly limited – in practically every situation it is easier to be towed out of trouble.

A winch is really designed to be used by a vehicle to pull other objects towards it – which allows you to position your vehicle accordingly. But when it comes to self-recovery it is unlikely you will be stuck in exactly the right position to take advantage of a front-mounted system. Snatch blocks are heavy-duty single line pulleys and go hand-in-hand with winches. Ensure that your snatch block is suited to your winch.

The main advantage of a winch is that it can give you the confidence to explore further off-the-beaten track, away from roads and tracks used by other vehicles. But if you plan to be that adventurous, it would be wise to team up with at least one other vehicle anyway.

A sensible compromise could be a good hand winch – the best is probably made by Tirfor. Another simple winching technique is to make use of a high lift jack. If this is chained to the vehicle at one end and a winching point, such as a tree trunk, at the other, you can slowly pull the vehicle out of trouble. The only drawback with this technique is that you can only winch the length of the jack at a time (1 metre/3 feet). If you are using a tree as an anchor, use canvas, or the purpose-made anchor straps available at most major equipment outlets, to protect the tree.

## High-lift jack

The high-lift jack is one of the most important tools that you will carry with you. It is indispensable and highly versatile. The classic high-lift jack is the red American-made one, which is simple and reliable. However, there are now numerous other makes on the market that are modelled on the original version and are just as good. Remember to use wooden blocks or some sort of base when jacking the vehicle up. Also ensure that your vehicle is in gear and that the handbreak is on. Older vehicles with heavy-duty bumpers make good jacking points, but you will find that a jacking point may need to be fitted to your vehicle if you have a newer model. If your jack is being stored outside, ensure regular cleaning as dust can get trapped in the oil. Cover the jack with canvas for further protection.

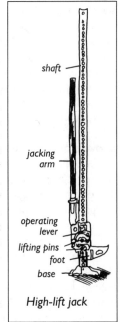

shaft

jacking arm

operating lever

lifting pins

foot

base

High-lift jack

## Hydraulic jack

Useful for smaller jobs or lifting the engine to change engine mounts.

## Sand ladders

With luck and careful driving you may not need a sand ladder at all, but it would be crazy to leave home without some means of getting out of soft sand. Various types of ladders and planks are available – including some made from lightweight alloys. We used aluminium alloy planks which were fine, but perforated steel sand ladders are just as good, although a little heavier.

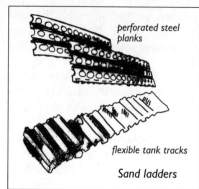

perforated steel planks

flexible tank tracks

Sand ladders

Another type is the flexible variety that looks a little like the tracks from a tank. These do not have to be laid flat like sand mats, so you can save yourself some digging.

## Towing points

Ensure you have adequate towing points on your vehicle, usually mounted below the vehicle at the back and front, making sure that they are easily accessible.

## Towing straps

There are two types available – static and kinetic. The kinetic type are basically slightly elastic, flat towing straps, otherwise known as snatch straps. A popular brand is Tuggum. These are specifically designed for pulling other vehicles out of a difficult situation. Snatch straps have a limited life of about 20 tugs and then the line becomes static. You should carry at least two towing straps of either type and sufficient shackles to connect them. Shorter, wider tree straps are also a good idea.

## Shovels or sand spades

An indispensable companion to the sand ladders. It may seem like hard work, but if you do not dig enough to free the vehicle properly and give yourself a flat surface to lay your sand planks on, you will only end up ploughing deeper and deeper into the sand – and that means even more digging.

D-shackles

bow shackles

Shackles – the only types that should be used on a vehicle

For sand, a long handled shovel with an angled blade is best, although in mud you want as flat an angle as possible. It is also worth considering a smaller shovel for rubbish – always burn or bury anything you are planning to leave behind, but be careful not to bury jagged cans or broken glass in game parks where animals may dig up your rubbish and injure themselves.

A garden trowel is useful for toilet trips.

## Jerry cans

You must use metal ones for fuel; storing petrol in plastic jerry cans is dangerous as it could explode. You can use either metal or plastic for water, though make sure you can distinguish between them if you choose all metal! Do not store water in jerry cans that were previously used for fuel as the taste never disappears. Opaque containers for water help prevent algae growing inside; a black container helps heat up some hot water. The number you take will depend on fuel consumption, tank capacity, route, load and how much you plan to take advantage of cheaper fuel supplies when you find them. For water, your route is the most important factor. Long stretches in the open desert will mean you need to carry substantially more.

## Oils

You are likely to get through more oil than in normal conditions – so be prepared. Engine oil is generally available but gear oil and brake and clutch fluid are more difficult to find. You will find everything you need in the bigger cities like Abidjan or Nairobi, but don't count on it elsewhere.

## Table and chairs

Depending on how long you intend to travel for, a folding chair and table are a good idea. When choosing, remember that they need to last as long as you might need them and will be used on a daily basis. We found that the canvas covered chairs (like a director's chair) have a much longer life and can also be washed regularly.

## Mosquito nets

Whatever type of sleeping arrangement you have decided upon when preparing your vehicle, it is very important that you equip your tent, rooftop tent or sleeping space inside the vehicle with a mosquito net. Even if you opt to find local accommodation it is advisable to carry your own mosquito net. Most places in Africa do provide nets but they are not always in the best condition.

## Sleeping gear

You will need a mattress, sleeping bag, a sheet for hotter climates, and pillows. If you have limited space, a roll-up mattress and fold-up pillow are useful. Sleeping bags can also be rolled into their covers and easily stored. A two-season sleeping bag should be adequate, but some parts of Africa can be cold. The sleeping bag should be washable. For the cover of your mattress and pillows we would suggest strong material, like canvas, of a dark colour, such as blue or green. This helps to avoid having to see every speck of grime you will accumulate!

## Lighting

Fluorescent striplighting is bright, convenient and doesn't put too much strain on the battery. Another popular option is a petrol lantern. Camping lights, which run on small gas canisters, are not such a good idea as, particularly in the desert and West Africa, replacement canisters are almost impossible to find and are extremely expensive.

Whatever you do, remember to bring a torch and spare batteries.

### Map light

A standard map light which can be attached to the car lighter is very useful when trying to read maps at night.

## Portable shower

This isn't essential, but it can make you feel infinitely more human after a long day's drive. The following are available: a plastic bottle, pump-action shower which holds enough water for a seven-minute shower, heating water on the stove to take the chill off in cooler weather; a solar-heated shower which heats four litres in about an hour; or a simple plastic tub filled with hot water from the kettle!

## Portable washing-machine (ie: a bucket!)

This idea was suggested to us by some friends, Sue and Steve Marshall, who did a trans-Africa trip in 1996. Use a bucket with a lid as a portable washing-machine. Before driving off, fill the bucket with washing detergent, water and dirty clothes and strap it in the vehicle. Remember to put the lid on! The motion of the vehicle will act as a washing machine, leaving you to rinse and hang up the clothes once you've reached your destination. Clothes pegs and a washing line are also useful.

## Compass and/or Global Positioning System (GPS)

Most travellers today use GPS as a navigational aid. GPS is great if you are going into really isolated areas, like the Sahara, and can set your co-ordinates accordingly. Most guidebooks specifically relevant to the Sahara and southern Africa have recorded co-ordinates of an area.

It is best to pack up your GPS when crossing borders as they can be misconstrued as a transmitter which can get you into trouble with the security forces. In general you will be quite surprised how little you actually use either the GPS or a compass, but both are useful tools and essential if you are heading into really remote areas.

A dash board mounted compass is the most ideal in a vehicle. Silva make an excellent selection of dash-mounted compasses that are designed specifically for use in a motorised vehicle. Remember that the electrics will throw off a normal compass so if you have a hand-held type stop and walk off a few paces for an accurate reading. Remember that neither a GPS or compass is a replacement for a good map. In fact without a good map the GPS or a compass are often useless.

## Other essential equipment

### Axe or machete
Very useful for chopping wood and hacking through vegetation.

### Warning triangles
Compulsory in some countries. We suggest you carry at least two.

### Foot or electrical tyre pump
Useful for repairing tyres, or pumping up an airbed.

### Tyre repair kit
Speaks for itself really!

### Blocks of wood
These are essential to place under a high lift jack. Particularly useful in soft sand or mud.

### Pressure gauge
A good pressure gauge is particularly useful in the desert where you will be deflating and re-inflating tyres continuously.

## FOOD AND COOKING
### Water and water purification methods
As discussed in storage units in this section (see page 38), your best bet for carrying water is either a 20-litre jerry can and another plastic container of 20 or 25 litres that is accessible at all times and can easily be filled with water. We found that using a plastic container with a tap was the easiest. These can be found at any major outdoor equipment retailer. Clear containers can promote algae growth so it's a better to go with a dark plastic container.

If the water looks cloudy – purify. For water purification we used Chloromyn-T. You only need a tip of a matchstick amount to purify 25 litres. Allow it to work for one or two hours, until the Chloromyn-T has settled. Micropur, puritabs and iodine are other purification methods. Iodine is an effective purifier but shouldn't be used on a long-term basis as your body absorbs it (see *Health*, page 141). The simplest and cheapest option is either to boil water or to use 'filter socks' – but neither method guarantees the killing of all evil goodies that might be lurking in the water.

We do advise that you take a water filter with you, particularly if you are going to be travelling in more remote areas, and cyclists should definitely have one. There are many filters on the market ranging from US$50 to $150. Top of the range are the Katadyne filters used by the Red Cross throughout Africa – though excellent they are pricey. Mountain Safety Research (MSR) (www.msrorg.com) also make a range of filters and we used the MSR MiniWorks, for which you can also purchase an additional virus filter, costing a total of US$50. Suppliers in the UK, South Africa and Australia include:

**First Ascent** Units 4 & 5, Limetree Business Park, Matlock, Derbyshire DE4 3EJ; tel: +44 1629 580484; fax: +44 1629 580275; email: info@firstascent.co.uk
**Outward Ventures** 14 Second Av, Claremont, 7700 Cape Town; tel: +27 21 683 3638; fax: +27 21 61 4157
**Grant Minervini Agencies** 19 Hindmarsh Av, PO Box 209, Welland, South Australia 5007; tel: +61 8 346 6061; fax: +61 8 340 0675

### Refrigerator
Refrigerators for vehicles run on either 12V DC, 240V AC or on gas – some refrigerators are built to run on all three. If you have the space and money, it is one of the first luxuries we would choose to take. They are particularly useful if you intend to carry a lot of film and of course they are extremely pleasant for cold drinks.

Ordinary camping shops can be a good source. Three-way or paraffin types need careful balancing to work properly. The Engel fridge has been recommended as an efficient but expensive option.

## Cooking equipment
### Petrol stoves
The wide variety of camping stoves available means you can exercise a fair degree of choice, though bikers and cyclists tend to opt for small, lightweight petrol stoves or burners. These can be fussy to light but are fairly reliable, depending on how much you are prepared to spend, though even expensive models can let you down. Several people have recommended Colman petrol stoves (one, two or three burners) as very reliable, though they are rather bulky and so not suitable for bikers or cyclists.

Disadvantages of petrol ovens are blackening of pots (though it does rub off much more easily if you smear the outside of your pans liberally with washing up liquid before you cook) and smoking when you first light it.

### Kerosene stoves
The Chinese-made kerosene wick stoves can be found almost everywhere in Africa. There is virtually nothing that can go wrong with them, and the small amount of fuel they burn means you can easily carry enough to last until the next source of kerosene.

### Meths burners
Beware of taking a meths burner as meths is not widely available.

### Gas stoves
Gas stoves are the easiest, cleanest and most reliable option. The small Camping Gaz cartridges (*cartouches* in French) are almost impossible to find, but refillable gas bottles can be filled in most larger towns. Many local families cook with gas (particularly in the Sahara) and most gas stoves have a choice of regulators to cover a range of gas fuels. If you are likely to be off the beaten track for long periods, it might be worth having large gas cylinders fitted in your vehicle.

### Open fires
Although open fires are harder to control for cooking, they are an instant focus when camping, particularly when it gets cold at night. If you don't have a fire grille, a few strategically placed rocks can provide a pot stand just above the flames, and potatoes and other vegetables can be roasted in no time, wrapped in foil with a few herbs or spices for extra flavour.

If you do build a fire, be sensible in dry areas where sparks may set grass or scrub alight. And never cut green wood for a fire, particularly in the desert and sahel areas or game parks – Africa has enough deforestation problems of its own without adding to them. If your transport allows you to carry firewood as you go, you can dry it out by lashing it to the roof rack or the front of your vehicle.

## COOKING WITH ONE BURNER?

If your choice of stove means you have only one burner you need not feel restricted to one-pot meals. Rice or pasta boiled for a few minutes will continue to cook sitting in the hot water while you make up a basic vegetable sauce. Or if you are cooking with meat or beans, start off your rice or pasta about half an hour before you plan to eat and set it aside while you finish off your other dish. Always bring rice or pasta back to the boil and check it is thoroughly cooked before straining.

If you are cooking two dishes you can always prepare them separately and heat them up just before you eat. In time you will get more than skilled at juggling pots. If you find yourself travelling in convoy, meeting up with other travellers in campsites or free camping, you can pool resources and end up with some really adventurous meals. Four one-burner stoves means four hot dishes to share.

### Matches
Matches are available almost everywhere but it is a good idea to carry a spare box. You can buy waterproof matches at most camping shops, though the only time we used them was for entertaining children!

## Cooking utensils
Like everything else it is best to keep these to a minimum. You will quickly learn to adapt what you have for a whole range of purposes, and cooking on the road is all about using your imagination.

Obviously you have more choice with a bigger vehicle. We brought a saucepan which doubled as a two-tier steamer, a deep, straight-edged frying pan, a cast-iron pot and a kettle. Other favourites are pressure cookers, woks and, particularly if you are in a reasonably sized group, big cast-iron cooking pots that can be left sitting on an open fire to stew away for hours.

Basics you need to consider are a decent sharp knife, a wooden spoon, something to strain boiled pasta or vegetables(unless you have a saucepan and lid that are suitable), a tin opener, a bottle opener, and possibly a chopping board, though this is not essential as there is very little skill involved in chopping vegetables straight into the pot. Go for enamel plates and bowls, but plastic mugs for tea and coffee as enamel gets frustratingly hot. We also took deep dishes rather than flat plates; they are easier to eat off without a table and safer for runny dishes. Take spares of cutlery – teaspoons love inaccessible corners in vehicles or to drop out of kit bags.

Anything else you use at home you can probably adapt from what you have brought with you. Whole spices can be ground-up successfully with a clean beer bottle in a saucepan; you can brew up tea or coffee in anything that holds hot water; garlic is just as good chopped as crushed; and a serrated knife will double as vegetable peeler and even as a grater.

## Food to take with you

Even if you are planning a shortish trip you will not be able to take everything you are going to eat, but it is a good idea to assemble a store box of basics and emergency supplies before you go. It will not take long before you realise what you need to carry, and what can be picked up on the road.

Good basic supplies to take with you include salt (extra fluid loss through perspiration means you will naturally salt your food more); some herbs and spices to liven up vegetables, though you will replace these with wonderful fresh local alternatives; tea and coffee; sugar (even if you do not normally use it – it has a high barter value and sweet tea is great if you are ill and cannot face food); rice and pasta; tomato puree (go for tubes rather than tins, which can be wasteful and have a tendency to splatter you in horror-film red if you open them in the heat!); stock cubes; oil in plastic screwtop bottles; and flour or cornflour for thickening. Dried beans are also good if your cooking equipment is up to the longer cooking times needed. If you have all of the above, even if all you can buy locally is tomatoes and onions, you will be able to cook up an acceptable meal. You will also be able to replace most of these basics in larger villages and towns on the way.

Slightly more luxurious items to take could include mustard; dried mushrooms or other vegetables to make pasta or rice dishes a bit more special; lemon juice in plastic bottles; dried fruit to nibble on; jam for a quick breakfast with local bread; biscuits or crackers; and boiled sweets for when you need a burst of energy, though better by far when you are flagging is Kendal mintcake (a high glucose bar that goes into the supplies for every major expedition).

We had a storage container called the 'glory hole' that housed more luxurious items such as a bottle of red wine, powdered custard, sweets and other goodies, specifically for those arduous days when you needed to spoil yourself.

You should also carry more substantial stocks to allow you to eat when you cannot buy local produce. We almost always had enough for four or five meals, just in case. With a vehicle you can afford to carry tins and if you have the space a few well-chosen tins can always be turned into a meal. Smaller tins of tuna or ham can be added to rice or locally bought vegetables, and instant mashed potato and dried milk is a useful filler with a vegetable stew. Small packets of parmesan cheese are a wonderful addition to basic pastas.

Unless you are extremely lucky there will be times when you will be unable to cook anything hot because the weather, circumstances or fate conspire against you. On these occasions you will feel a whole lot better for having some provisions that can be turned into a cold meal. One of our great standbys was a tin of beans (the flageolet beans available in French supermarkets in West and central Africa are best, although kidney or haricot beans are also good), mixed with a tin of tuna in oil, lemon juice, fresh chopped onion or tomato if you have it, mustard and herbs.

## Storing food

Choose storage containers with care. Rough driving conditions will shake things around so much that jars will literally unscrew themselves, plastic lids will pop off, and tubes of tomato puree will puncture. You can minimise these nightmares by packing loose spaces with towels so things do not jump around so much, but it is also worth thinking about having the right containers in the first place.

Plastic jars and bottles with deep screw tops are best. Tupperware-style boxes should have very tight seals. Do not buy oil in a flip top bottle – it can get flipped just when you don't want it to. If you can't get oil with a screw top then transfer it to a safer jar. You are only likely to forget this once! Another good option is old tins with plastic sealing lids which can be washed out and used for storing things like sugar, tea and coffee.

Food storage boxes need to be kept reasonably clean. You'll know when it's time for a clean out. Fresh vegetables are best kept out of plastic bags, which make them sweat and start to rot. An open cardboard box is a good idea, or tie them up in a cloth local-style to keep them as dry as you can.

## Washing up

For washing up we used a square plastic bowl which doubled up as our personal washbasin. Washing-up liquid, a cloth and a scourer are the essentials. Some travellers wash their dishes in Milton (a gentle disinfectant), which we didn't find necessary. Giving all your dishes, cutlery and pots a good clean when hot water becomes available is sufficient to keep the germs at bay. If you are struggling to clean that burned-on mess at the bottom of the pan, use sand – it's the best scourer you could ever find.

A drying-up cloth is an option. We took one and used it regularly, but it does need frequent washing as it gets really filthy. Most travellers we met either left their dishes to dry or would flap them vigorously to dry them off. You will see a lot of organised tours doing this – usually to the amusement of others.

## PERSONAL EQUIPMENT

We have listed a few personal items that we found useful. Remember that overloading of a vehicle is easily done, so take care when making your choices.

## Clothes

Take as few as possible – you will not need much once you are on the road. You'll need warm clothing for nights in the desert and in the highlands and something to keep the rain out is also useful. Otherwise, lightweight cotton is the general rule. Dark and patterned fabrics don't show stains and rips.

You should also be aware of local dress customs. In some Islamic countries women in particular should take care – even the tops of your arms can be regarded as provocative. To make sure you are not offending anyone, look at what local people are wearing. Their reactions will soon let you know if you have crossed acceptable levels of modesty.

We found that taking one 'smart' item of clothing helped when having to deal with a very conservative embassy, as in Sudan, or even at a border crossing. With the amount of people you meet along the way you never know to where you might be invited.

**THE 'CLOTHES BOX'** *(for a couple travelling together)*

- two pairs of jeans
- five T-shirts
- two pairs of light cotton trousers
- one skirt
- one sleeveless dress
- one light cotton overshirt
- one pair of 'smart' trousers and shirt
- two swimming costumes
- two wraparound skirts (double up as a towel/sarong)
- light cotton scarf or shawl (useful against wind, dust, insects and sunburn)
- two sweatshirts
- two thick sweaters
- two woolly hats
- two pairs of hiking boots
- two pairs of sandals
- two raincoats
- socks and underwear

## Other items
### Short-wave radio
A short-wave radio with plenty of short-wave bands is great for picking up news both from home and on conditions in countries you may be visiting. It is a good idea to take something that is not fixed to the vehicle – both for security and portability.

### Camera
Photographic equipment and photography is discussed in detail on pages 88–9. In addition to your usual camera equipment we highly recommend taking a Polaroid camera, which can be of real help when wanting to take photos of people. If you first take a photo with a Polaroid and give them that photograph, more often than not, they will then be happy for you to take as many pictures as you wish with your usual camera. And the delight of adults and children alike as they watch the picture develop in front of their eyes is an added bonus.

### Fun and games
We found it quite useful to carry a variety of games with us, such as a pack of cards or backgammon, for those lonely nights in the middle of nowhere.

You will also find that it's loads of fun to get into the local games that are played on street corners. The most popular game throughout Africa is a kind of backgammon, most commonly known as *woaley*. It changes its name from country to country, however; other names it goes by are *awalé* in the Ivory Coast, *ayo* in Nigeria, *aju* in Togo and Benin, *ouri* in Senegal, and *aware* in Ghana. Rules of play also change slightly from country to country, so always ask locals before delving into the game.

### Pocket calculator
Useful for working out fuel consumption and exchange rates.

### Swiss army knife or Leatherman's knife
Either one will always come in handy.

### Hammock
This is a non-essential item, but one we would highly recommend. After a hard day's driving, if you are intending to stay a few days, there is nothing like stringing up the hammock and relaxing under the African sun.

### Gifts
It is quite amazing just how important a small supply of inexpensive gifts can be – particularly for children who are desperate to help you fill your jerry cans at wells, guard your vehicle, or give directions. On the other hand, you should never hand out gifts just for the sake of it. Constant handouts can mean that the local economy comes to depend on them, and later travellers will suffer because the same will be expected of them.

There will, however, be occasions when people have greatly helped you – either in deed or in material terms. This is particularly true for overlanders, who have far more than just a backpack to consider. Generosity can be thanked with a simple gift. We were often asked if we had anything from our home country. Wherever you are from, something small and personal always makes a valuable gift; for example anything with a Union Jack on it, from pens to postcards, is always welcomed. Other items we were often asked for were magazines or newspapers, ballpoint pens, cotton and needle (particularly in the Sahara for the local nomadic women), and recycled goods from your own supplies. Empty containers of any kind which can be used to carry water are highly sought after in many areas.

However, often your friendship and the chance to swap addresses can be the most appropriate response, but don't make promises you don't intend to keep.

## SPARES AND TOOLS
Working on your vehicle before you leave will give you some idea of what you are likely to need. Check through your workshop manual or talk to a friendly mechanic or off-road enthusiast to find out if you are missing something essential regarding spares and tools.

In many cases you will be able to limp along to the next big town where spares are available – but at an inflated price. In general, labour is cheap but parts are expensive – so it pays to be as well equipped as possible.

Too many heavy parts, like springs, are likely to damage your suspension. It is better to take more lightweight spares than you think you will need – like gaskets, oil seals or bearings – which can then be sold or exchanged for heavier parts.

Some places in Africa are better than others for picking up spares. The high cost of imported parts means second-hand spares will almost always be the only viable option. Even official dealers for your vehicle are not guaranteed to have what you need, although they will generally direct you to the best second-hand source. The hammering a vehicle takes on African roads means most sizeable towns have a second-hand yard that can either come up with what you need or with a good alternative.

## Spares

Deciding what spares to take with you is not easy. The decision is dependent on the make, model and age of your vehicle as well as the amount of space available in it. It is also a bit of a guessing game as you must try and think beforehand what might go wrong and what spares might be available locally en route.

If you have managed to use your vehicle on a few trips before you head off then you should have an idea of problems specific to your vehicle and take spares accordingly. You should also get advice from a good mechanic who may know of typical problems regarding the model and make of your vehicle. Always remember to take all your workshop manuals with you.

Before we left we had parts of our vehicle (an FJ45 Landcruiser with diesel engine and Ford transit top) replaced that were on their last legs or that we thought might break once on the road. These included the brake master-cylinder, water pump, fuel lift pump and engine mounts. We kept the old versions of everything that was replaced as an emergency spare.

Consider also consumable spares, ie: items you will have to replace as part of a service: oil filters, fuel filters, air filters, etc. Most consumable parts will be available in larger towns, but you may not get the brand you usually use and quality can vary greatly. We roughly calculated how many kilometres we were going to cover and brought sufficient filters, etc with us. As a bare minimum carry two or three of each type you require and try to replace them whenever you can. We also carried 20 litres of engine oil which gave us two oil changes, ie: one emergency change (broken sump) and one regular change.

The following is a list of suggested spares which should be tailored to your requirements.

### Consumable spares

- two oil filters
- two fuel filters
- two air filters
- engine oil (enough for two changes)
- 5 litres of gear box and differential oil
- grease
- 1 litre of brake and clutch fluid oil
- 2 litres of radiator coolant

### General spares

- glow plugs/spark plugs
- set of engine gaskets
- set of all oil seals
- set of wheel bearings
- set of engine mounts

### TIMING CHAINS

If you go for a vehicle that has a timing chain fitted, you should get it replaced before departure. Even if it is not causing you any problems before you set off, you could get into big trouble if it were to break while you are on the road.

- set of radiator hoses
- accelerator cable
- two fan belts
- set of brake pads
- brake master-cylinder rubbers
- water pump
- suspension rubbers and bushes
- condenser
- distributor cap
- spare fuel cap
- spare radiator cap
- contact breaker points
- light bulbs
- U bolts for leaf springs
- clutch plate
- fuses

### Useful bits and pieces

- funnel (make sure it fits the filler of your fuel tank and has a gauze filter)
- jubilee clips
- cable ties
- electrical tape
- electrical wires
- masking tape
- assortment of wire
- assortment of nuts, bolts and washers
- contact adhesive
- Pratly putty
- 2 metres of fuel hoses (long enough to be used as a siphon)
- flexible 'bathroom' sealant
- instant gasket paste
- exhaust repair putty
- gasket paper
- can of WD40 or Q20

## Tools

Ensure you pack a good and comprehensive set of tools. The tools required vary from vehicle to vehicle and many jobs need 'special service tools'.

However, there are general tools that will cover most jobs and with a bit of lateral thinking can be used in place of special service tools.

### Suggested list of tools
- a good set of spanners (imperial or metric as required by your vehicle)
- a good set of sockets with a power bar and ratchet
- assortment of screw drivers
- adjustable spanner
- mole wrench
- pipe wrench
- grease gun
- metal and rubber hammers
- torque wrench (essential for alloy engines)
- pliers
- circ clip removers
- multisize puller
- jumper leads
- set of feeler gauges
- hacksaw
- multi-meter electrical tester
- flat metal file
- small round file
- hand drill and bits (9V cordless drills can be connected directly to your battery)
- tyre levers
- tyre valve tool
- wet and dry sandpaper
- length of pipe (to extend your power bar for those stubborn nuts)

## CHOOSING A MOTORBIKE
### Alex Marr

For those prepared to sacrifice comfort and space, travelling by motorbike offers a very exciting alternative. Although frequently physically demanding, most bikes also give the traveller an unparalleled freedom to explore off-the-beaten-track Africa. A bike can cope in a number of situations that a 4X4 vehicle cannot. Whether crossing rivers by canoe, negotiating narrow, rocky climbs or simply weaving a line along a badly pot-holed road, two wheels beats four nearly every time.

Another factor, often overlooked, is that bikes are not perceived by locals as great symbols of wealth (unlike cars) and they tend to be friendlier as a result. It helps at checkpoints and border crossings too – there is something about turning up at a remote road control tired and dirty that generates a sort of sympathetic admiration in all but the most heartless of officials. Someone getting out of a shiny new Landcruiser is a lot more likely to be invited to participate in some underhand redistribution of wealth.

Of course, travelling by bike has its downside. It's hard to convince yourself it's a good way to travel if you get a puncture in a thunderstorm the day after you've had your tool-kit stolen. Also note that bikes are not allowed into any national parks in Africa and must be left behind while you make alternative arrangements.

## Which motorbike?

In virtually all of Africa a bike with some degree of off-road capability is essential. Two-stroke bikes are not suitable for long trips as they are generally small, impractical and unreliable. These days there is a myriad of four-stroke bikes which are given an 'off-road' label by the manufacturers. The degree of 'off-roadability' varies enormously, ranging from superlight enduro bikes (designed for racing), which can tackle virtually any terrain, to large twin-cylinder bikes which are given trendy off-road styling but are really more designed for touring in comfort in easy conditions. The large middle ground is made up by versatile 'trailbikes' offering varying degrees of compromise between comfort, features, weight and off-roadability.

(Just to confuse the issue, note that trailbikes are often called 'enduros' in Germany and are also sometimes referred to as 'dualsport bikes', particularly in America. What the British call enduro bikes – for competition use – tend to be called 'hard enduros' in Germany.)

Listed below is a (non-exhaustive) selection of models which a fairly adventurous traveller who is not content with sticking to the main roads could consider.

### Yamaha

The legendary reliability and unsophisticated engines of the XT500 and subsequently the XT600 meant Yamaha were the most popular overland bikes from the 1970s to the 1990s. The XT600 Tenere models, with their 27-litre tank and bullet-proof simplicity, were for a long time the bike to use in Africa. Now discontinued, they are rarer, but there are still those who would never use anything else. Unfortunately, finding decent second-hand models can be a problem. One big advantage of their popularity is that a number of XTs are still found in Africa, having been sold by overlanders at the end of their trips, and scavenging spares is a reasonable possibility.

The recent electric-start XT600E is heavy at 164kg (360lb) and not as popular. Heavier still is the XTZ660, a water-cooled single. The XTZ750 Super Tenere is Yamaha's twin-cylinder offering.

The TT range (250 and 600cc) are truer raw off-roaders than the XT, but are more limited in availability. They are a good choice but can be hard to find as they not imported officially into some countries like the UK.

Yamaha's WR400, which in 1998 revolutionised the 4-stroke competition scene, is a superlight bike, but as a high-revving out-and-out racer it is hardly designed with luggage carrying in mind – strengthening the rear subframe would be essential. It is an unlikely choice and definitely not suitable for those doing long distances on tarmac, but it may suit someone travelling light and regularly in very tough conditions.

## Honda

The Honda XR600, and since 1996 the XR400, are extremely robust off-roaders and utterly dependable. Offering the usual Honda high standard of quality, they are an excellent choice, with no frills – air cooled and no electric start, not even an ignition key. Comfortable they may not be, but they are built to last. Partly due to their use in desert rallies, a good range of accessories, such as large tanks, are available (see below).

The XR650L is a more street-legal version of the XR600 (but over 20kg/44lb) heavier) with a high seat that suits tall riders. The NX650 'Dominator' is slightly more road-oriented, but also a good candidate.

The all-new Honda XR650R replaced the XR600 in 2000. With an aluminium frame and compact engine, this is an incredibly light bike for the power it produces, weighing in at under 130kg (285lb). It looks to have all the makings of a good overlander but only time will tell if it is as reliable as its ancestor.

The Transalp and Africa Twin are comfortable, larger, twin-cylinder bikes, but due to their weight most people would consider them to be too cumbersome for a trans-Africa trip. Note they also have expensive fairings which would almost certainly not withstand the rigours of Africa travel.

## Suzuki

The long established DR350 and DR650, simple air- and oil-cooled machines, have their fair share of fans, the smaller version having a reasonably low seat and particularly popular with female riders. Unfortunately the 650 has a 17-inch rear tyre. The new DR400 was introduced in 2000, with a water-cooled motor which comes in both kick- and electric-start versions.

## Kawasaki

Not so frequently seen in Africa, the water-cooled KLX range (300 and 650cc) are very capable off-roaders, although, as with the DR, the larger model takes a 17-inch rear. The KLR650 is heavier and more road-oriented.

## KTM

The R640 'Adventure' is the closest you can get these days to a dedicated overlander's bike. With a 28-litre tank, twin tripmeters and options like side panniers, this bike is almost ready to go straight from the crate. However, they are expensive and there are question marks over engine vibrations and long-term reliability.

## BMW

The F650 'Funduro' is BMW's single-cylinder trailbike, but at close to 190kg (420lb) it is more at home on the road.

The GS series of large twin-cylinder bikes have been available throughout Africa for years. These creamy smooth, shaft-driven machines are a pleasure to ride on the road, but for most people their sheer weight makes them a real handful in tough-going terrain. Even so, the latest R1150GS is certainly marketed as a real off-road machine and the GSs will probably never lose their faithful band of supporters, who will continue to manhandle them around the continent for years to come. Needless to say they are not cheap and a massive range of equally expensive accessories is available from a number of German manufacturers (see pages 59–60).

## Checklist

Your choice of bike depends upon a number of factors:

- Your intended route. Generally speaking, the harder the terrain the more suitable a lighter bike will be. For example someone crossing central Africa in the rainy season would have a gruelling, if not impossible, time on an Africa Twin. At the other extreme, if you are going to be cruising around southern Africa, most of the time on tarmac roads, you may find a Honda XR400 slow and uncomfortable.
- Those short on leg-length will not enjoy the comparatively high seat of an XR650L. Also very important for those travelling alone in remote areas, you have to be able to pick the bike up on your own – and you have to be pretty strong to right a fully loaded Africa Twin lying on its side in a pile of mud. Try it before you go – if you can't manage it, get a smaller bike or get down to the gym!
- The availability of extra equipment, such as large tanks and luggage carriers. Yamaha XTs, Honda XRs and BMWs are the most popular overland bikes and so offer the best choice in this respect (see page 59).
- How much the standard bike has to be modified – especially important for those people short on time or not mechanically inclined.
- Your budget.

## MOTORBIKE PREPARATION

*Alex Marr*

Pre-trip preparation is the key to a successful time in Africa. Cutting corners at this stage is likely to result in problems en route and you can almost guarantee this will happen in the most remote and inconvenient places. As well as having a mechanically sound engine, considerable thought should be given to any peripheral items, such as mounting racks for luggage. These are the things that are going to break or cause problems.

Whatever bike you use, it goes without saying that it should be given a thorough mechanical overhaul before you leave. At the very least, you should start with new oil, filters (air, oil and fuel), spark plugs, chain, sprockets, tyres, inner tubes, brake pads and cables. Items which you know are going to get considerable wear, such as the clutch and the non-engine bearings (wheel, swingarm, steering) should be thoroughly checked. It would be prudent to fit new ones before you leave. Whether or not you go for a complete engine strip down depends on the age of the bike, how long you have owned it yourself and its general condition.

## Tools

It is a good idea at this stage to think about what tools you intend to take with you. With a view to keeping things as light as possible, select the smallest number of tools you think you will need on the trip and prepare the bike confining yourself to using only these tools. It will soon become obvious what you do and don't need.

## Bike modifications/additions

How you go about modifying the bike really depends on the length and intended route of your trip. When planning a trans-continental trip, for example, the following essential points need to be addressed:

### Fuel tank

Generally speaking the ideal fuel tank size is around 25–30 litres. This is a good compromise between not being overly heavy or bulky and giving a decent range, around 500–600km (300–380 miles) for most bikes. This will be sufficient in all but a few circumstances. Realistically you are more likely to be constrained by what large tanks are available for your particular bike. Companies like Acerbis (Italy), a leading developer and manufacturer of plastic components for all applications for major corporations or individuals involved in the motorcycle, sporting or industrial sector, make large plastic tanks for a wide range of off-road bikes, though most of them tend to be slightly small, in the 18–24-litre range. Acerbis Italia's website is www.acerbis.com. Contact details for distributors in the UK, South Africa, USA and Australia are as follows:

**Bert Harbins Racing (UK)** Unit 6, Townsend Centre, Houghton RE, Dunstable, Beds LU5 5JP, UK; tel: +44 1582 472374; fax: +44 1582 472379; emaiol: mail@bertharkinsracing.co.uk

**PRO Action KTM Husaberg (South Africa)** Cambridge Manor Office Park, Witkoppen Rd, Paulshof, Sandton, Johannesburg/Gauteng 2056, South Africa; tel: +27 11 807 8718; fax: +27 11 807 8717

**Acerbis USA** 13200 Gregg St, Poway, California 92064, USA; tel: (800) 659 1440 (free dial number) or +1 619 679 5220; fax: +1 619 679 3912

**Off Road Imports (Australia)** 4/17 Rob Place, Vineyard, NSW 2156, Australia; tel: +61 2 4577 7022; fax: +61 2 4577 7408; email: offroad@zeta.org.au

Some people try to fabricate their own tank, usually out of aluminium, but considerable skill and expense is required to produce a product of high enough quality.

It's worth pointing out that in areas where you actually need more fuel than this, such as certain parts of the Sahara, for safety reasons you are more than likely going to be travelling with at least one other vehicle (a 4X4 or truck) which will be able to carry extra fuel in jerry cans or plastic containers for you.

For a long trip in the desert you will also need a considerable amount of water, say 20 litres, which just adds to the difficulty of carrying fuel on your bike. If there is no extra vehicle and if you don't have jerry cans to carry extra fuel, you can usually find cheap plastic containers. They often break but

*Previous page* West African mask, Senegal

*Above* Tuareg making tea in the Sahara, near Timbuktu, Mali

*Right* Drummer on Gorée Island, Senegal

*Below* Muslim man in an alley in Lamu, the most traditional of Kenya's coastal towns

*Below right* Woman making dough-balls, Djenné market, Mali

*Above* Initiation ceremony, Senegal

*Left* Gabbra hut, Kenya

*Below left* Fishing market, M'Bour, Senegal

*Below right* Traditional dhow, Lamu, Kenya

*Above* Kokerboom after dusk, Kakamas,
Northern Cape, South Africa

*Right* Paintings inside Debre Birhan Selassie
Church, Gonder, Ethiopia

*Below* Zimbabwe Ruins (great enclosure)

should usually last until you can pour the fuel into your main tank. Another way is to use water 'bags', such as those made by Ortlieb. They are very resilient and are fine for carrying fuel for short periods – and of course they take up very little space when not in use.

## Hard luggage

There are essentially two ways of carrying your gear and the debate among experienced overlanders will continue forever about which is the better system! Hard luggage usually involves mounting hard aluminium side-boxes at the rear of the bike on to some sort of steel rack attached to the mainframe and subframe. This method is very popular in Germany and a number of companies manufacture the equipment (see pages 59–60).

Aluminium boxes have two big advantages over soft luggage: they are waterproof and they offer a much greater degree of security from theft. However, they are also heavy and unwieldy and annoyingly hard to mend if they break in a crash. You can find steel welders everywhere in Africa but specialist aluminium welders are rare. Over time, friction on the aluminium creates a dark-grey dust which means clothes and other sensitive items have to be kept covered.

## Soft luggage

Soft material side-panniers (Cordura, leather or similar) are also fitted at the rear side. Unless the contents are very light, they cannot just be thrown over – some sort of frame is needed to support the weight.

Much cheaper and lighter, soft luggage is most people's choice on a short trip. Actually, good-quality panniers are surprisingly hard wearing and provided they are well supported, should easily last a long trip. If damaged they can easily be repaired with stitching. The obvious disadvantages are that they get wet in the rain and it is easier for people to pinch things from them. It is also harder to access the contents easily through a single zip on the top.

Whatever method you choose, it is very important to keep the weight as low down and as between the axles as possible. If the bike's centre of gravity is too high or too far back it makes riding in difficult conditions, such as soft sand even harder.

For my long trip on an XR400, I settled on a compromise of soft panniers at the sides and a small, lockable, 100% waterproof, aluminium topbox for camera, films, important documents, etc. This was designed so a spare rear tyre could fit perfectly around it. I had a waterproof Sealine drybag for camping gear sitting across the rear seat and panniers. I found this system worked very well – the key was fabricating a very strong steel framework which provided support and transferred a lot of the weight onto the mainframe. It also meant I could strap a 10-litre jerry can under either pannier. The non-waterproof factor was not such a problem – I generally tried to avoid rainy seasons, but when it was wet I kept my clothes in dustbin liners. Maybe I was just lucky, but I never found security a big issue: in 23 African countries I never had anything stolen.

Within the luggage, it is important to protect all your belongings from the constant vibrations they will receive – most things can be neatly stored in small tupperware boxes and clothes within plastic bags. Apart from the main luggage, lightweight items can also be secured in front of the headlight.

Most riders also carry either a tankbag or a small rucksack for essential items which need to be accessed quickly.

## Tyres

One important point to realise is that trailbikes which take anything other than a 53cm (21in) front and a 45cm (18in) rear tyre will have a restricted choice.

On a long trip, tyre choice requires careful thought, mainly because sourcing decent tyres in Africa is a perennial headache. Apart from in some places in southern Africa, finding decent tyres is not easy. Tyres are always available in big cities but they tend to be very thin (for 125cc bikes) and some of them look like they would melt if you went over 40km/h (25mph). With a bit of persistence you can usually find something, but in West and Central Africa, generally speaking, it is very difficult.

Ultra-knobbly motocross tyres offer the best grip in rough terrain, but they are not really practical because of their very limited life, particularly when ridden on tarmac, which is more often than you think. A better choice in tough conditions are tyres like Michelin Desert, Pirelli MT21 or Metzeler Karoo. They have much harder-wearing knobbles which are spaced closer together and consequently have a much longer life, although they still wear fast on the road.

More versatile 'trail tyres' – such as Metzeler Sahara, Avon Gripster and Dunlop Trailmax – with a broader, shallower tread pattern, are generally a good compromise, offering a longer life and an acceptable amount of grip in sandy or stony conditions – they are not so good in mud, however.

For those entering north Africa and crossing the Sahara, it is best to leave southern Europe with a pair of new Michelin Desert tyres and to carry a spare at the rear, space permitting.

## Miscellaneous

Other essential modifications are:

- A bash plate, to protect the crankcase from flying stones.
- Rim locks (or security bolts) which prevent tyres creeping round the rim at low pressure settings used in soft sand.
- An O-ring (or X-ring) chain. Stronger than normal chains, the inside of the links is constantly lubricated, increasing longevity.
- Good-quality handguards (such as Acerbis) which protect your levers in a fall.
- A fuel filter, if your bike doesn't have one

Desirable modifications include:

- Fitting an oil-temperature gauge, and for those bikes with a small oil-cooler (or none at all) replacing it with a larger unit.

## TOOLS AND SPARES LIST

- spare rear tyre
- front and rear heavy-duty inner tubes
- good-quality puncture repair kit with lots of patches
- small mountain bike pump
- a few spare spokes
- connecting links for chain
- clutch lever
- brake lever
- clutch cable
- throttle cable(s)
- air filter
- three oil filters
- fuel filter
- two spark plugs
- fuel hose and jubilee clips
- bulbs and fuses
- electrical wire and connectors
- assorted nuts, bolts and washers
- main gaskets
- duct tape
- assorted cable ties (lots)
- spare bungee rope/straps
- instant gasket
- silicon sealant
- epoxy glue
- liquid steel
- Loctite (for nut threads)
- small tub of grease
- about 1 litre of engine oil (for top up and oiling air filter)
- standard small toolkit (combination spanners, $^3/_8$ inch drive ratchet + relevant sockets, screwdrivers)
- Leatherman's or Swiss army knife
- feeler gauges
- file
- spark plug spanner
- tyre levers
- repair manual

- For those who intend using a GPS (geographical positioning system), some sort of mounting bracket on the handlebars is necessary.
- Bland looks. The less new and shiny a bike looks, the better. Removing stickers from new bikes helps.

## Spare parts

For those who have never travelled in Africa, one of the problems is not knowing in advance what spares you are likely to be able to pick up on the way. Generally speaking very little is available for large bikes north of South Africa. In some large capitals you may find basic items, like oil filters, for popular models, but not much more – there simply isn't the demand. In the more westernised capitals like Harare, Windhoek and Nairobi (and most of South Africa) you will find more choice, especially non-model-specific items such as tyres and chains.

What spares you take with you is a compromise between trying to cover all eventualities (the wrong approach) and taking as little as you can get away with (the right one). Only take what there is a good chance you will probably need. This may sound naïvely optimistic, but it is really a case of logical risk evaluation. If you have a fundamentally good bike, well prepared and properly looked after, it is pretty unlikely that anything seriously mechanical will go wrong – and if it does, how can you possibly know what it is going to be and plan for it? If the worst does happen in the middle of nowhere, you will be able to get your bike to the nearest town eventually – although it may require hiring help and will take a while – where you can try to repair it. You may need the right spares to be couriered out from your home country and you should be able to convince customs that, as you'll be exporting the spares again as part of your bike, you should not have to pay any duty. It is a good idea to have some arrangement set up in advance with your local dealer back home in case this is required.

Much more likely problems concern luggage carriers etc, so lots of bodge-it items such as glue, duct tape and plenty of cable ties are invaluable for temporary repairs.

## Clothing

Choice of riding gear is yet another compromise – protection versus practicality. While some degree of protection against a crash is essential, don't underestimate the amount of time you'll be off the bike, walking around villages or cities. A strong cordura enduro jacket with built in shoulder- and elbowpads is a good choice. A simple spine protector with a waistband provides back support and protection without being too restrictive or uncomfortable.

Most riders use full-length motocross-style boots – an excellent safety measure – although some people find them too cumbersome when not actually riding and prefer the flexibility of normal strong walking boots which cover the ankle. This is a something of a risk given how vulnerable feet and legs are in the event of a crash, but again it boils down to personal preference.

As with the bike, the blander you look the better – unfortunately nearly all off-road gear these days is distinctly unbland.

## Helmet

Off-road style helmets with a peak and requiring goggles (which are easily lost) are best in dusty conditions, but normal road helmets are usually more comfortable and offer better all-round vision, though the visor can become scratched after a while.

## Camping

### Tents

A lightweight tent, sleeping bag and mosquito net are essential. Some sort of mattress is highly desirable. Thermarest make one which can be packed to an incredibly small size.

### Stove

A high-quality petrol stove (such as MSR) is the most practical way to cook.

### Water

A camelback-style water system (a hose coming from a 'bladder' on your back) can be very useful when you need to drink often in hot and difficult conditions.

A filter bag (made of a material such as Millbank cloth) is the most space-economic method of filtering.

## Personal items
Clothes, hygiene, books, etc are of course subjective things, but it is really a question of common sense based on the available space. Most people take far too much at the start of a long trip. A good general rule is to sort out what you would like to take with you and then halve it.

## Further information
### Books
*Adventure Motorcycling Handbook* by Chris Scott
*Afrika-Motorrad-Reisen* by Bernd Tesch, a German biker who has ridden right across Africa on several occasions, and has his own website (see below).
*Desert Biking* by Chris Scott

### Magazines
*Trailbike and Enduro Magazine* (TBM) A UK-based monthly publication with up-to-date information on the latest trailbikes. For information and subscriptions, tel/fax: 080 8840 4760.

### Websites
A mass of enlightening information is available from the following websites (and their links), dedicated to overland motorcycle travel:

www.adventure-motorcycling.com
www.berndtesch.de
www.horizonsunlimited.com

### For luggage and accessories
www.acerbis.com
www.touratech.de
www.wunderlich.de
www.xr-only.com

## BICYCLE SELECTION AND PREPARATION
*David Mozer of Bicycle Africa Tours*
## Types of bicycle
Most people cycling across Africa use mountain bikes, although some do still prefer tourers, and hybrid (or cross-bikes) are also possibilities.

I have a preference for mountain bikes (MTBs) over touring bikes for most excursions in Africa. The MTB is versatile, durable, stable and the disadvantages are few. I have found that once the bike is loaded with gear, a couple of extra kilograms in the frame are immaterial. The tyres and wheels are probably more of a factor, because that is where you'll find a lot of the extra weight. But for most excursions in Africa you won't want to give up the fat tyres.

In my opinion the hybrids, or cross-bikes, are crossed the wrong way. Instead of narrow tyres and straight bars, I would select fat tyres and drop bars as a better cross. The fat tyres increase stability and the drop bars increase control and the number of hand positions, as well as reduce wind resistance. This is especially useful if you know you will be doing some big mileage on paved roads, but also some challenging terrain on dirt roads. With narrow tyres you loose stability. The straight bar also tends to raise the centre of gravity, which further diminishes control. If you are looking for less rolling resistance and straight bars, put narrower tyres on an MTB.

If you already have an MTB and want to increase your grip options, two come to mind. Get some bar extenders (there is quite a wide variety available), or replace the whole handlebar assembly with the set-up you prefer. I have put drop-bars on an MTB with good results.

There are many good mountain bikes on the market and the choice comes down to personal preference. Though their names are different, many are made in the same factory, with the same inputs. Basically you get what you pay for. A rule of thumb is to pay enough to get what you feel you need.

## Preparing your bicycle
### Frames
In addition to the geometry and size of the frame, there are other important factors: the size (diameter and thickness) of tubing; the quality of workmanship; the kind of metal; and the size of wheel that the frame uses. Many of these factors play more of a role in how comfortable the bicycle is to ride than how durable it is under normal use. Under normal conditions there is little or no performance difference between frames with high top tubes (men's bikes) and slanted top tubes (women's bikes).

Generally, new models have more efficient frame geometry than older bikes. Once you have the right style you probably won't have to worry too much about the specifics of the frame angles. In considering the kind, size and quality of the tubing, it is not necessary to get sucked too far up-market. Low-end bicycles, above the lower mass-market levels, simply don't fall apart very often.

Our advice is to not overlook the cost effectiveness and advantages of the solid US$300 bike with a frame of a weldable metal (chrome-moly steel). In the unlikely event that it should break, you usually don't have to go far to find someone who can fix it in some fashion. I have seen steel frames brazed over a blacksmith's bed of coals! On the other hand be wary of expensive frames made of materials or assembled with adhesive that might be weakened by vibration. I have seen expensive bikes shake apart even on 'paved' roads. Aluminium frames have the same problem of being difficult to repair if they break in a remote areas.

An important variable dictated by the frame is wheel and tyre size. Not all frames use the same size of wheel and not all wheels have the same selection of tyres. For remote areas consider a frame with a wheel that takes a sturdy tyre.

Collectively, in terms of geometry, tubing, tyre availability and workmanship, this suggests a modest MTB as a starting point.

## Size

A bicycle that is too big or too small for the user can be a safety hazard. Bicycles are sized, in inches or centimetres, by the measurement along the seat tube from the top tube to the bottom bracket (theoretically, it varies by brand). The final determination of a safe size comes when the bicyclist straddles the top tube, stands with both feet flat on the ground, and checks the clearance between the top tube and his/her crotch. The recommended clearance depends on the type of riding you will be doing – 3–5cm (1–2in) for road riding and double that for off-road riding. Your crotch and 7.5cm (3in) below it is a fixed distance above the ground, but because the bottom bracket isn't the same distance above the ground on all bicycles and 'sizing' varies by brand, the 'right size' may be different from bicycle to bicycle. Typically, people use MTBs 5–10cm (2–3in) smaller than they use touring bicycles.

## Speeds

Once upon a time there were only one-speed bikes, then there were 3 speeds, and that expanded to 5, 10, 12, 15, 18, 21, 24 and 27 speeds. Is there a difference? Sometimes. Is it important? Sometimes. Between 1, 3, 5, 10 and 15 speeds there are functional differences that can be important. In a flat area, with short trip distances and no loads, a one-speed might be sufficient and cost effective. In hilly terrain, on rough roads, over long distances and/or when hauling a load, 15 speeds are advantageous. Each additional chainring (front gear) you combine with a basic five-gear freewheel cluster (the rear gears) creates a substantial increase in range of gear ratios. It's the 'range' that is important! The same is not true for changing from a 5-, 6-, 7- or 8-gear freewheel. The incremental difference between speeds is smaller, but the range is usually unchanged. At the efficiency level that most people ride, the benefits from reducing increments between gears is not measurable. In fact, the fancy freewheels can cause new problems.

## Freewheels, hubs and axles

There are two systems for attaching the gears to the rear hub; traditional threaded freewheel units which screw on to the hub, and rear hubs with built-in freehub mechanisms that use cog cassettes. These are not interchangeable. To change from one system to the other you must change the hub, which requires rebuilding the entire wheel. In terms of remote area maintenance, the main significance of this is on the rear axle. Mountain bike rear hubs with screw-on freewheels generally use an axle similar to those on Chinese bicycles (and local knockoffs) found around the world. If you break this axle you can get a replacement axle almost anywhere. Good luck finding an axle for a freehub. If your freewheel should self-destruct you are more likely to be able to find a fill-in freewheel than cog cassettes.

Traditional hubs are available with solid nutted axles or hollow quick-release axles. Unless you need to take a wheel off frequently, solid axles are an economical and practical choice. Hollow axles can be replaced with solid axles and vice-versa.

Hub bearings can be loose or sealed. Loose bearings may require adjusting (use standard size bearings) and can be serviced and rebuilt easily with a set of cone wrenches. Sealed bearing hubs are difficult to service and require special parts and tools.

### Protecting freewheels and hubs from dust, grit and rain

Usually the manufacturer's instructions tell you to lubricate most of the ball bearings on a bicycle (the headset, bottom bracket and hubs) with grease, but lubricate the freewheel with light machine oil. In some extreme climates and cycling conditions it also may be practical to protect the bearings in your freewheel by packing them with grease.

If you are cycling in conditions where dust or a lot of water are likely to get into the freewheel you should consider packing your freewheel with grease. This is done by screwing a fitting (freewheel grease injector, US$25) on to the back of the freewheel. It has an 'O' ring so it seals against the back. You then use a grease gun to pump grease into the injector. The injector directs the grease into the freewheel. When the chamber of the freewheel is full, grease will begin to come out of the front of the freewheel.

Problems can be created from doing this, so care is necessary. (This could be more of a problem when installing the grease in a cold climate. We have never had a problem during any of our activities in the tropics.) First a description of a freewheel: a traditional freewheel is essentially two frustums (cones with the top cut off by a plane parallel to the base), one nested in the other. There is a race and a ring of ball bearings at each end of the frustums to keep the two pieces evenly spaced and able to rotate independently. The outer frustum is grooved and threaded on the outside to support the gears and the inside is notched all the way around. The inside frustum screws on to the rear hub and has spring-loaded teeth sticking out of it. The springs are very small and not particularly strong. When a bicycle is coasting the teeth slip over the notches and creates the familiar clicking sound. When the bike is pedalled the notches come up to the teeth and engage them, pulling the rear wheel along.

When you pack a freewheel the entire space between the frustums is filled with grease. As you ride the bike the bearings and the teeth carve out a path for themselves within the chamber of grease. Within their 'chambers' they are protected from dust and moisture. The potential problem lies in the strength of the small springs behind the teeth and the stiffness of the grease. If the grease is too stiff the teeth may not extend fully and may break off. You need to use a soft grease in the freewheel and start off coasting and riding easily after you pack the bearings. It will help if you do the process in warm weather.

On hubs (usually older) where the dust cap doesn't rotate with the axle, you can keep foreign material out of your bearings by wrapping the exposed part of the cone with a pipe cleaner and then twisting the two ends back on each other so that it fits snugly. This technique can also be used on the bottom bracket.

## Chains

It used to be that all chains more or less fitted all bicycles. No longer! The new 7-speed freewheels require narrower chains, and some of these chains require their own special tools, replacement rivets and service techniques for maintenance and repair. The high-tech chains are hard to repair if they fail on the road. Unless you have a certified mechanic working on your bike you may want to stay away from some of the advanced technology. You will maintain more options if you stay with 5- or 6-cog freewheels and the standard chains that fit these assemblies.

An ongoing concern for chains is lubrication. Africa is dusty. If you over-oil your chain will get caked up. And once you get into the desert you will have to run dry as oil quickly attracts sand and this will destroy even the very best equipment.

## Derailleurs

Derailleurs are now built to close tolerances so that a specific movement of the shiftlever moves the derailleur to a specific gear (indexing). To use this system the derailleur and shifter have to be matched. Generally, most models of derailleurs from one manufacturer are interchangeable. The main differences between the derailleurs within one manufacturer are weight, price and quality. As the weight goes down the price goes up. But a higher price doesn't necessarily mean better quality. Grams are shaved by using more plastic or alloy metals, but this can also compromise strength. Generally at the level of performance at which MTBs are ridden a few ounces of weight is not as important as durability. Unless you are certain of their durability, derailleurs with plastic parts should be avoided. For remote locations, a high-quality, all metal derailleur can be sufficient and is preferable. To continue to use an index system, any replacements should be the same brand as the original equipment. Whatever you use, if you go far enough on bad roads it will take a beating.

## Gear shifters

For years gear shifters have been disks with a lever sticking out. The shift lever rotates through a continuous range of settings. To shift gears the user moves the lever to the desired setting and the disk stays in place by friction. Any shifter would work with any derailleur. Engineers have now calculated the distance the disk needs to rotate for a specific derailleur to shift gears and have put stops (indexing) at these locations on the shifters. As long as the index systems continued to use over-the-bar shifters with both 'index' and 'friction' modes, even if the system came out of calibration from cable stretch or some other reason, you could switch to friction mode and things would work. Even if you needed to replace the derailleur with an incompatible model, you could move a lever, release the indexing, return to the friction system and continue on your way.

The world is no longer as interchangeable. The latest 'advance' is grip shifters which twist, and two-lever, under-bar ratchet systems (eg: 'rapid-fire' or 'express-shifting'). Just push a lever to ratchet up a gear, push another lever to release down a gear. Neither system offers a friction option. To work, the systems must be calibrated. If the derailleur breaks and you can't get a compatible replacement the shifter is useless. Furthermore, the shifters are virtually impossible to repair. The best thing about a broken ratchet shifter is the opportunity to replace it with a dual-mode, over-the-bar shifter. 'Grip shifters' don't protrude out from the handlebars as far and have fewer moving parts to jam and break, so they are less prone to malfunction. But they are still single mode. If you are selecting a new bike, shifting systems with a friction mode alternative are highly recommended. Short of this, grip shifters are the choice.

## Bottom brackets

The bottom bracket is the mechanism inside the frame, between the two crank arms that hold the pedals. There are bottom brackets with sealed bearings and bottom brackets with free-bearings. The former is more expensive and harder to service. In contrast, the latter can be serviced world-wide and the bearings are available in many remote areas, assuming there are bicycles in the area.

## Brakes

It is said that a bicycle will always stop – brakes just let you determine where. If you want that choice, choose your brakes carefully. The heavier the loads and the more downhill, the stronger the brakes need to be. Among the strongest type of brakes are cantilever, v-brakes, u-brakes, roller-cam and drum brakes.

Drum brakes are expensive and usually found only on tandems. V-brakes, u-brakes and roller-cam brakes have tended to be problematic and clog with mud very fast under those conditions. The most cost-effective brakes on the market today are cantilever brakes. The simplest designs use a standard brake cable from the brake lever to the cable hanger between the brakes. Standard brake cables are widely available. The more unique part of cantilever brakes is the way the two sides are connected. The simplest use a straddle-cable between the brakes, with a fixed anchor at one end and an adjustable cable-pinching plate on the other. These can be repaired with a short piece of standard brake cable.

## Wheels and spokes

There are alloy rims and steel rims. Alloy rims are more effective when wet, easier to keep true and easier to tap dents out of, but they dent easier. Steel rims are strong, but they are dangerous in wet weather and when they start having problems they can be tough to get true.

Spokes are available in different gauges. The standard ones are 15g spokes, but 14g spokes are stronger. Double butted 14/15/14 spokes are strong and light. The preferred material for spokes is stainless steel.

## Tyres

One of the major features of MTBs is their durable wheels and tyres. The wheel is a small diameter and the rim is wider, so they are stronger, more trouble free and more stable than comparable touring bike wheels. The beefy tyres on MTBs are also relatively trouble free and if properly inflated they are very effective at protecting the rims from dents. The wider the tyre the higher the rolling resistance, so if you will be doing a lot of riding on smooth roads this is a drawback. If you will be cycling on both paved and unpaved surfaces, consider combination knobby tyres with a solid raised centre bead. The centre bead makes easier rolling on paved roads and the knobby tread will help you in the dirt.

Though the supply line for good tyres may be long, the longer life, less down time and additional versatility usually make them a good choice. MTB tyres are becoming more widely available in Africa's large cities. With a little planning ahead it is not hard to keep a sufficient number of spares on hand.

The price bears very little relation to suitability. Cheaper, gum-walled tyres can be better than skin walls at taking the weight on bad roads. On desert pistes deflate your tyres so they bulge, increasing the surface area in contact with the ground. Skin walls invariably split under this kind of treatment. Tyres with little tread proved to be the best at sitting on top of the sand – Chan Sheng and Michelin road tyres are particularly good.

### Inner tubes

Inner tubes can be made out of a variety of materials and there are at least three types of valves. Airless tubes are also available. The construction material of pneumatic tubes may affect its puncture resistance and will determine what type of glue and patches you need to repair a puncture. The most common inner tube material is butyl rubber, which can be repaired with the glue and patches found in patch kits around the world.

'Thornproof' tubes are probably better labelled 'puncture resistant.' They are usually two to six times as expensive as regular tubes. Puncture-resistant tubes can be made of extra thick butyl rubber, or of totally different materials, such as polyurethane plastic. When this punctures it requires its own special patch kit (twice as expensive as kits for butyl tubes). Combination latex/butyl tubes are an expensive hybrid (eight times the price of regular butyl) that can be patched with a standard patch kit.

Puncture-resistant tubes may be of the greatest advantage where there is a lot of glass or short, sharp objects on the road. If there are no sharp objects on the route all tubes are about equal. If you have long thorns to contend with, the best thing to do is avoid them!

Automobile tyres and tubes and most US bicycles use a 'schraeder valve'. European cyclists often use a 'presta valve'. The Chinese bikes use a third type of valve. One solution to the valve issue is to make sure that every bicycle has a pump that fits the valve of the tubes on that bicycle. A little more coverage can be gained by using one of the pumps that can be switched from schraeder to presta. If schraeder valves are used, make sure that every pump for automobiles can also be used to inflate the bicycle's tyres.

Airless tubes solve some problems, but they offer a harsher ride, are six to ten times as expensive as regular tubes, at least twice as heavy, have twice the rolling resistance and don't carry heavy loads well. It is still probably most practical, for remote sites, to use butyl compound tubes that are repairable.

## Tube protectors

Some people praise tube protector strips. I know of several cases where the edge of the strips wore a line of holes in the tube, causing unrepairable punctures. For off-pavement riding, there is no final decision on the effectiveness of protective strips. I have never used them in Africa and have only rarely had problems with a flat that I think a tube protector would have prevented.

## Pedals and toe-clips

If you are likely to be dismounting in dirt (anything from dust to mud) it is best to stay away from any pedals that have hardware on the bottom of your shoes that can clog. This pretty much eliminates cleats and clipless pedals. Conventional pedals give you the flexibility to use multipurpose shoes, which cut down on the number of pairs of shoes you will have to pack.

You can gain some efficiency as you pedal by using toe-clips. If you are trying them for the first time, or don't have a high level of confidence, don't tighten the straps initially nor when you are in urban traffic, sand, mud, rocks and other technical situations.

## Saddles

You are going to have an intimate relationship with your saddle – get one that is comfortable. Those that are too narrow or too wide may not support your pelvic bones properly or comfortably. Spring saddles will have you bouncing about all day. Gushy soft and rock hard can also leave you constantly searching for a comfortable way to sit. If you are not used to riding a bike, almost any saddle will leave you sore to begin with. Gel covers on saddles help to reduce saddle soreness, along with a comprehensive application of Vaseline or something similar over the relevant parts of your body!

The angle of the seat and what you wear also play a role in saddle comfort. Thick seams and bunched clothing between you and your saddle quickly take their toll. Wear padded cycling shorts, which are designed to be worn without underwear.

## Accessories

The best advice on accessories is, be sure they are strong enough to take the beating they are sure to get. And, attach them securely. If accessories fail while in use it may not be fatal, but it can be very frustrating. Buy equipment that is properly designed and sufficiently durable for its intended use. One way to minimise lost screws is to apply Loctite (medium strength) or tyre patch cement to the threads before bolting on racks and cages.

## Racks and packs

Do not carry anything on your back in a rucksack or backpack. Your back will ache very quickly and you will overheat sooner. Even water packs can be a problem for some people, though they have their advocates. Waistpacks (bumbags) are more manageable, but can still be annoying. I like the versatility of a waistpack, but rig it to handlebars while I am riding.

To carry large loads you need a sturdy rack and saddlebags (panniers). Racks and packs can wear fast and screws loosen quickly when rattled about on a daily basis. Choose racks and packs that are sturdy and stable enough to handle the conditions they will be subjected to. The weak points on racks tend to be the welds and eyelets. The weak points on panniers tend to be where the hooks screw into the backing.

Bicycles travel best if the weight of any load is distributed evenly and kept low. Four slim packs, two front and two rear, are better than two giant bulging ones. If you are travelling with only a moderate amount of baggage (say 10kg/22lb) you can get by with just a rear rack and medium-size panniers on each side. If the weight is too heavy in the rear the front wheel becomes hard to handle and you will expend extra energy trying to keep the bike under control. For heavy loads split the weight between front and rear.

There are two choices for strength with lighter weights: racks made with aluminium rod or with steel alloy tubing. I have seen a lot of aluminium racks break and they tend to be hard to fix. I have never seen a steel alloy tubing rack break, though if it did it would be easier to get it repaired.

The best mount is to screw the rack directly onto the frame. Look for a frame with rack braze-ons on the seat-stays and threaded eyelets on the axle drop-outs. If you anticipate riding on roads, trails or streambeds with high rocks or roots DO NOT USE low-rider racks. Low-riders will give your packs more of a beating than on racks that hold them higher. And if one of those rocks or roots gets hold of your pannier you may take a beating as well.

If you will be travelling on rough roads, it is preferable that the attaching system for the packs consists of strong hooks and non-stretch webbing straps with buckles or Velcro fasteners. Packs with suspension systems that rely solely on elastic cords and springs can bounce off when you hit bumps and potholes. Similar advice applies for attaching articles to the top of the rack: you will have more flexibility and fewer problems if you use non-elastic nylon webbing straps with buckles instead of elastic straps, shock cords or bungee cords. Webbing is also lighter.

Handlebar bags, frame packs or waistpacks are not essential, but they are very convenient for cameras, snacks, sun lotion, notepads, etc. As they sit so high, you don't want to carry too much weight in a handlebar bag.

The advice on water bottle cages is the same as for racks – they should be sturdy enough to handle the conditions they will be subjected to. It's best if they mount into braze-ons on the frame.

### Fenders and kickstands

Fenders and kickstands can be more of a disadvantage than an advantage: on trains, planes, buses and during the course of a normal day, fenders get knocked out of alignment. They are inconvenient to detach, reattach and keep adjusted. In dry weather they keep a little sand off the chain. In rain they will keep you happy and stop the chain from being washed, but if you ride off paved roads, they can quickly clog with mud and become a major aggravation.

If you have a rear rack, a less fragile (although less thorough) protection is available from snap-on commercial products which can be fitted to the top of the rack. Alternatively, you can improvise by cutting up a 1.5-litre water bottle and taping it on to the racks to provide a splash guard which keeps body, drive train and baggage drier.

The disadvantage of kickstands is thay they are often not designed to support the weight of a loaded touring bike. If your bike is going to be fully loaded most of the time most kickstands are not worth the bother.

## Mirrors

Rear-view mirrors are not a substitute for good cycling technique, but they are useful. They tend to lead a rough life on tour. Whether they are attached to the handlebar, helmets or glasses, they tend to good bashing and have a short life span.

## Lights

Every effort should be made to stay off the roads at night. A disproportionate number of accidents happen at night, and they are often fatal. If you have to be on the road after dark, lights and reflectors are essential. Plan ahead for your lighting system. If you don't expect to be riding at night much, you won't need a particularly elaborate system.

There is a choice of four kinds of power source. In ascending order of initial cost, they are: battery, generator, rechargeable battery, and combo generator/rechargeable battery. Prices can range from US$2 to US$100. Your budget, location and pattern of use will dictate which is the best system for you.

A versatile solution is to use a headlamp. These strap around your helmet or head and provide hands-free light on or off the bike. If you decide on battery power, choose a model that uses batteries that are easily replaced ('D' is most common world-wide). Remember that rechargeable batteries need an electrical current or a solar cell to recharge.

## Locks

It seems that the further you are from the New York cities of the world, the less sophisticated the bike thieves, the rarer the bolt cutters and the less need there is for heavy locks and chains. While on tour, my bike is usually loaded and conspicuous, securely stored at the hotel, or left for only a few minutes while I run an errand. In the latter cases I lock it. I use a rather ordinary lock and long cable. The long cable is attached to a fixed object to prevent snatch-and-ride.

## Tools and spare parts

To fully enjoy the self-sufficiency and independence that a bicycle can provide, you need to carry a few tools and spare parts. They do not add much weight and could prevent you from having to push your bike on a long walk or having a long wait for a taxi. Select the tools and spare parts you need to do basic adjustments and maintenance on your bicycle and any special tools if your bicycle has esoteric components.

For a long solo trip, or any kind of group trip when supply lines could be long, bring enough tools and spare parts to be able to completely overhaul your bike and repair everything, short of a broken frame or rim. Essentially turn yourself into a mini-portable bike shop! If you are in a group of fewer than ten, usually only one set of these tools needs to be brought on a trip. The group leader or their designate is responsible for organising this kit, and other participants need not worry about these items.

If you should need a spare part or tool sent to you in an emergency, DHL and other worldwide package services are now available in most African capitals and many other major African cities. You will need a contact back home who can buy a replacement part and send it out via courier. Unfortunately, the shipping is not cheap.

## Water
Dehydration can hit very quickly. Feeling thirsty is not a good indication, you could well be in serious trouble already. Basically there is no substitute for drinking plenty of water in a timely manner.

### Water bottles
It is essential to take a water bottle on every trip. In hot weather you will be drinking a litre of water or more every 15km (10 miles.) For long trips you need a large water supply, such as water bags. Be sure you have sufficient water capacity for the kind of travel you plan. Safe drinking water is getting increasingly available in Africa, but it is still problematic. It is also possible that some areas have no water during the dry seasons. Even when there is water you may find the pump you expect to use is broken.

A tip is to use white-coloured water bottles as the water inside doesn't heat up quite as much.

### Water purification
A heavy, relatively expensive and high-tech option is to carry a filtering water pump. There are several brands of differing quality available, priced from US$30 to US$200. If you don't have a filter and are out of water, a few water purification tablets can save your life. Carry a few on every trip. I don't like to rely on water purification tablets because they can 'purify' your system the same way that they purify the water – some of the organisms they kill are beneficial. You don't want a purified intestinal track.

## Food and cooking utensils
Even if you start the day with a good breakfast and full of energy, as the day goes on you will burn it up. If you do not eat again, the calories will be consumed and you will reach a state of hypoglycaemia, or low blood sugar. It can hit you very quickly and leave you dead in your tracks. On any trip have extra food with you at all times. It needs to provide not just quick, but also sustainable energy. Breads, local pastries, biscuits and bananas are widely available and are good choices. You should carry emergency packets of dried

food for times of need. The dehydrated meals available from camping and outdoor shops are expensive, none too generous in size and do not offer much in the way of choice, so unless you are rich with a small appetite and not particularly interested in food, you will have to look at alternatives. Good buys, particularly if weight is a problem, are packet soups, packets of instant Chinese noodles and other dried 'instant' food.

There's a wide range of lightweight billycan sets, though if you go for collapsible pots and pans pay particular attention to handles and how they clip or hook on. If some plastic slot-on handles chip you will never get them to stay put again.

## Personal equipment
### Helmets and gloves
Many sports present a risk of head injury. Bicycling definitely has this hazard and warrants precaution. Scrapes and broken bones heal, but scrambled brains may not. Helmets won't prevent an accident but they can reduce the severity of the consequence. Compared to the lifetime cost of a head injury or even death, the cost of wearing a helmet is small. I know of several crashes in remote locations of Africa where the cyclist's helmet took a hard hit and the cyclist rode on. None of these cases involved an automobile.

In sun a helmet also serves to protect your head, which significantly reduces fatigue.

The value of gloves is similar to that of a helmet. Gloves don't prevent accidents but they can reduce injuries, such as the amount of gravel embedded in your palms. They are also invaluable in reducing road vibration.

### Clothing
On extended tours all clothing – and bodies – get really filthy as there can be a long time between washing opportunities. Perhaps the hardest aspect of travelling by bike is going for two weeks at a time without a decent wash – sweating every day in the same smelly clothes. As the trip progresses, it is easy to get increasingly sloppy about things, for example cycling in flip-flops after shoes become too smelly and start falling apart. Leather gloves get forgotten for the same reasons.

In choosing your clothes consider comfort, visibility and social standards. You can never make yourself too visible as a cyclist. Brightly coloured cotton T-shirts work well. Special cycling shorts have padding in the crotch, relatively long legs and no heavy inseams. Leather in cycling shorts is less durable than shorts with towelling or synthetic material.

If you are going to be cycling at dawn, dusk or at night, an oversize, long-sleeved white shirt is an excellent item. It can be slipped on over anything and does not take up much space. A long-sleeved shirt also doubles during the day as protection from the sun. By covering your arms, you will reduce the amount of moisture you lose (for more information see *Chapter 7, Health*). Worn separately or together, a medium-weight sweater (or pile jacket) and nylon wind jacket will prepare you for variety of changes in temperature and weather conditions. A pair of loose trousers or a wraparound skirt that can be slipped on over your cycling shorts will make you more presentable (for more information see *Chapter 7*).

You can get shoes specially designed for cycling, but they tend to be uncomfortable to walk in. If you have a pair of shoes that you can cycle in without getting cramp in your feet and also walk in, then they are probably fine for general bicycle touring. As a rule cheaper athletic shoes have stiffer soles, so are better for cycling. If your feet get cramp using multipurpose shoes to cycle in then you will need to have two pairs of shoes.

Dust and exhaust are another problem. The irritation from exhaust can be the worst. When pollutants reach a choking level a bandana over the mouth and nose helps considerably.

### Sunglasses

If you are used to sunglasses, you will want to wear them most days. They will not only protect your eyes from the sun but also keep dust out of your eyes and reduce eye-fatigue from the drying wind. DO NOT wear sunglasses with side blinders. They restrict peripheral vision, which is very important if you have to manoeuvre in traffic or swerve to avoid a hazard. In the afternoon, just when you are ready to take off your sunglasses, a new irritant appears: gnats and small bugs. If you are going to be riding at dusk, it is worth buying a pair of glasses with clear lenses.

### First-aid kit

When people are in unfamiliar surroundings they can receive more injuries than usual. A lot of these are cuts and scrapes. Carry a first-aid kit and be able to give minor first aid. Prompt attention to even the smallest scratch is very important.

For an extended tour you should also prepare a medicine kit with prescription medicine and remedies for headaches, colds, upset stomachs, allergies and other common ailments. If possible get pills in 'blister packs' or individually packaged forms. Bulk-packed pills tend to vibrate into dust on long cycle tours. If you take a prescription drug, carry a duplicate prescription that gives the generic name. (See the list of suggested kit on page 73.)

### Camping equipment

You only need camping gear if you are going to camp. If you are taking a tent and/or stove, make sure you have all the pieces before you leave.

One of the problems with camping on a cycling tour is the security of your belongings – you're pretty much tied to your camp. A second problem is when it rains in Africa, it generally rains buckets, so no tent is going to be as nice as the simplest hotel room. When it is not the rainy season, what you really need, including in many hotel rooms, is a free-standing bug net. The most practical of these is made by Long Road Travel Supplies (111 Avenida Drive, Berkeley, CA 94708, USA; tel: (800) 359 6040 (USA or Canada) or +1 510 540 4763 (USA only); fax: +1 510 540 0652 (USA only); email: sales@longroad.com; web: www.longroad.com). If you take either a tent or plan to sleep under the stars in your bug net, it is useful (if not essential!) to have a dedicated ground cloth, ie: a piece of plastic, a woven mat, an old sheet, etc.

To self-cater you not only need a cooker, but also the pots, pans and utensils to use with it. You will also need space to carry some staples that you will need frequently but won't want to buy for every meal, like cooking oil, salt, pepper, sugar and spices.

The most versatile stoves are multi-fuel designs. Mountain Safety Research (MSR) (see page 42) make one that is highly regarded. You will need a safe container for carrying fuel. Sigg bottles work well for this. Make sure you have enough fuel storage capacity to last between fuelling points.

## Other items for bicycle touring

Depending on your plans there are a number of other special items worth taking:

- If you will be staying in local housing or small hotels that don't necessarily provide linen, take sheets and a towel.
- If you are going to be sleeping in the highlands or travelling during the cold season, you might want to take a sleeping bag or blanket as well as the above.
- Rubber thong sandals for wearing into the shower provide a buffer against slimy situations.
- A flat, rubber universal sink stopper for doing laundry in hotel sinks.
- Small gifts for new friends you'll make.
- A stack of business cards is an easy way to honour any requests for your address.
- Extra passport pictures of yourself are also a welcome gift and may be useful if the red tape invents an unexpected new form or you need to apply for an additional visa.
- Binoculars if you are going to a bird or wildlife area – if not, they are probably just extra weight.
- Camera, lens, flash, film and batteries – be self-sufficient because these may be hard or expensive to supply en route.
- Reading and writing materials will help you pass slower times and remember good times.

## Other tips for cyclists
### Accommodation and food

If you plan to stay overnight outside major cities and tourist destinations, which is the norm for bicycle tourists, it is usually difficult to plan your accommodation too specifically without the help of a travel consultant who has been there. In small towns and villages you may find you have no choice at all. You will get to stay in the best – and probably only – hotel in town. Where there is a choice it is often determined by price, so your selection will be dictated by your budget.

Many budget African hotels only have a few rooms and beds, so if you are travelling with a large group your choices may already be narrowed and the group may exceed the capacity of a village hotel. While camping is an option, we tend not to camp for a combination of reasons: you have to carry more gear

## SUGGESTED CYCLE KIT LIST
### Spares and tools
- panniers eg: Overlander by Carradice
- two spare tyres
- ten inner tubes
- a puncture repair kit
- cables
- brake pads
- grease and oil
- bearings
- wires and straps
- pliers

- a set of Allen keys
- cable cutter
- spoke tensioner
- a set of spanners
- screwdriver
- bottom bracket tensioner
- front bearing spanner
- spokes
- box of nuts and bolts, etc
- chain link extractor
- toothbrush

### Medical
- rehydration mix and spoon
- gauzes, bandages and creams
- suture kit
- anti-malaria tablets

- antibiotics
- eye ointment
- Paracetamol
- tooth repair kit

### Water
- two Travelwell military water purifiers

- two 10-litre water bags

### Cooking
- Coleman's multifuel cooker
- two spoons
- two plastic bowels

- two plastic cups
- a saucepan
- a penknife

### Camping equipment
- a tent
- two sleeping mats
- two sleeping bags

- nylon string
- a towel
- a torch

### Miscellaneous
- two whistles (as a warning and signal)
- binoculars

- a compass
- a camera

(both shelter and cooking) or include a support vehicle (which negates much of any savings); it takes time to set-up and takedown a camp that is better spent on being more involved in seeing Africa; camping tends to be on the outskirts of towns and separated from the community.

I prefer to be more immersed in the village. The modest cost of most accommodation and meals does more to help the village economy and may be no more expensive than camping. Furthermore, many parts of Africa don't lend themselves to camping and there can be more security problems. Meal planning is similarly influenced by budget and by the availability of markets, cooking facilities and restaurants. In rural areas selection may be so limited as to constitute no choice. But if you are in an area where any Africans are travelling cooked food is usually available.

### Seeing wildlife
One of the best experiences is seeing free-range animals from the freedom of a bicycle seat. If you know where to look it is possible to see a wide variety of wildlife and birdlife from a bicycle, but with the continuing encroachment on wildlife habitats by man this is further and further away from inhabited areas.

If you choose to search for wildlife, be selective about your objectives. These are wild animals and when threatened can be very dangerous. They have their own ideas on how to handle intrusions into their personal space. I have seen baboons and elephants from a bicycle in Burkina Faso, Togo and Zimbabwe, watched giraffes, zebras and gazelles in Kenya and Cameroon and enjoyed monkeys jumping overhead in Ghana and Liberia. I once heard the growl of a lion while on a bicycle and an elephant has chased me – not a relaxing experience.

Without an experienced guide *do not* go in search of cape buffaloes, lions, elephants or rhinos by bicycle or on foot. Most countries help you with this by not allowing bicycles or foot travel in the major game parks. To see the big game you will have to store your bike and get into vans for a day or two. Unless you pre-arrange it, you will not find transport for game drives waiting at the park entrance. Usually game-watching safaris begin from major cities, so you need to plan accordingly.

## SHIPPING YOUR VEHICLE
### Vehicles
If you are planning to ship your vehicle back at the end of the trip (or indeed start your journey by shipping one out), this can be a major expense. The lowest prices from Mombasa, Dar es Salaam, Accra or Cape Town to Europe are all over US$1,000 for a container (there are a lot of other African countries that also offer freight service but the above are the largest and most popular). Also beware of all the hidden extras, these can add as much as another 50 percent.

However, travellers we talked to who had shipped their vehicles from Europe to South Africa found the shipping companies and agencies fair, even with all the hidden costs, which were quoted in advance. When they then wanted to ship their vehicles either to East or West Africa, hidden costs were not an issue, but the red tape resulted in them having to pay a fortune in bribes.

It is advisable to try and find other travellers who are wanting to ship their vehicle as a container can be shared, depending on the size of the vehicle.

Whether in east, west, central or southern Africa, you will be encouraged to use a shipping agent – but this does add considerably to the cost. You will always be able to deal directly with the shipping line if you persevere – the agents are often more trouble than they are worth.

## Motorbikes
Of course, shipping a bike can be much cheaper – particularly if you share a container. It is even possible to hitch a lift by putting a bike inside a vehicle already being shipped. Air freight for motorbikes is also pretty reasonable.

## Bicycles
It is generally possible to take a bicycle as luggage on most airlines.

## Websites
The following is a list of good website addresses for shipping lines, agents and costs:

**An Mbendi Profile – African Shipping Industry**
www.mbendi.co.za/indy/trns/shipaf.htm
**The South African Shop** – shipping charges information
www.sashop.com/shop/shipping.htm
**Complete online freight services** (international) www.freightquote.com

**AFRICA**

| | | | |
|---|---|---|---|
| Zimbabwe / Botswana Adventure<br>Vic Falls to Harare | 2 wks | £240 |
| Wildlife Discoverer<br>Vic Falls to Cape Town | 3 wks | £360 |
| Gorillas & Game Parks<br>Nairobi to Nairobi | 3 wks | £360 |
| Lakes & Game Parks<br>Nairobi to Vic Falls | 4 wks | £480 |
| Delta Desert and Game Parks<br>Harare to Cape Town | 4 wks | £480 |
| African Contrasts<br>Nairobi to Cape Town | 7 wks | £795 |
| Livingstone's Trail<br>Nairobi to Harare | 8 wks | £895 |
| Grand African Explorer<br>Nairobi to Harare | 9 wks | £995 |
| Trans African Expeditions<br>London to Cape Town | 28 wks | £2170 |

*Also available, overland expeditions in Middle East & South America*

**BUKIMA**
ADVENTURE TOURS

**01234 871 329**
e-mail: bukima@compuserve.com
**CALL NOW FOR FULL COLOUR BROCHURE**

**absolute Africa**
**Budget CAMPING SAFARIS**
**From 3 – 29 Weeks • For Ages 18 – 40s**
www.absoluteafrica.com   email: absaf@atual.co.uk   Phone: +44 (0) 20 8742 0226

# Unique Tours to Special Places for Memories of a Lifetime

**TUNISIA - SENEGAL - GAMBIA - GUINEA - MALI
BURKINA FASO - IVORY COAST - GHANA - TOGO
BENIN- CAMEROON   - ERITREA - ETHIOPIA
KENYA - UGANDA - TANZANIA -   MALAWI
ZIMBABWE -   BOTSWANA -   SWAZILAND
LESOTHO -     SOUTH   AFRICA   &   MORE**

Unique, two- and four-week village-based cross-cultural tours to all regions of Africa for ordinary active people. Cycling difficulty is moderate. The itineraries and activities focus on the diversity and complexity of the history, economy, culture, environment and society. Highlights include meeting local people, exploring historical sites, stays in traditional villages, first-hand contact with the culture and beautiful cycling.

**Unique Tours
Since 1983**

**ibike tours
4887 Columbia Drive South
Seattle WA 98108-1919 USA
Tel/Fax: 1-206-767-0848
E-mail: ibike@ibike.org
Internet: www.ibike.org/ibike**

# Organised Tours

*Warren Burton and Kath Larsen of Encounter Overland*

Many of the advantages of travelling in your own vehicle can also be enjoyed by joining an organised overland tour, and with a lot less trouble and expense. Of course, you will need to sacrifice a degree of independence and be prepared to live and travel with a large group, but there are many compensations provided by this means of travel.

One of the main advantages is that you can leave all of the preparation and planning to the tour company. Although planning can be a lot of fun in its own right, if you don't have the time this could be the answer to your prayers. The company should brief you in good time with specific information on anything you need to do before you leave: visas, vaccinations and insurance, etc, and will advise on what you should pack for the trip. After that, all you have to do is turn up at the departure point and join in with the fun.

Overland tours are also worth considering for those with limited time available to travel and with limited finances. Because the same route has normally already been taken by your driver or by another driver with the same company, it is possible to travel much faster. Experience also means the driver tends to know the best places to visit or to stay in each area and the best ways around bureaucratic hurdles, all making the journey more efficient than it would be for independent travellers in their own vehicle.

Those who do opt for an organised tour will probably never realise just how much they have been protected from African bureaucracy. While they sit in the truck at a border post they will probably have no idea of the amount of paperwork and hassles being dealt with by the driver or courier. The experience of expedition leaders in dealing with borders also means that trucks tend to have fewer problems with officials than independent travellers who are facing things for the first time.

Economies of scale mean that whatever trip you choose it will be possible to do it for less with an organised tour. Fuel is one of the biggest expenses of any trip. Even allowing for the higher fuel consumption of a large truck, it works out a lot less to spread this between 20 than it is share it between two (the most common number sharing a smaller vehicle) or even four (the maximum). The cost of all equipment and spares is similarly spread across a much larger group.

As all trucks operate some kind of rota system, travellers can even find themselves with more spare time to explore at the end of the day than their independent counterparts. If you travel independently you have to take personal responsibility for all the daily tasks of vehicle minding/guarding, motor maintenance, shopping, pitching camp, making a fire, purifying water, cooking, cleaning and so on. But in a large group such tasks can be more efficiently divided and shared out, which means that some days you will be working and some days you won't.

Security is one of the most significant differences between the two options. The biggest headache for independent travellers is the need for constant vigilance over their vehicle and its contents. This makes it very difficult to get away from the vehicle, thus reducing the possibilities for hiking and visiting more inaccessible spots. This is one time when the cramped conditions of travelling with four people in a vehicle pays off, as it is possible to split into pairs taking alternate responsibility for it.

With an organised tour there are always enough people around to ensure a permanent security rota which allows members to leave their gear behind and take off by foot, canoe, train or bus. Individuals can generally leave the tour at any time and travel independently (at their own expense) to a pre-arranged rendezvous point.

So, with all the above in favour of organised tours, it would seem that independent travellers with their own vehicles must need their heads examining. Why travel any other way? Of course there are disadvantages to organised trips, which may cause you to think again.

First and foremost comes the lack of independence, which is why most of us consider doing a trip to Africa in the first place. Most tour companies will do their utmost to accommodate individual preferences in the itinerary, and most journeys are pretty well planned. Once the journey gets underway, the leader/driver will generally allow a measure of democracy, allowing the trip to deviate a little from the published route, but that isn't the same thing as finding a particularly nice beach and deciding to hang around for a week or so, or deciding to miss out countries altogether and take a completely different route across the continent from the one you may have originally planned. Only independent travel gives you complete freedom to really do what you want. If you are on an organised tour, your preferences will always be subject to the approval of all the other people on the trip – and people are the other potential problem.

However well you feel you can get along with other members of the human race, there will come a time during the course of a six-month trip when you really don't want to spend every day with that group of 20 people. You will always have one thing in common with the other people on a trip, you all want to travel through Africa, but beyond that there are no guarantees you will get along with them.

The truth is, you are very unlikely to be landed with an entire group that you can't stand, and if you do maybe they aren't the problem anyway! It's also well worth making sure that you treat yourself to time out from the group whenever you get the chance.

You should certainly make a point of getting away from the group if you want to spend time mixing with local people, and there can't be many people who don't want to get a taste of African culture while they are travelling. But the safety and protection offered by a large group can also do a great deal to distance you from that culture. People will approach a large group in a very different way than they would if you were on your own, or in a group of two or three people, and you are far less likely to make genuine friendships if you don't break out of the group from time to time.

## The routes

There is an incredible variety of trips to choose from, both shorter tours and the original trans-African expeditions. The longer trips are typically from London to Nairobi, Harare, Johannesburg or Cape Town and can be combined with a number of optional extensions. The eastern route has also opened up over the last couple of years and a few companies are now running trips between southern Africa and Cairo via Ethiopia, or southbound via the same route. It is possible to link these with extensions into the Middle East and Asia.

The traditional trans-African route via the Sahara, the Sahel, West Africa to Central Africa, the Democratic Republic of the Congo (DRC – formerly Zaire) and on to East Africa is not achievable safely at the time of writing. While there are a few reports of independent travellers 'sneaking through' the Central African Republic and DRC, it is not presently being considered by overland companies. The constant state of unrest and armed conflict, especially in the Congo, rules it out.

Most companies who still operate a trans-African route will include an overflight alternative route taking in more of West Africa (probably Ghana, Togo, Benin and possibly Gabon). Overflights are generally taken from Accra in Ghana, Douala in Cameroon or Libreville in Gabon to Nairobi where the trip will continue around East Africa before continuing south.

There is also presently no safe and practical route through the Congo and Angola to southwest Africa – Namibia. However, a few operators have recently pursued an alternative from Niger into Chad then crossing into Sudan following a northerly route to Ethiopia before turning south to Kenya. This route is very much in its exploratory stage and is subject to seasonal restriction and still somewhat unpredictable owing to political instability.

Algeria (the former trans-Saharan route) is still unstable, especially in the northern, more populated half, making it an impractical journey. The alternative route via Morocco and Mauritania to Mali is still the one followed by all operators.

New trips by a few operators have recently taken in Libya and Tunisia. Often, as one region closes off, others open up; that's the beauty and intrigue of Africa.

The expense and bureaucratic difficulties of West Africa mean that few companies offer comprehensive tours of this most colourful and lively part of the continent. Some shorter tours are available, but this is likely to remain an area that is best explored independently. Southern and eastern areas, however, offer a huge choice of excellent shorter tours.

There has been a big growth in these shorter tours over recent years, allowing you to fly into a region for a few weeks and get a taste of it in a concentrated burst. These days such tours represent the biggest part of the overall market. The most popular starting points are Nairobi, Harare and, more recently, Johannesburg or Cape Town.

Shorter expeditions also mean you can add them into your schedule once you arrive in a particular area, so giving you even greater freedom of movement. An organised tour could easily fit in with other parts of your journey by combining it with a hired car.

It is worth bearing in mind that a wide range of expeditions are available when you arrive in the main centres and so do not necessarily need to be booked in advance. Local tours can respond to changing conditions much faster than the London-based operations and so can sometimes provide a more interesting trip, the downside being that you have no way of assessing the quality of their operation until you arrive, and you probably have no 'come back' options should you have a major complaint. Smaller companies in South Africa and Zimbabwe are now offering a variety of expeditions, including South Africa, Mozambique, Namibia and Botswana.

## What to expect

Of course, the precise way in which the tours are organised varies from company to company. The tour company will generally organise briefing sessions to introduce themselves and explain how the trip will work, the everyday practicalities and precisely what you need to arrange in advance in the way of documents, vaccinations and so on. They will usually also offer or suggest a comprehensive insurance policy, a must for any form of travel (see page 91).

Most tour operators aim to make the experience feel as close to independent travel as possible. There is, therefore, a fairly democratic approach to deciding on day-to-day details. Members of the group will normally set up a rota to cope with all the daily chores, especially cooking and security.

Two or three people each day will be responsible for cooking all meals, although there will often also be a rota for cooks' helpers. Even when a company provides a cook as part of its team, you will be expected to help out with much of the actual work, with the cook acting more as an adviser.

Everyone on the trip will also be expected to volunteer for an additional job. These vary from company to company and according to the number of people on the trip, but they might typically include responsibility for things such as stores, fire-lighting, water purification, security, first aid and rubbish collection. Many drivers will also suggest the option of setting up a bar, which tends to be a popular job!

You will normally have to pay a deposit on booking. Most companies ask for a kitty at the beginning of the trip to cover food and other communal expenses, but others include this within the overall cost of the trip. It is important to be clear what is and what is not included in the basic price. This greatly varies from transport only through to all food, camping, game park fees and other admission charges. Others may require a Local Payment which often covers direct costs en route such as national park entrance fees, etc. Also remember to add in the cost of any airfares when you are budgeting your trip. These will not be included in the tour operators' cost.

The truck will stock up with staples before it sets off and wherever supplies are easy to get, but most food is bought locally and shopping will generally be the responsibility of those on cooking duty for the day.

You will generally have to supply your own bedding, but tents are normally provided. Sleeping is generally in shared, two-person tents. Check the availability of campbeds and mosquito nets as most do not supply these.

Most companies use Bedford, MAN or Mercedes trucks, customised with their own seating configuration. They have very different layouts, but all of them can accommodate a group of around 20 to 24 people.

A few trucks pack luggage and tents into a separate trailer, making more space in the truck itself, as luggage is generally locked away by all companies during the day anyway (with access only at the beginning and end of the day). This makes little difference to access but it does make things a bit more comfortable.

It is worth checking out the seating design of trucks in which you are thinking of travelling. Has it been organised simply to fit in the greatest number of bodies, or does it look relatively comfortable and possible to get a reasonable view of your surroundings? Try to get a sense of the relative merits of forward-facing and inward-facing seats, different companies offer different combinations. You will be spending a long time in that truck so you ought to be quite sure you are happy with the layout.

More than anything else, the success or failure of your journey will largely be in the hands of your leader/driver. This is an incredibly demanding job – the encumbent has also to be a motor mechanic, a diplomat, an actor, a social worker, an expert on everything and a friend to everyone. The larger companies have extensive training programmes for their drivers, including both workshop experience and travelling with another leader/driver. Other companies without the infrastructure to offer that kind of training are forced to rely more on the individuals on the tour – that means *you*!

Some companies also provide couriers or cooks, although it is not always clear just how useful these are. On a short journey a good all-round leader/driver should be adequate, but on a longer trip a second team member is invaluable in order to help with visas and bureaucracy, sometimes travelling ahead to deal with the paperwork, and helping out with some of the driving.

## Choosing a tour

You can pay anything between £2,000 and £5,000 for a full trans-African trip, but the variations between them are not just a matter of cost. The range of choices offered can be quite bewildering. Make sure that you find out exactly what is included in the price and how the trip is organised.

Cost is an important factor to bear in mind. As with most things, the general rule is that the more you pay the more you get. The cheaper end of the market can also tend to have less experienced leaders/drivers and use older and less dependable vehicles. Leaders/drivers with the larger operators keep in constant touch with full-time staff, who can help out in the event of problems or emergencies.

One-off expeditions are less secure when the going gets tough, but it may well be that you are not looking for the gold star treatment. If your idea is to set off on an adventurous expedition and to make the trip as independent as possible, to the extent of accepting the possibility that the truck may not even make it through, then the cheapest end of the trans-African market may well suit your purposes.

It is also worth noting that, although operators generally claim precise departure dates, some smaller companies may sometimes change these in order to make sure they can fill the seats. So if time is a priority, in particular on shorter journeys, it is worth going with one of the more established operators.

## UK-based overland companies
Many of these companies also have representatives in South Africa and Nairobi.

**Absolute Africa** Swanscombe Rd, London W4 2HL; tel: 020 8742 0226. A company with 21 years' experience. Average age 18–35. Also offer gorillas and game park tours. Nairobi to Cape Town – 77 days £880 + £450 kitty; London to Cape Town – 28 weeks £1,600 + £810 kitty; Mombasa to Cape Town – 44 days £520 + £340 kitty

**Acacia Adventure Holidays** 23a Craven Terrace, London W2 3QH; tel: 020 7706 4700; fax: 020 7706 4686; email: acacia@afrika.demon.co.uk. Operating since the 1980s in specially designed Mercedes vehicles with padded seats – 12 forward and 8 inward facing. Rolldown sides. Average age 20–40 and maximum group size 20. Tour leader, driver and cook (on trips under three weeks). Overland safari prices include all game parks, ferry crossings, etc. Video available on request. Also operates short adventure holidays such as diving, cycling, rafting, trekking and lodge safaris. Nairobi to Harare – 29 days £895 + £140 kitty; Nairobi to Cape Town – 7 weeks £1,395 + £270 kitty; Cape Town to Harare – 3 weeks £645 + £110 kitty.

**Africa Overland Club** 11 Woodland Mews, Sedgefield, Cleveland TS21 3EH; Freephone 0800 7311 8841 or 01740 623633; email: ron@africa-overland.com. Budget camping expeditions throughout Africa from two weeks to 26 weeks, for those who are free spirited and have a passion to experience the real Africa. Gorilla safaris, visiting Kenya and Uganda – 2 weeks £349 + £100 kitty; Nairobi to Cape Town – 8 weeks £600 + £180 kitty; 'Africa All The Way' UK to Cape Town via West Africa 26 weeks £1,600 + £400 kitty.

**Africa Travel Centre** 21 Leigh St, London WC1H 9QX; tel: 020 7387 1211; fax: 020 7383 7512. Offers a wide range of long and short overland options including truck tours, rail tours, self-drive in southern Africa, camping and coach tours, motorbike safaris, balloon safaris and game lodge safaris. Because the Africa Travel Centre represents a range of companies it can be a good place to start when shopping around for a trip that suits you.

**African Trails** 3 Flanders Rd, Chiswick, London W4 1NQ; tel: 020 8742 7724; fax: 020 8742 8621; email: aftrails@globalnet.co.uk. Has been running trips since 1980

with one driver and courier. No age limit quoted – most passengers 18–35. Seats face inwards. Also offers a gorillas and game parks tour, and shorter trips in southern Africa. Nairobi to Cape Town – 7 weeks £550+ 260 kitty

**Bukima Africa** 15 Bedford Rd, Great Barford, Milton Keynes MK44 3JD; tel: 01234 871329; fax: 01234 871866. 4WD expedition vehicles with a driver/leader and a co-driver/mechanic. Some seats face forward, some inwards. Also offers a gorillas and game parks tour out of Nairobi, and Victoria Falls to Harare in ten days. London to Cape Town – 28 weeks £1,795 and US$850 kitty; Nairobi to Cape Town – 7 weeks £645 + US$426.

**Dragoman** Camp Green Farm, Kenton Rd, Debenham, Suffolk IP14 6LA; tel: 01728 861133; fax: 01728 861127. Running trips for 16 years using uniquely designed 16-ton Mercedes trucks with a crew of two. Seats face forward. Discounts sometimes available on full tour prices. Phone for details of weekly slide shows at Nomad Traveller's Centre, 3–4 Turnpike Lane, London N8 0PX; tel: 020 8889 7014; fax: 020 8889 6529. Talks also held around the UK. Offers a very wide range of shorter tours including the bushlands of the Kalahari and Namibia, and the Kenyan game parks, and combinations of individual tours and tours of Asia and Africa. Also run trips which feature visits to community projects helping local people to maintain their culture and benefit from tourism. All programmes are paid for at a fair rate. Nairobi to Harare – 5 weeks from £1,055 + US$485 kitty; UK to Harare – 19 weeks £3,520 + US$1,715 kitty; Tunis to Cairo – 4 weeks £835 + US$505 kitty.

**Economic Expeditions** 29 Cunnington St, London W4 5ER; tel: 020 8995 7707; fax: 020 8742 7707; email: ecoexped@mcmail.com. Small company with 29 years experience specialising in budget tours. Average age 18–mid-30s. London to Nairobi – 22 weeks £1,280 + kitty; Nairobi to Johannesburg – 6 weeks £380 + kitty; Cairo to Nairobi – 12 weeks £850 + kitty; Gorilla trek – 2 weeks £180

**Encounter Overland** 267 Old Brompton Rd, London SW5 9JA; tel: 020 7370 6951; fax: 020 7244 9737; email: adventure@encounter.co.uk; web: www.encounter-overland.com. Company with over 30 years' experience running overland trips and safaris throughout Africa. Vehicles all 4WD with inward-facing seats and towed baggage/equipment trailers. They operate expedition-type trips with only one leader/driver, so 'passengers' must be willing to participate fully. Age guideline 18–45, most in their 20s and 30s. Trips sold globally so groups of an international mix. The following prices are inclusive with no food kitty: London to Nairobi – 18 weeks £2,495 + Local Payment US$1,020; London to Cape Town – 28 weeks £4,320 + Local Payment US$1,690; Casablanca to Accra – 13 weeks £1,665 + Local Payment US$680; Nairobi to Cairo – 9 weeks £1,545 + Local Payment US$595; Cairo to Tunis via Libya – 6 weeks £1,075 + Local Payment US$470; Harare to Cape Town – 5 weeks £1,175 + Local Payment US$545

**Exodus** 9 Weir Rd, London SW12 0LT; tel: 020 8675 5550; email: sales@exodustravels.co.uk. Company with over 25 years' experience using Mercedes trucks. Three leader/drivers on shorter trips, a crew of two on longer expeditions. Age range 17–45 on trips of four weeks or longer. Mixed seating. Phone for dates of slide shows held once a fortnight in London at 19.00. Also offers Nairobi to Victoria Falls,

Victoria Falls to Windhoek, a 24-day Rift Valley trip out of Nairobi and shorter tours in north Africa. Nairobi to Cape Town – 11 weeks £2,500 (includes game parks) + £190 food kitty; Kenya, Tanzania and Uganda – 4 weeks from £1,200; Kenya and Tanzania – 2 weeks from £700.

**Explore Africa** Rose Cottage, Summerleaze, Magor, Newport, NP6 3DE; tel: 01633 880 224; fax: 01633 882 128. Company with 18 years' experience using Bedford trucks, with a crew of two on longer trips. Average age is 18–35. Older passengers accepted if 'young at heart'. Also offers a gorillas and game parks safari, a 5-week tour of southern Africa and a 3-week tour of Morocco. Exploratory tours, eg: Nairobi to Cape Town – 16 weeks £1,250 + £300 kitty; Return trip Mombasa to Victoria Falls – 5 weeks £490 + £110 kitty.

**Explore Worldwide** 1 Frederick St, Aldershot, Hampshire GU11 1LQ; tel: 01252 319448; fax: 01252 760100. Small group holidays using a mix of hotels, lodges and camping in north Africa, Kenya, Tanzania, Uganda, Malawi, Zimbabwe, Zambia, Botswana and Namibia. Phone for details of slide shows in London and around the UK. East Africa Game Park and beach break safari – 2 weeks £290 + £120 kitty; 3 weeks £390 + £160 kitty.

**Guerba Adventure and Discovery Holidays** Wessex House, 40 Station Rd, Westbury, Wiltshire BA13 3JN; tel: 01373 826611; fax: 01373 858351. Overland expeditions and shorter safaris for over 20 years. Uses Mercedes trucks with inward-facing seats and three crew. Offers a wide range of treks, lodge safaris and 4WD tours with comfort-added camping and no camp chores. Also a wide range of short safaris in East and southern Africa, and accommodated tours and coastal extensions. Nairobi to Cape Town – 11 weeks £1,830 + £475 kitty; Nairobi to Harare – 7 weeks £1,300 + £260 kitty; Cape Town to Harare – 4 weeks £810 + £180 kitty

**Kumuka Expeditions** 40 Earls Court Rd, London W8 6EJ; tel: 020 7937 8855; fax: 020 7937 6664. Uses MAN trucks with a crew of two. Age limits on some tours. Twelve seats face forwards, six face inwards. Cook included on some tours. Discount for early bookings sometimes available. Videos screened at 18.30 every Wednesday. Kenya, Tanzania and Zanzibar – 3 weeks £795 + £170 kitty; Nairobi to Cape Town – 9 weeks including Uganda £2,095 + £430 kitty; Johannesburg to Cape Town (via Zimbabwe, Botswana and Namibia) – 5 weeks £1,095 + £260 kitty.

**Oases Overland** 5 Nicholsons Cottages, Hinton St, Mary, Dorset DT10 1NF; tel: 01258 471155; fax: 012558 471166; web: www.oasis-overland.co.uk. Small company offering tours in Africa and the Middle East. Uses Scania and Leyland trucks with a driver/mechanic and courier. Seats face inwards. Passenger ages generally 18–40. Trips from 3 weeks to 7 months. Also offers London to Accra and Victoria Falls to Cape Town. London to Cape Town – 29 weeks £1,675 + £660 kitty; Nairobi to Cape Town – 51 days £575 + £260 kitty; Nairobi to Victoria Falls – 28 days £370 + £120 kitty.

**Phoenix Expeditions** College Farm, Far St, Wymeswold, Leics LE12 6TZ; tel: 01509 881818; fax: 01509 881822; email: phoenix.expeditions@ukonline.co.uk; web: www.phoenixexpeditions.co.uk. Camping safaris and expeditions for the adventurous budget traveller. Transport is in custom-built Scania or Bedford safari vehicles with the expertise of a tour leader and driver/mechanic. Zimbabwe and Botswana Explorer – 18 days £325 + US$270 kitty; Great Rift Valley Expedition (Istanbul to Cape Town) – 20 weeks £1,450 + US$1,140 kitty.

**Truck Africa** 6 Hurlingham Studios, Ranelagh Gardens, Fulham, London SW6 3PA; tel: 020 7731 6142; fax: 020 7371 7445; email: sales@truckafrica.com; web: www.truckafrica.com. Tours from three weeks trans-Africa to tours of West Africa for 30 weeks. Three crew on all East and southern Africa tours including camp helper/cook. Scanias and Leyland Freighters used with combination inward- and forward-facing seats. Average age 27. Video showings every Wednesday and Saturday or by appointment. Group discounts for five people booking together. Kitty covers three meals a day, services of camp helper (except on trans-Africa tours), game park entrance fees, campsite fees, group excursions, and end of trip meal. Parks and Primates – 3 weeks £465 + £180 kitty; Victoria Falls to Cape Town – 5 weeks £550 + £270 kitty; Kenya to Zimbabwe – 6 weeks £610 + £390 kitty; Eastern Explorer – 4 weeks £575 + £390 kitty; Trans-Africa – 20 weeks £2010 + £470 kitty.

## Other overland companies

Many of the above-mentioned companies also have representatives in Nairobi, Harare and South Africa, as well as Australia and the US. There are also other expedition companies worldwide. Here are some to look out for:

**The Adventure Centre** 1311 63rd St, Suite 200, Emeryville, CA 94608, USA; tel: 800-227 8747 or 510/654 1879; or 17 Hayden St, Toronto, Ontario, M4Y 2P2, Canada; tel: 416/922 7584.

**Himalayan Travel** PO Box 481, Greenwich, CT 06836, USA; tel: 800/225 2380.

**Afriesj Expedities** Hemonystraat 33, 1074 BM Amsterdam, The Netherlands; tel: (020) 662 3953.

There are many companies offering specialist overland tours specific only to southern Africa, with representation in South Africa only. You will need to shop around and your best bet is to visit a local travel agent for further information. Here are some companies we came across while travelling.

**Affordable Adventures** Johannesburg; tel: (011) 465 9186; email: adventures@global.co.za; www.tourism.co.za/adventures

**Tribe Safari** Pretoria; tel: (012) 996 0288; email: info@tribesafari.com; www.tribesafari.com

**Karibu Safari** Natal; tel: (031) 563 9774 or Johannesburg; tel: (011) 462 6414; email: karibusa@iafrica.com; www.karibu.co.za

**Africa Tours** Pretoria; tel: (012) 333 7110; email: dat@global.co.z; www.destination.co.za

For a personal view on a 22-week expedition with an organised tour from Morocco to Kenya, have a look at a website called 'Hey Africa! Do you mind if we camp here?' The address is www.heyafrica.com.

86

**ENCOUNTER**
ASIA • AFRICA • SOUTH & CENTRAL AMERICA

# ARE YOU A STICK IN THE MUD?

## COME WITH ENCOUNTER YOU AINT SEEN NOTHING YET

Trust Encounter's 35 years of experience to completely involve you in a world of adventure

FOR YOUR BROCHURE RING

## 020 7370 6845

OR VISIT

**www.encounter-overland.com**

# Practicalities

## PAPERWORK
### Passports
Make sure you have plenty of spare pages in your passport! Most visas that you will get along the way are one-page visas, rendering the page useless for other stamps or visas. Most African countries are extremely 'stamp happy', and use up a lot of space. Throughout the continent you will come across checkpoints where all your documents will be scrutinised and your passport stamped, sometimes over and over again. Some countries, like the Sudan, write a report of vehicle and personal details in the back of your passport.

If you have dual nationality, take both passports as visas are often charged according to nationality. If you have two to choose from, you can always go for the best deal! And remember that if you have an Israeli stamp in your passport you will not be allowed to travel to Arab countries.

### Passport photos
You will find when applying for visas that a lot of embassies demand two, and sometimes three passport photos to attach to your visa application. We took over 50 passport photos with us, but this is optional as it is relatively cheap to have your passport photo taken in most capital cities of Africa.

### Carnet de passage (*carnet*)
The *carnet* is an essential and expensive document for everyone taking a vehicle (including a motorbike) across Africa. It is a system that allows you temporarily to import a vehicle into a country without paying customs duty – in some cases this can be many times its actual value.

A *carnet* is a book containing details of yourself and your vehicle on each of three sections of every page. When you first enter a country, the first section is stamped and removed and the third section (which you keep in the book) is also stamped. On leaving the country, the second section is stamped and removed and the third section is stamped again.

The idea is for customs to collect two matching halves; if not they will claim customs duty through the issuing authority. You must collect a complete set of entry and exit stamps – if you fail to get an exit stamp for a country where you got an entry stamp, you are likely to have a lot of explaining to do later on. This is completely dependent on where your *carnet* was issued. We found that *carnets* issued in Germany or the UK were a lot stricter when it came to entry

## PHOTOGRAPHY
*Ariadne Van Zandbergen*

Your Africa trip will most likely be a once-in-a-lifetime experience, and while photography might seem like a minor detail among your other preparations, a small amount of forethought will help you take the best advantage of the many photographic opportunities that will come your way.

**Equipment** The simpler the camera, the less there is to go wrong – complex electronic gadgetry can be sensitive to rain, dust and heat. For landscapes and portraits, a solidly built manual-focus camera will be adequate. An auto-focus camera will, however, focus with greater precision than any person can hope to on a regular basis, which is particularly useful for moving subjects, such as animals.

For most purposes, the combination of 28-70 and 70-300 or similar magnification zoom lenses will be ideal. A higher magnification than 300 is useful for wildlife but very expensive; for a small loss of quality, teleconverters are a cheap way to get around this: a 300 lens with a 1.4x converter becomes 420mm, and with a 2x it becomes 600mm.

It is possible to buy one lens that covers the full range from 28-300, but such lenses are generally of inferior quality and bulky by comparison to a 28-70 when shooting at low magnifications.

The best way to protect equipment from dust, heat, water, vibrations and bumps is to store it in a Pelican case (any camera shop can order one). On foot, a backpack-style camera bag is more convenient and less likely to attract attention than a normal camera bag. A tripod will allow you to photograph on foot in low light conditions. I cannot overstate the importance of supporting your camera on a beanbag when you photograph wildlife from a car – you can make this yourself from strong fabric, and fill it with beans or rice.

**Film** Print film is the preference of most casual photographers, slide film of professionals, serious amateurs, and anybody else who hopes to have pictures published. Slide film is the more expensive, but is much cheaper to develop.

Most serious photographers working outdoors in Africa favour Fujichrome slide film, in particular Sensia 100, Provia 100 (the professional equivalent to Sensia) or Velvia 50. Slow films (ie: those with a low ASA (ISO) rating) produce sharper and less grainy images than fast films. Velvia 50 is extremely fine grained and shows stunning colour saturation; it is the film I normally use in soft, even light or overcast weather. For hand-held photography in low light, Sensia or Provia 100 is preferable because it allows you to work at faster shutter speeds. 100 ASA film is more tolerant of contrast, and thus preferable in harsh light.

For print photography, a combination of 100 or 200 ASA film should be ideal. It is advisable to stick to recognised brands. Fujicolor produces excellent print films, with the Superia 100 and 200 recommended.

It is important that you try to develop your film as soon as possible, but avoid developing print film outside major cities, and slide films anywhere but South Africa and Nairobi. One solution is to post or courier film home every few weeks.

**Some basics** The automatic programmes provided with many cameras are limited in the sense that the camera cannot think, but only make calculations. A better investment than any amount of electronic wizardry would be to buy or borrow a photographic manual for beginners and get to grips with such basics as the relationship between aperture and shutter speed.

Beginners should also note that a low shutter speed can result in camera shake and therefore a blurred image. For hand-held photographs of static subjects using a low magnification lens (eg: 28–70), select a shutter speed of at least 1/60th of a second. For lenses of higher magnification, the rule of thumb is that the shutter speed should be at least the inverse of the magnification (for instance, a speed of 1/300 or faster on a 300-magnification lens). You can use lower shutter speeds with a tripod or beanbag.

Most modern cameras include a reliable built-in light meter, and give users the choice of three types of metering: matrix, centre weighted or spot metering. You will need to understand how these different systems work to make proper use of them.

**Dust and heat** Dust and heat are a constant problem in Africa. Keep your equipment in a sealed bag, stow films in an airtight container (such as a small cooler bag) and avoid changing film in dusty conditions. Bring a cleaning kit and take care of your equipment. Regularly clean the inside of your camera with a small brush or air blower. A small grain of dirt inside your camera can scratch a whole film.

**Light** The light in Africa is much harsher than in Europe or North America, which is why the most striking outdoor photographs are often taken during the hour or two of 'golden light' after dawn and before sunset. Shooting in low light may enforce the use of very low shutter speeds, when a tripod or beanbag will be required to avoid camera shake. With careful handling, side-lighting and backlighting can produce stunning effects in soft light and at sunrise or sunset.

Generally, however, it is best to shoot with the sun behind you, which means most buildings and landscapes are essentially a 'morning shot' or 'afternoon shot'. If you spend a bit of time in one place, you'll improve your results by planning the best time to take pictures of static subjects (a compass can come in handy).

When photographing people or animals in the harsh midday sun, images taken in light but even shade are likely to look better than those taken in direct sunlight or patchy shade, since the latter conditions create high contrast. Avoid photographing a shaded subject against a sunlit background, which also creates contrast. Fill-in flash is essential to capture facial detail of dark-skinned people in harsh or patchy light.

**Protocol** Attitudes to photography vary greatly from one country to the next, and travellers should take heed of local sensibilities. As a rule, it is considered offensive to photograph people without asking first. Some people will refuse, some will agree enthusiastically, while others will expect a small payment. Even the most willing subject will often pose stiffly when a camera is pointed at them; relax them by making a joke, and take a few shots in quick succession to improve the odds of capturing a natural pose.

In most parts of Africa, official attitudes towards photographing government installations have relaxed over the last decade, but this too varies from one country to the next – be circumspect about pulling out your camera at border posts, near military installations and on bridges.

and exit stamps. Ours was issued in South Africa through the AA and other than proving that we had a final exit stamp out of Africa and an entry stamp into the UK, endorsed by a local police station in the UK, our funds were returned with minimal hassle.

The existence of *carnets* is the main factor that makes selling a vehicle at the end of your journey far more difficult than you might think. When you sell, you have to get your *carnet* discharged by the local customs – that means some form of duty will need to be paid before the deal can go through. If you do not work this out at the time, you are likely to be hit with a hefty bill later on.

*Carnets* are issued by national motoring organisations. They are expensive because these authorities need to know they will be able to recover the money if a vehicle has been sold without duty being paid.

Different countries have different regulations on the issue of *carnets*. Unfortunately, however, you cannot just shop around on the international markets, unless you go to the trouble of re-registering your vehicle. The *carnet* must be issued by an authority in the country where the vehicle is registered.

In the UK you will either need to lodge a bond equivalent to several times the current value of the vehicle or take out a special insurance policy against your defaulting on the *carnet*. The amount of cover required is one and a half times the value of the vehicle for most countries, but up to four times the value for Egypt, Nigeria and Kenya. Insurance is available from Campbell Irvine Ltd (43 Earls Court Road, London W8 6EJ; tel: 020 7937 6981; fax: 020 7938 2250) for a *carnet* issued by the **AA** (Automobile Association (UK), Fanum House, Basingstoke, Hampshire RG21 4EA; tel: 0870 5448866; web: www.theaa.co.uk), or from R L Davison & Co Ltd for one issued by the **RAC** (Royal Automobile Club (UK), RAC House, 1 Forest Road, Feltham, Middlesex TW13 7RR; tel: 020 8917 2500; fax: 020 8917 2525). Even if you do sell without discharging your *carnet*, the insurance company is still entitled to recoup the duty from you.

You should make absolutely sure your *carnet* has been validated for all the countries you have requested. Customs officers will check carefully to ensure their country is listed. You may as well play safe and request absolutely every country you may possibly wish to visit – the number of countries covered does not affect the cost.

Although a *carnet* is likely to come in useful everywhere, it is not absolutely essential in north and West Africa. If you do not have a *carnet* here, a *laissez-passer* will be issued when you enter the country, for a small fee. You should be able to cover most of western and southern Africa without a *carnet*. In central countries, a *carnet* is advisable; in East Africa it is essential.

## International certificate for motor vehicles

Known as a *carte grise* (grey card) wherever French is spoken – even though it is white! – it costs a few pounds, but is a vital investment. Available from motoring organisations, it provides an official-looking summary of the details and serial numbers of your vehicle. You will be asked to produce it at just about every border, police check and rain barrier you come across.

## Insurance
### Medical
Medical insurance is essential. Shop around for a good deal as prices and cover can vary substantially.

### Vehicle and personal belongings
Policies generally include some cover for personal belongings – but this is unlikely to include theft from a vehicle.

Comprehensive vehicle insurance is less important. You can get insurance through Campbell Irvine, 43 Earls Court, Kensington, London, W8 6EJ; tel: 020 7937 6981. They are experienced in meeting the insurance needs of overlanders.

Third party vehicle insurance is not available in advance for most areas – although you can extend UK insurance with a Green Card as far as Morocco or Tunisia. After that it is both advisable and compulsory (policed to varying degrees) to buy third party insurance locally. Once you reach Niger or Mali it is possible to buy a single policy which will cover you for the whole of West Africa. Similarly, you can get another single policy covering Central CFA countries (Cameroon, Chad, Central African Republic, Equatorial Guinea, Gabon and Congo). You will have to shop around for a short-term policy in Kenya. Third Party Insurance Certificates are available at the border in some countries, including Zimbabwe and Zambia.

Alternatively you could make up your own policy, get a rubber stamp made up (Kenya has loads of street vendors for just the job) and ask a friend to sign it for you. This is clearly not legal and you do run a slim chance that an official will check up on it, but more than likely you will just be told to buy the local policy if they don't like the look of it. The document we made up got us all the way to Morocco before we had to buy a policy. We felt no guilt over this as your chances of making a successful claim against a local policy are small, to say the least. We have yet to meet somebody who managed to claim successfully from a local policy.

## International driving licence
These are available from national motoring organisations (such as the AA or RAC) on production of a current driving licence. You must get your international licence in the country that your licence was issued.

## Personal references
References can be useful if you are up against big bureaucratic problems. A reference from a bank or other financial representative can be used to prove that you will not be stranded through lack of funds. A character reference may also be helpful if you are in a tight corner. If at all possible, get a character reference translated into French.

## VISAS

Try to get as many visas as you can before leaving. This is easier said than done, as most are valid only for a short period so will be out of date before you arrive. Most visas are issued as you go, from embassies in capital cities or consulates in larger towns. Consulates are often a better bet as embassies can sometimes take several days to process an application – which can mean an enforced lengthy stay in an expensive city if you have several visas to get.

Generally speaking you should be able to pick up a visa in the capital of a neighbouring country – but do not count on it. For example, there is no Cameroon Consulate in N'djamena, Chad – despite being only a few kilometres from the border. Major cities – Dakar, Abidjan, Nairobi, Dar es Salaam and Harare – have embassies for most other African states. Addis Ababa has the most representation when it comes to embassies and consulates. As the founder of the OAU (Organisation of African Unity) in 1963 and the establishment of UNECA (United Nations Economic Commission of Africa) in 1958, most countries have some type of representation in Addis Ababa. The moral: if all else fails, go to Addis Ababa.

If you can, write to the embassies of those countries you intend to visit several months before you leave, asking for information on the latest entry requirements (you can also pick up some interesting background material and tourist information from them). Where there is no embassy in your country, write to the nearest embassy.

### Visa requirements

Specific visa requirements vary according to nationality. Most requirements for European travellers have now been harmonised – apart from special arrangements for UK travellers in most Commonwealth countries and similar arrangements for French nationals in former French colonies.

Other travellers, such as those from Australia, New Zealand and the USA will have different requirements – for example, Australian, New Zealand and USA citizens need visas for Niger, and Australian and New Zealand citizens need one for Togo. If in doubt contact your own embassy for further information.

There are many varying factors that need to be considered when applying for a visa. Firstly, costs can vary considerably from one country to the next depending on your nationality and where you applied for your visa. On reaching a certain border you might find that your embassy, and every guidebook, has told you that you are exempt from needing a visa, but that you will still have to pay to have your entry stamped in your passport. This is true when it comes to most Commonwealth nationals. Once again, ask other travellers or locals about the latest status on visa applications regarding the next country you might be going to visit.

## EMBASSIES AND CONSULATES

Below is a list of embassies and consulates in the UK, South Africa, USA and Australia (there is a good website if you need further information – www.embassyworld.com).

## African embassies and consulates in the UK

**Algeria** 54 Holland Park, London W11 3RS; tel: 020 7221 7800

**Benin** Dolphin House, 16 The Broadway, Stanmore, Middlesex HA7 4DW; tel: 020 8954 8800; fax: 020 8954 8844

**Botswana** 6 Stratford Place, London W1N 9AE; tel: 020 7499 0031; visas: 0891 600335

**Burkina Faso** 5 Cinnamon Row, Plantation Wharf, Battersea, London SW11 3TW; tel: 020 7738 1800; fax: 020 7738 2820

**Cameroon** 84 Holland Park, London W11 3SB; tel: 020 7727 0771/3; fax: 020 7792 9353

**Congo** Alliance House, 12 Caxton St, London SW1H 0QS; tel: 020 7222 7575; fax: 020 7233 2087

**Democratic Republic of the Congo (DRC)** 26 Chesham Place, London SW1X 8HH; tel: 020 7235 6137; fax: 020 7235 9048

**Egypt** 26 South St, London W1Y 8EL; tel: 020 7499 2401; fax: 020 7355 3568

**Eritrea** 96 White Lion St, London N1 9PF; tel: 020 7713 0096; fax: 020 7713 0161

**Ethiopia** 17 Prince's Gate, London SW7 1PZ; tel: 020 7589 7212–5

**Gabon** 27 Elvaston Place, London SW7 5NL; tel: 020 7823 9986; fax: 020 7584 0047

**The Gambia** 57 Kensington Court, London W8 5DG; tel: 020 7937 6316–8; fax: 020 7937 9095

**Ghana** 104 Highgate Hill, London N6 5HE; tel: 020 8342 8686; fax: 020 8342 8566

**Guinea** 22 Gilbert St, London W1Y 1RJ; tel: 020 7333 0044

**Guinea-Bissau** 8 Palace Gate, London W8 4RP; tel: 020 7589 5253

**Ivory Coast** 2 Upper Belgrave St, London SW1X 8BJ; tel: 020 7235 6991

**Kenya** 45 Portland Place London W1; tel: 020 7636 2371/5; fax: 020 7323 6717

**Lesotho** 7 Chesham Place, London SW1 8HN; tel: 020 7235 5686; fax: 020 7235 5023

**Liberia** 2 Pembridge Place, London W2 4XB; tel: 020 7221 1036

**Malawi** 33 Grosvenor St, London W1X 0DE; tel: 020 7491 4172/7

**Mauritania** 140 Bow Common Lane, London E3 4BH; tel: 020 8980 4382; fax: 020 8556 6032

**Morocco** 49 Queen's Gate Gardens, London SW7 5NE; tel: 020 7581 5001/4; fax: 020 7225 3862

**Mozambique** 21 Fitzroy Square, London W1P 5HJ; tel: 020 7383 3800; fax: 020 7383 3801

**Namibia** 6 Chandos St, London W1M 0LQ; tel: 020 7637 6244; fax: 020 7637 5694

**Nigeria** Nigeria House, 9 Northumberland Av, London WC2 5BX; tel: 020 7839 1244; fax: 020 7839 8746

**Rwanda** 58/59 Trafalgar Square, London WC2N 5DX; tel: 020 7930 2570; fax: 020 7930 2572

Embassy addresses and telephone numbers in the UK are regularly updated and published by HMSO in *The London Diplomatic List* (ISBN 0-11-591746-2, price £3.95). The closest embassy in Europe is normally given for countries which have no embassy in the UK.

**Senegal** 11 Phillimore Gardens, London W8 7QG; tel: 020 7937 0925/6
**Sierra Leone** 33 Portland Place, London W1N 3AG; tel: 020 7636 6483-6
**South Africa** South Africa House, Trafalgar Square, London WC2N 5DP; tel: 020 7930 4488; fax: 020 7321 0835
**Sudan** 3 Cleveland Row, London SW1A 1DD; tel: 020 7839 8080
**Swaziland** 58 Pont St, London SW1X 0AE; tel: 020 7581 4976–8; fax: 020 7589 5332
**Tanzania** 43 Hertford St, London W1; tel: 020 7499 8951-4; fax: 020 7491 9321
**Tunisia** 29 Prince's Gate, London SW7 1QG; tel: 020 7584 8117; fax: 020 7225 2884
**Uganda** Uganda House, 58/59 Trafalgar Square, London WC2N 5DX; tel: 020 7839 5783; fax: 020 7839 8925
**Democratic Republic of the Congo** 26 Chesham Place, London SW1X 8HH; tel: 020 7235 6137; fax: 020 7235 9048
**Zambia** 2 Palace Gate, London W8 5LS; tel: 020 7589 6655; fax: 020 7581 1353
**Zimbabwe** Zimbabwe House, 429 Strand, London WC2R 0SA; tel: 020 7836 7755

## African embassies and consulates in France and Belgium
**Burundi** Square Marie Louise 46, 1040 Brussels, Belgium; tel: 230 45 35
**Central African Republic** 30 Rue des Perchamps, 75016 Paris, France; tel: 142 24 42 56
**Chad** Boulevard Lambermont 52, 1030 Brussels, Belgium; tel: 215 19 75
**Djibouti** 26 Rue Emile Ménier, 75116 Paris, France; tel: 147 27 49 22
**Equatorial Guinea** 6 Rue Alfred de Vigny, 75008 Paris, France; tel: 147 66 44 33
**Mali** Av Molière 487, 1060 Brussels, Belgium; tel: 345 74 32/345 75 89
**Niger** 154 Rue de Longchamp, 75116 Paris, France; tel: 145 04 80 60
**Rwanda** Av des Fleurs 1, 1150 Brussels, Belgium; tel: 763 07 38; fax: 763 07 53; 12 Rue Jadin, 75017 Paris; tel: 147 66 54 20; fax: 142 27 74 69

## African embassies and consulates in South Africa
**Algeria** 950 Arcadia St, Hatfield, PO Box 57480, Arcadia 0007, Pretoria; tel: (012) 342 5074; fax: (012) 342 5087
**Angola** CPK Building, 153 Olivier St, Brooklyn, PO Box 8685, 0001, Pretoria; tel: (012) 466 104; fax: (012) 466 253
**Botswana** 24 Amos St, Colbyn, PO Box 57035, Arcadia 0007, Pretoria; tel: (012) 342 4760; fax: (012) 342 1845
**Burundi** 1315 Church St, PO Box 12914, Hatfield 0028, Pretoria; tel: (012) 342 4881; fax: (012) 342 4885
**Congo** 960 Arcadia St, PO Box 40427, Arcadia 0007, Pretoria; tel: (012) 342 5507; fax: (012) 342 5510
**Democratic Republic of the Congo** 423 Kirkness St, PO Box 28795, Sunnyside 0132, Pretoria; tel: (012) 344 1478; fax: (012) 344 1510
**Egypt** Drostday Building, 270 Bourke St, Muckleneuk, PO Box 30025, Sunnyside 0132, Pretoria; tel: (012) 344 6043; fax: (012) 343 1082
**Eritrea** 1281 Cobham Rd, Queenswood, PO Box 11371, Queenswood 0121, Pretoria; tel: (012) 333 1302; fax: (012) 333 2330
**Ethiopia** Southern Life Plaza, 2nd Floor, 1150 Schoeman St, PO Box 11469, Hatfield 0028; Pretoria; tel: (012) 342 6321; fax: (012) 342 8035

**Gabon** Southern Life Plaza, corner Festival and Schoeman St, PO Box 9222, Hatfield 0028, Pretoria; tel: (012) 342 4376; fax: (012) 342 4375

**Ghana** 1038 Arcadia St, PO Box 12573, Hatfield 0028, Pretoria; tel: (012) 342 5847; fax: (012) 342 5863

**Ivory Coast** Infotech Building, Suite 106, 1090 Arcadia St, Hatfield, Pretoria; tel: (012) 342 6913; fax: (012) 342 6713

**Kenya** 302 Brooks St, PO Box 35954, Menlo Park 0102, Pretoria; tel: (012) 342 5066; fax: (012) 342 5069

**Lesotho** Momentum Centre, 6th Floor, West Tower, 343 Pretorius St, PO Box 55817, Arcadia 0007, Pretoria; tel: (012) 322 6090; fax: (012) 322 0376

**Madagascar** 14 Greenfield Rd, Greenside, PO Box 786098, Sandton 2146, Johannesburg; tel: (011) 646 4691; fax: (011) 486 2403

**Malawi** 770 Government Av, Arcadia 0007, PO Box 11172, Brooklyn 0011, Pretoria; tel: (012) 342 0146; fax: (012) 342 0146

**Mali** Infotech Building, Suite 111, 1090 Arcadia St, Hatfield 0028, Pretoria; tel: (012) 342 7464; fax: (012) 342 0670

**Morocco** 799 Schoeman St, Arcadia 0007, Pretoria; tel: (012) 343 0230; fax: (012) 343 0613

**Mozambique** 199 Beckett St, PO Box 40750, Arcadia 0007, Pretoria; tel: (012) 343 7840; fax: (012) 343 6714

**Namibia** Tulbagh Park, Suite 2, Eikendal, 1234 Church St, Colbyn, PO Box 29806, Sunnyside 0132, Pretoria; tel: (012) 342 3520; fax: (012) 342 3565

**Nigeria** 138 Beckett St, Arcadia, PO Box 27332, Sunnyside 0132, Pretoria; tel: (012) 343 2021; fax: (012) 343 1668

**Rwanda** Infotech Building, Suite 113, 1090 Arcadia St, Hatfield, PO Box 55224, Arcadia 0007, Pretoria; tel: (012) 342 1741/2; fax: (012) 342 1743

**Sudan** 1187 Pretorius St, Hatfield, PO Box 25531, Monument Park 0105, Pretoria; tel: (012) 342 4538; fax: (012) 342 4539

**Swaziland** Infotech Building, Suite 105, Arcadia St, Hatfield, Pretoria; tel: (012) 342 5782; fax: (012) 342 5682

**Tanzania** 845 Government Av, PO Box 56572, Arcadia 0007, Pretoria; tel: (012) 430 4383; fax: (012) 342 4375

**Tunisia** 850 Church St, PO Box 56535, Arcadia 0007, Pretoria; tel: (012) 342 6282; fax: (012) 342 6284

**Uganda** Infotech Building, Suite 402, 1090 Arcadia St, PO Box 12442, Hatfield 0028, Pretoria; tel: (012) 342 6031; fax: (012) 342 6206

**Zambia** Sanlam Centre, 353 Festival St, PO Box 12234, Hatfield 0028, Pretoria; tel: (012) 342 1541; fax: (012) 342 4963

**Zimbabwe** 798 Merton St, PO Box 55140, Arcadia 0007, Pretoria; tel: (012) 342 5125; fax: (012) 342 5126

## *African embassies and consulates in the USA*
**Algeria** 2118 Kalorama Rd, NW, Washington DC, 20008; tel: 202 265 2800

**Benin** 2737 Cathedral Av, NW, Washington DC, 20008; tel: 202 232 6656/7/8; fax: 265 1996

**Botswana** 3400 International Drive, Suite 7M, NW, Washington DC, 20008; tel: 202 244 4990/1; fax: 244 4164

**Burkina Faso** 2340 Massachusetts Av, NW, Washington DC, 20008; tel: 202 332 5577/6895

**Burundi** Suite 212, 2233 Wisconsin Av, NW, Washington DC, 20007; tel: 202 342 2574

**Cameroon** 2349 Massachusetts Av, NW, Washington DC, 20008 tel: 202 265 8790–4

**Central African Republic** 22nd St, NW, Washington DC, 20008; tel: 202 483 7800/1; fax: 332 9893

**Chad** 2002 R St, NW, Washington DC, 20009; tel: 202 462 4009; fax: 265 1937

**Congo** 4891 Colorado Av, NW, Washington DC, 20011; tel: 202 726 0825; fax: 726 1860

**DRC** 1800 New Hampshire Av, NW, Washington DC, 20009; tel: 202 234 7690/1

**Djibouti** Suite 515, 1156 15th St, NW, Washington DC, 20005; tel: 202 331 0270; fax: 331 0302

**Egypt** 3521 International Court, NW, Washington DC, 20008; tel: 202 895 5400; fax: 244 4319/5131. Consular section: tel: 966 6342

**Equatorial Guinea** Suite 405, 2522 K St, NW, Washington DC, 20005; tel: 202 393 0525; fax: 393 0348

**Eritrea** Suite 400, 910 17th St, NW, Washington DC, 20006; tel: 202 429 1991; fax: 429 9004

**Ethiopia** 2134 Kalorama Rd, NW, Washington DC, 20008; tel: 202 234 2281/2; fax: 238 7950

**Gabon** Suite 200, 2034 20th St, NW, Washington DC, 20009; tel: 202 797 1000; fax: 332 0668

**Gambia** Suite 1000, 1155 15th St, NW, Washington DC, 20005; tel: 202 785 1399/1379/1425; fax: 785 1430

**Ghana** 3512 International Drive, NW, Washington DC, 20008; tel: 202 686 4520; fax: 686 4527

**Guinea** 2112 Leroy Place, NW, Washington DC, 20008; tel: 202 483 9420; fax: 483 8688

**Ivory Coast** 2424 Massachusetts Av, NW, Washington DC, 20008; tel: 202 797 0300

**Kenya** 2249 R St, NW, Washington DC, 20008; tel: 202 387 6101; fax: 462 3829

**Lesotho** 2511 Massachusetts Av, NW, Washington DC, 20008; tel: 202 797 5533–6; fax: 234 6815

**Liberia** 5201 16th St, NW, Washington DC, 20011; tel: 202 723 0440

**Madagascar** 4 Massachusetts Av, NW, Washington DC, 20008; tel: 202 265 5525/6

**Malawi** 2408 Massachusetts Av, NW, Washington DC, 20008; tel: 202 797 1007

**Mali** 2130 R St, NW, Washington DC, 20008; tel: 202 332 2249 or 939 8950

**Mauritania** 2129 Leroy Place, NW, Washington DC, 20008; tel: 202 232 5700

**Morocco** 1601 21st St, NW, Washington DC, 20009; tel: 202 462 7979–7982; fax: 265 0161

**Mozambique** Suite 570, 1990 M St, NW, Washington DC, 20036; tel: 202 293 7146; fax: 835 0245

**Namibia** 1605 New Hampshire Av, NW, Washington DC, 20009; tel: 202 986 0540; fax: 986 0443

**Niger** 2204 R St, NW, Washington DC, 20008; tel: 202 483 4224–7

**Nigeria** 1333 16th St, NW, Washington DC, 20036; tel: 202 822 1500

**Rwanda** 1714 New Hampshire Av, NW, Washington DC, 20009; tel: 202 232 2882; fax: 232 4544

**Senegal** 2112 Wyoming Av, NW, Washington DC, 20008; tel: 202 234 0540/1

**South Africa** 3051 Massachusetts Av, NW, Washington DC, 20008; tel: 202 232 4400; fax: 265 1607

**Sudan** 2210 Massachusetts Av, NW, Washington DC, 20008; tel: 202 338 8565–70; fax: 667 2406

**Swaziland** 3400 International Drive, NW, Washington DC, 20008; tel: 202 362 6683/6685; fax: 244 8059

**Tanzania** 2139 R St, NW, Washington DC, 20008; tel: 202 939 6125; fax: 797 7408

**Togo** 2208 Massachusetts Av, NW, Washington DC, 20008; tel: 202 234 4212; fax: 232 3190

**Tunisia** 1515 Massachusetts Av, NW, Washington DC, 20005; tel: 202 862 1850

**Uganda** 5909 16th St, NW, Washington DC, 20011; tel: 202 726 7100/1/2 or 0416

**Zimbabwe** 1608 New Hampshire Av, NW, Washington DC, 20009; tel: 202 332 7100; fax: 483 9326

**Zambia** 2419 Massachusetts Av, NW, Washington DC, 20008; tel: 202 265 9717–9; fax: 332 0826

### *African embassies and consulates in Australia*

**Egypt** 1 Darwin Av, Yarralulma, ACT, 2600; tel: 06 273 4427; fax: 06 273 4279

**Gabon** 42 Quinton Rd, Manly, NSW, 2095; tel: 02 9977 0599; fax: 02 9977 0185

**Kenya** 6th Floor QBE Building, 33–35 Ainslie Av, Canberra, ACT, 2601, GPO Box 1990, Canberra City, ACT, 2601; tel: 06 247 4788; fax: 06 257 6613

**Lesotho** 294 Old South Head Rd, Watsons Bay, NSW, 2030; tel: 02 9398 3798

**Liberia** 36 Yarravale Rd, Kew, Victoria, 3101; tel: 03 9862 1392; fax: 03 9862 3563

**Madagascar** Level 7, Jardin-Fleming House, 19–31 Pitt St, Sydney, NSW, 2000; tel: 02 9252 3770; fax: 02 9247 6384

**Morocco** 11 West St, North Sydney, NSW, 2060; tel: 02 9922 4999; fax: 02 9923 1053

**Nigeria** 7 Terrigal Crescent, O'Malley, ACT, 2606, PO Box 241, Civic Square, ACT, 2608; tel: 06 286 1322; fax: 06 286 5332

**South Africa** Corner State Circle and Rhodes Place, Yarralumla, ACT, 2600; tel: 06 273 2424; fax: 06 273 3543

**Tunisia** 27 Victoria Rd, Bellevue Hill, NSW, 2028, PO Box 805, Double Bay, NSW, 2028; tel: 02 9327 1417; fax: 02 9327 1855

## HEALTH
*with Dr Felicity Nicholson*

Nomad Pharmacy in the UK supply all organised tours with their medical kits and are experts in what you will need when travelling in Africa. You can choose from a mini-kit or full truck kit. A full medical kit from Nomad Pharmacy costs about US$500 (3–4 Turnpike Lane, London N8 0PX; tel: 020 8889 7014).

· We would also suggest that you go over your previous medical history with your local GP and take the appropriate medication with you. Hopefully you won't be needing it – but better be safe than sorry.

For women travellers it's important to carry all relevant medication regarding vaginal infections. See *Chapter 7* for more detailed information on health and women's issues.

The medical kit list on pages 100–1 includes everything we think you might need, but this does not necessarily mean that every item needs to be taken with you. The list should be discussed with either your local GP or travel clinic, who can advise you on what you are more likely to need. Malaria, bilharzia, diarrhoea of varying kinds, constipation, skin infections, flu and irritable eyes and ears from the dust are the problems you need to consider. Most of the travellers we spoke to while on the road had suffered from at least one of these.

It is also a good idea to attend a first-aid course for your own safety and security. In terms of intravenous (IV) treatment, it's best not to undertake this unless you are a qualified medic, doctor or nurse. Most travel kits include IV treatment packs as many medical institutions in Africa do not have these supplies. If you are seriously injured you should always take all of your own medical equipment with you. Medical staff in Africa do not find this offensive and in fact welcome good equipment.

Carry a medical self-help book with you. The one most travellers carry is *Where there is no doctor – a village health care handbook* by David Werner, Carol Truman and Jane Maxwell. This book can be ordered through amazon.co.uk and is also available at Nomad Pharmacy, 3–4 Turnpike Lane, London N8 0PX; tel: 020 8889 7014. There are many other choices of self-help books (see *Chapter 7* page 149), so you should shop around and take whichever one suits your needs.

## Vaccinations

To ensure a healthy trip to Africa check on your immunisation status. You must be up to date on tetanus (ten-yearly), polio (ten-yearly), diphtheria (ten-yearly), hepatitis A and typhoid. For many parts of Africa vaccinations against yellow fever, meningitis and rabies are also needed. The majority of travellers are advised to be vaccinated against hepatitis A with a hepatitis A vaccine (eg: Havrix Monodose, Avaxim). One dose of vaccine lasts for one year and can be boosted to give protection for up to ten years. It is now felt that the vaccine can be used close to the time of departure and is nearly always preferable to gamma globulin, which gives immediate but partial protection for a couple of months.

The newer typhoid vaccines last for three years and are about 85% effective. You should have this unless you are leaving within a few days for a trip of a week or less, when the vaccine would not be effective in time.

Immunisation against cholera is currently ineffective, but a cholera exemption certificate is required when crossing land borders in sub-Saharan Africa and may also be required by individual countries (eg: Tanzania, Zanzibar and Uganda). Cholera certificates can be obtained from your local travel clinic who are aware of the obstacles you might face in Africa.

Hepatitis B vaccination should be considered for longer trips (two months or more) or for those working in situations where risk of contact with blood is increased. Three injections are ideal, which can be given at 8, 4 and 0 weeks prior to travel.

Vaccination against tuberculosis is also advised for trips of two months or more.

Go to a travel clinic a couple of months before departure to arrange all these.

## Malaria prevention

There is no vaccine against malaria, but using prophylactic drugs and preventing mosquito bites will considerably reduce the risk of contracting it. Seek professional advice for the best anti-malarial drugs to take. Mefloquine (Lariam) is the most effective prophylactic agent for most countries in sub-Saharan Africa. If this drug is suggested then you should start at least two and a half weeks before departure to check that it suits you. Stop immediately if it seems to cause depression or anxiety, visual or hearing disturbances, severe headaches or changes in heart rhythm. Anyone who is pregnant, has been treated for depression or psychiatric problems, has diabetes controlled by oral therapy, is epileptic (or has suffered fits in the past) or has a close blood relative who is epileptic should not take mefloquine. The usual alternative is chloroquine (Nivaquine/Avloclor) twice weekly, and proguanil (Paludrine) twice daily. Although this is less effective it is often used for trips of short duration (two weeks or less) or where there is no time to try mefloquine. In Namibia and the game parks of South Africa, this is the prophylactic regime of choice.

The antibiotic doxycycline (100mg daily) is considered by many to be better than chloroquine and Paludrine in areas where resistance to these drugs is high. It need only be started one day before arrival. It may also be used by travellers with epilepsy, unlike the other regimes, although the antiepileptic therapy may make it less effective. Users are warned that allergic skin reactions in sunlight can occur in about 3% of people. The drug should be stopped if this happens. Women using the oral contraceptive should use an additional method of protection for the first four weeks when using doxycycline.

All prophylactic agents should be taken with or after the evening meal, washed down with plenty of fluid and continued for four weeks after leaving Africa.

There is no malaria above 3,000m; at intermediate altitudes (1,800–3,000m) there is a low but finite risk. Much of South Africa is free from the disease, although it is a risk in some parts; elsewhere the risk to travellers is great. It is unwise to travel to malarial areas of Africa when pregnant or with children: the risk of malaria is considerable and these travellers are likely to succumb rapidly to the disease. See also page 143.

## Medical institutions
### UK

**British Airways Travel Clinic and Immunisation Service** 156 Regent St, London W1; tel: 020 7439 9584. This place also sells travellers' supplies and has a branch of Stanford's travel book and map shop. There are now BA clinics all around Britain and four in South Africa. To find your nearest one, phone 01276 685040.
**MASTA** (Medical Advisory Service for Travellers Abroad) Keppel St, London WC1 7HT; tel: 09068 224100; web: www.masta.org. This is a premium-line number, charged at 50p per minute.
**Nomad Travel Pharmacy and Vaccination Centre** 3–4 Wellington Terrace,

## MEDICAL KIT

With any of the following medicaments, it is vital that, if in doubt, you seek medical advice before use and read the instructions.

### Analgesics (pain killers)
- Aspirin for sore throat and mild pain
- Paracetamol for mild pain and temperature
- Ibuprofen for joint inflammation and pain
- Paracetamol/Codeine for moderate pain

### Antibiotics
- Amoxycillin for chest, ear and urinary tract infection (general antibiotic)
- Ciprofloxacin for gut and urinary tract infections
- Tinidazole for amoebic dysentery and giardia
- Flucloxacillin for skin infections
- Erythromycin for skin and chest infections (if allergic to penicillin)
- Mebendazole for thread-, round- and hookworm infections

### Malaria prevention and treatment
- Anti-malarial tablets (see page 99)
- Quinine sulphate and Fansidar
- Quinine sulphate and doxycycline
- Fansidar

### Bilharzia
- Biltracide

### General medical items
- Buccastem for severe nausea, vomiting and vertigo
- Loperamide for acute diarrhoea
- Oral dehydration sachets for rehydration
- Senokot tablets for constipation
- Merocaine lozenges for sore throats
- Indigestion tablets for excessive acid and indigestion
- Loratidine for allergies
- Pseudoephedrine for nasal and sinus congestion
- Clove oil for toothache (apply in very small amounts)

### Eye, ear and nose
- Chloramphenicol for eye infections
- Normal saline sachets for an eye wash
- Eye bath as an eye-wash unit
- Ear drops
- Nose drops

### Sterile surgical equipment
- Sterile surgical gloves
- Scalpel (disposable)
- Mersilk suture of varying sizes
- Suturing forceps
- Stitch cutter
- Dental needles
- Syringes of varying sizes
- Variety of needles
- Pink and green Venflon for intravenous administration
- Sterile gauze to cleanse area of sterilisation
- Medical set for intravenous administration

### Powder and creams for the skin
- Hydrocortisone for skin allergies and insect bites
- Lactocalamine for sunburn, itching and rashes
- Daktarin cream for fungal infections
- Cicatrin powder for wound infections (antibiotic)
- Magnesium sulphate for treatment of boils

### Comprehensive first-aid kit
- Granuflex dressing for tropical ulcers
- Gauze swabs for cleaning wounds
- Melolin of varying sizes for non-sticky wound dressing
- Micropore or zinc-oxide tape used as surgical tape
- Assortment of plasters
- Crepe bandage for muscular injuries
- Steristrips for wound closures
- Wound dressing for heavily bleeding wounds
- Triangular bandage for securing broken limbs
- Safety pins
- Steripods (disposable antiseptic sachets)
- Water gel or Jelonet dressing for burns
- Scissors
- Tweezers
- Disposable gloves
- Lancets (which can be used as sterile needles and for popping blisters)
- Betadine as antiseptic solution

### Other things to consider taking
- Thermometer
- Permethrin mosquito-net treatment
- Flu medication

Turnpike Lane, London N8 0PX; tel: 020 8889 7014.

**Thames Medical** 157 Waterloo Rd, London SE1 8US; tel: 020 7902 9000. Competitively priced, one-stop travel health service. All profits go to their affiliated company InterHealth which provides health care for overseas workers on Christian projects.

**Trailfinders Immunisation Centre** 194 Kensington High St, London W8 7RG; tel: 020 7938 3999. Also 254–284 Sauchiehall St, Glasgow G2 3EH; tel: 0141 353 0066. Non-profit-making private clinic with one-stop shop for vaccines, insurance, etc.

## USA

**Centers for Disease Control** 1600 Clifton Road, Atlanta, GA 30333; tel: 877 FYI TRIP; 800 311 3435; web: www.cdc.gov/travel. This organisation is the central source of travel information in the USA. Each summer they publish the invaluable *Health Information for International Travel* which is available from the Division of Quarantine at the above address.

**Connaught Laboratories** PO Box 187, Swiftwater, PA 18370; tel: 800 822 2463. They will send a free list of specialist tropical-medicine physicians in your state.

**IAMAT** (International Association for Medical Assistance to Travelers) 736 Center St, Lewiston, NY 14092. A non-profit organisation which provides lists of English-speaking doctors abroad.

### Australia

**TMVC** tel: 1300 65 88 44; website: www.tmvc.com.au. TMVC has 20 clinics in Australia, New Zealand and Thailand, including:

*Brisbane* Dr Deborah Mills, Qantas Domestic Building, 6th floor, 247 Adelaide St, Brisbane, QLD 4000; tel: 7 3221 9066; fax: 7 3321 7076

*Melbourne* Dr Sonny Lau, 393 Little Bourke St, 2nd floor, Melbourne, VIC 3000; tel: 3 9602 5788; fax: 3 9670 8394.

*Sydney* Dr Mandy Hu, Dymocks Building, 7th floor, 428 George St, Sydney, NSW 2000; tel: 2 221 7133; fax: 2 221 8401.

### South Africa

There are four **British Airways travel clinics** in South Africa: *Johannesburg*, tel: (011) 807 3132; *Cape Town*, tel: (021) 419 3172; *Knysna*, tel: (044) 382 6366; *East London*, tel: (0431) 43 2359.

**Glaxo Wellcome** Experts in malarial prophylactics. PO Box 3388, Halfway House, Johannesburg 1685; tel: 011 403 3586.

## MONEY

From a security point of view it would make sense to take most of your money as travellers' cheques, but in fact it is useful to take as much hard currency in cash as you feel you can safely carry. You may wish to take advantage of changing money on the street (a decision for each individual to make – be extremely careful if you do). Some banks will not change travellers' cheques and in some areas there may be no banks at all and you may have to rely on changing money with local traders. Some countries will demand payment for certain services in hard currency.

**NOTE**
The West African CFA and the central African CFA are not interchangeable. However, sometimes Air Afrique, Air Gabon or Air Cameroon will change one CFA to the other as they find both currencies useful.

It is worth bringing both small and large denomination notes with you. Do not under any circumstances carry US$100 bills; most banks will not accept them because of the number of fakes in circulation. In any case, small notes are useful when you have to pay low charges in hard currency – otherwise you end up getting your change in local money. Bring a mix of currencies to take advantage of swings in exchange rates. You will also find that only certain currencies will be acceptable in some countries. The two most important currencies to carry are US dollars and French francs. The dollar is the international currency of exchange, but in some banks in West Africa, particularly small towns, French francs are the only currency accepted.

Make sure you also have either French francs or CFA francs (Communauté Fiscalière de L'Afrique de L'ouest (CFA) is the common currency of the West African Monetary Unit) with you when crossing the Sahara into Niger or Mali, as you must have these to pay various charges at the border. There are two CFAs – the west African CFA and the central African CFA. The latter is used in Cameroon, the Central African Republic (CAR), Chad, Congo, Equatorial Guinea and Gabon.

If you have travellers' cheques, make sure you carry your receipt of purchase as many banks in Africa will not exchange them without it. You are not supposed to carry it with your travellers' cheques (for security), but you do not have much choice. Keep it in a separate pocket or bag, but carry it with you if you want to change money. Carry a photocopy and keep the original securely elsewhere.

You do not necessarily need to take all the money you are likely to need. American Express cardholders can buy US$1,000 worth of travellers' cheques at any of their offices with a cheque guaranteed by an Amex card. It is sometimes even possible to buy hard currency with your credit cards (shop around – different banks in the same town will have different rules).

You can also have money wired to a bank in Africa, although it can take some time – sometimes up to 12 days! Have someone taking care of your financial affairs back home. They should be able to help smooth the way for any transfer of funds.

## SUPPLIERS AND USEFUL ADDRESSES
### Vehicle selection
#### Internationally
*Autotrader* magazine can be found at major newsagents. It has information on used and new vehicles to sell or buy, or look in local papers.

### In the UK
**Westfield 4x4** Lancaster, LA2 OHF; tel: 1524 791698; fax: 1524 792653; email: sales@west-4x4.demon.co.uk; web: www.westfield.com Spare part suppliers specific to Mercedes Benz Type 411 and all makes of Unimogs worldwide.

## Vehicle preparation
### Internationally
**Superwinch** (world-wide suppliers of winches and recovery gear); web: www.superwinch.com

### In the UK
**Africa Travel Centre** 4 Medway Court, Leigh St, London WC1H 9QX; tel: 020 7387 1211.

**Black Diamond Warrington Transmission Centre Ltd** Unit 2–7, Guardian St, Warrington, Cheshire WA5 16J; tel: 01925 416619; fax: 01925 230472; technical hotline: 0345 125914; email: sales@wtc.co.uk; www.wtc.co.uk/p4x.htm. One of the largest independent re-manufacturers of gearboxes, differentials and axles. Nationwide delivery and they speak English, French and German.

**Brownchurch Ltd** Bickley House, 1A Bickley Rd, London E10 7AQ, tel: 020 8556 0011. The largest suppliers of rooftop tents in the UK.

**Drive Africa** PO Box 26705, London SW12 8WG; tel/fax: 020 8675 3974; email: mail@driveafrica.com; web: www.driveafrica.co.uk/main.html. Drive Africa will help you plan your holiday, ensure that your route and itinerary is carefully worked out, familiarise you with road conditions, answer your questions regarding planning and preparation, and can even book accommodation and activities.

**Expedition Advisory Centre (Royal Geographical Society)** Kensington Gore, London SW7 2AR; tel: 020 7581 2057

**Gumtree Enterprises** (specialists in Land Rovers) Fallbrook Workshop, Plumpton Lewes, East Sussex, BN7 3AH; tel: 01273 890259; email: gumtree@ukonline.co.uk; www.gumtree.com

**Nomad** 3–4 Turnpike Lane, London N8 0PX; tel: 020 8889 7014 fax: 020 8889 9529.

**North Staffs 4X4 Centre** Stafford Rd, Stone; tel: 01785 811 211; email: info@ns4x4.co.uk; www.ns4x4.co.uk

### In South Africa
**ARC** (general fitment centre) 45 Main Rd, Edenvale, Johannesburg; tel: (011) 452 5298.

**Avnic Trading** (suppliers of Garmin GPS 11 Plus); Johannesburg; tel: (011) 701 3244; fax: (011) 701 3270.

**Brakhah 4X4** (specialist vehicle equipment centre) Centurion, Pretoria; tel: (012) 663 4506; fax: (021) 663 5492.

**Cape Off Road and Safari** (one stop 4x4 shop) Epping, Western Cape; tel: (021) 934 3554.

**Northern Off-Road Equipment** (specialising in stainless steel, long-range fuel tanks) Strydom Park, Randburg, Johannesburg; tel: (011) 791 1611.

**Outdoor Warehouse** (specialists in outdoor equipment) Randburg, Johannesburg; tel: (011) 792 8331/6818. Also in: Pretoria; tel: (012) 661 0505; Durban; tel: (031) 579 1950/70; Cape Town; tel: (021) 948 6221.
**SA Surplus** (roof-top tent suppliers); Johannesburg; tel: (011) 316 4777.
**Safari Auto Tent** (roof-top tent suppliers); Beaufort West, Cape Town; tel: (0201) 3732.
**Safari Centre** (the best-known and longest-established 4x4 outfitter) Main Rd, Bryanston, Johannesburg; tel: (011) 465 3817 fax: (011) 465 2639. Also at: 36 James Crescent, Halfway House, Midrand; tel: (011) 805 3316 fax: (011) 315 7866; corner Durbanville and Church St, Durbanville, Cape Town; tel: (021) 975 3180 fax: 975 3114; Plot 22021, Kgomokasitswe St, Gaborone West Industrial Site, Botswana; tel/fax: (09627) 372390.

## Off-road driving courses
### In the UK
**David Bowyer's Off Road Centre** East Foldhay, Zeal Monochrum, Crediton, Devon EX17 6DH; tel: 01363 82666.
**The Ian Wright Off-Road Driving Centre** West Sussex; tel: 0800 731 7192; www.ianwrightorg.com
**Lee James 4X4** (countrywide); tel: (0115) 911 3201; www.leejames4x4.cwc.net

### In South Africa
**Safari Centre** offers off-road driving training and guided trails.

## Off-road websites
**www.ultimate-offroad.co.uk** Internet magazine with the latest news on all four-wheel-drive issues – particularly good is the link to 'expedition and equipment'.
**www.4x4mag.co.uk** Internet magazine – particularly good classified section on used vehicles.
**www.4x4offroad.co.uk/index.htm** Of general interest regarding off-road issues.
**www.4xforum.co.za** Offering information on all aspects of four-wheel driving in Africa.

FOR ALL YOUR OVERLANDING SUPPLIES

NOMAD TRAVELLERS STORE
* EQUIPMENT *CLOTHING
*MEDICAL *VACCINATIONS
CALL 020 8889 7014 FOR COLOUR BROCHURE
3-4 Wellington Terrace, Turnpike Lane, London N8
40 Bernard St, Russell Square, London WC1
*New Clinic:* 43 Queens Road, Clifton, Bristol
Email: sales@nomadtravel.co.uk  www.nomadtravel.co.uk

## ECONOMIC EXPEDITIONS
For the best value expeditions through Africa
30 weeks London-South Africa £1560  22 weeks London-Kenya £1280
12 weeks Nile Expedition £850  6 weeks Kenya-South Africa £380
5 weeks Middle East £380  2 weeks Gorilla Safari £180
PRICES INCLUDE FOOD   Tel: (020) 8995 7707   Fax: (020) 8742 7707
Email: ecoexped@cwcom.net  Website: www.economicexpeditions.com

**MOROCCO & WEST AFRICA OVERLAND ADVENTURE**
Expeditions from 2–10 weeks
Countries visited: Morocco/Mauritania/Senegal/Mali/
Burkina Faso/Ghana/Togo/Ivory Coast
For your free brochure call
**NOMADIC EXPEDITIONS LTD.**

Fully bonded

Travel Trust
Association
No. R6352

Tel 0870 220 1718 (24 hours) Fax 0870 220 1719
Email info@nomadic.co.uk Website: www.nomadic.co.uk

**Truck Africa**

## Adventure Overland Tours
3–30 weeks from only £410 visiting the best of
Africa with the African specialists.
For brochure tel: +44 (0)20 7731 6142; www.truckafrica.com

## *Wanderlust*
### THE ULTIMATE TRAVEL MAGAZINE

Launched in 1993, *Wanderlust* is an inspirational magazine dedicated to
free-spirited travel. It has become the essential companion for
independent-minded travellers of all ages and interests, with readers
in over 100 countries.

A one-year, 6-issue subscription carries a money-back guarantee – for further details:

**Tel.+44 (0)1753 620426**
**Fax. +44 (0)1753 620474**

or check the *Wanderlust* website, which has

details of the latest issue, and where

you can subscribe on-line:

## www.wanderlust.co.uk

# Part Two

## On the Road

# Your Vehicle

The long-awaited day finally arrives and you are ready to hit the road. The African experience is about to begin!

This section provides you with some useful information while driving through Africa. It includes information on driving and recovery techniques and an overview of daily maintenance, breakdown and repairs. It also deals with African bureaucracy and the challenges you will face along the way. Finally it covers day-to-day issues regarding accommodation, meals, health, security and how to stay in touch with family and friends.

Once again, remember to respect other cultures, their dress and the environment in which they live. In doing so your experience of Africa and its people will be that much more fulfilling.

## DRIVING TECHNIQUES

This section aims to give you an insight into the different conditions you can expect to encounter and the best way to tackle them. There are a few basics common to all terrains that you should be aware of.

Be familiar with the four-wheel-drive capability of your vehicle ie: does it have permanent or selectable four-wheel drive, what differential locks does it have and how are they engaged and does it have freewheel hubs or not? All this information will be in the vehicle handbook and is essential knowledge to help prevent you getting stuck in difficult terrain.

Driving in Africa can be exhausting because of the difficult conditions and long days behind the wheel, so it is preferable to share driving as much as possible. If you do this from the outset all the drivers will have an opportunity to experience different conditions and become familiar with the vehicle.

The benefits of walking through an obstacle before driving through should never be underestimated, particularly when faced with water, mud holes and rocks, as the chances of getting stuck or causing major damage because of an unseen object can be greatly reduced. With most bad conditions it is preferable to coax the vehicle to go in the right direction rather than fight the wheel and risk damage.

Night driving, unless completely unavoidable, is not usually worth the hassle. There are very few fences along the side of roads, so cattle and people are always on the roads, and other vehicles often don't have or don't use their headlights.

Finally it is important to keep your thumbs out of the steering wheel rim because when the vehicle hits an object the steering wheel can kick back with enough force to bruise or even break them.

There are three main conditions you will face: mud, sand and corrugations. Each requires a different technique and presents its own set of unique problems. In general the majority of main roads in Africa are not in very bad condition (with the exception of the Democratic Republic of the Congo), although you will inevitably encounter one or all of the following situations depending on where and when you go. We found the most important thing to remember when driving long distances in Africa is to take it easy and be vigilant. We never drove over 80km/h (50mph), because at this speed we could anticipate and react to bad sections of road. A slower speed also helps to reduce wear and tear and is more economical on fuel.

## Mud

It is essential that you engage four-wheel drive and select the appropriate gear before hitting the muddy section. For vehicles with large engines third-gear low-range or first-gear high-range is appropriate and for smaller engines second-gear low-range. It is also important to limit wheelspin, which will just make you bog down deeper. If the wheels start to spin, ease off the accelerator until you get more traction, then accelerate gently again, trying to avoid wheelspin. If wheelspin continues even after decelerating, it is better to stop and use a recovery technique (see below) than to dig yourself in deeper by spinning the wheels.

Should you encounter a water-filled boghole, always stop and walk through the boghole first. Logs and rocks are often put in the hole by other drivers, and these can do serious damage to the underside of your vehicle. A walk through will help to locate these and plot the best course. Nine times out of ten it is better to drive through the middle of deep bogholes rather than to try to skirt round them, as you usually end up sliding sideways into the hole and possibly overturning, or getting stuck as it is usually muddier on the edges.

## Sand

Momentum in sand is the key. We found high-range four-wheel drive to be more appropriate for most of our desert crossings. We only used low-range when we could see a particularly soft patch ahead or we were already stuck. If you see a section that you feel needs low-range, make sure you give yourself room for a run up, and try to get into low-range third before you hit the soft sand – this gives you momentum.

Changing gear in soft sand can bring you to a stop as quickly as braking and should be avoided. Try not to use the brakes at all, as you will build up a wall of sand in front of your tyres, which makes starting up harder. If you need to stop it is better to look for a harder area and just take your foot slowly off the accelerator. If you feel yourself getting stuck a good trick is to 'waggle' the steering wheel from side to side, as this makes the front wheels act as a snow plough, helping to remove the build-up of sand. If you do come to a halt, don't try too hard to extricate yourself with the power of the engine alone as this will either cause wheelspin and bog you deeper in, overheat the engine, damage the engine or snap a half shaft.

## Corrugations

Corrugations are probably the most irritating and most common driving obstacle in Africa. They are constant ripples on dirt roads or other hard surfaces, caused by vehicles travelling at speed. They often occur when a reasonable stretch of road occurs after a soft section and previous vehicles have taken the opportunity to speed up.

There are only two ways of coping with corrugations – very fast or very slow. Neither option is particularly pleasant. Driving fast, you can skip across the tops of the bumps. This is generally the favoured approach, although it does give your suspension a hard time and removes much of your steering and braking control. The slower option can be quite tortuous but is often the only way. You will sometimes notice tracks running parallel to badly corrugated roads which are an indication of the surface local traffic prefers – though often there is not a great deal to choose between them.

## Wading a vehicle/river crossings

Don't even consider this if you haven't prepared your vehicle properly (see *Chapter 2*, Vehicle Preparation). Always walk across first to gauge the depth and plot a route. If you feel the water is too deep or fast flowing, DON'T CROSS. Wait for the water level to drop or find another route.

If you decide to cross, here are a few tips. On older vehicles, take off the fanbelt to prevent damage to the fan blades. Don't stall the engine. If you do, do not attempt to restart your engine as you will cause even more damage. If you do stall you will need to winch or tow the vehicle to dry ground. Water and mud will probably have been sucked into the engine via the exhaust which means you have a major job on your hands. You will need to strip and clean the entire engine; if at all in doubt, get some professional help.

Always keep a constant speed and do not change gear – correct gear selection is essential. A footmat placed over the radiator helps to create a larger bow wave and larger draw down in the engine bay, which keeps more of the engine out of water.

## RECOVERY TECHNIQUES

With luck and sensible driving you shouldn't need to use recovery techniques too often, but when you do get stuck it can save a lot of hard work (often in deep mud and extremely hot conditions) if you have the right equipment and know a few recovery techniques. See *Chapter 2*, Vehicle Equipment for the choice of recovery equipment.

There are many factors involved in how you go about extricating your vehicle from a tricky spot. These are: what you are stuck in, the availability of anchorage points, what equipment you have and what's available locally (manpower, other vehicles, blocks of wood, etc). Every recovery requires some common sense and usually hard work. In almost all situations a certain amount of digging will be required. This is probably the most important part of all recoveries and it is always worth doing properly. That said, here are a few basic recovery techniques that can be adapted as conditions dictate.

## Sandmats

Sandmats are most often used to get out of deep sand, but can also be used in mud, as a jacking plate for high-lift jacks and for repairing holes in damaged bridges. They can also be very dangerous, especially in sand. When the vehicle accelerates off the end of the mats they have a tendency to be spat up and out by the back wheels and can easily cause serious bodily harm, so make sure you stand well clear of them. The most important part of recovery with sandmats is the digging. The sand must be cleared away from all wheels, and the chassis if the vehicle is grounded. When the sand has been moved the mats should be placed in front of the wheels with the least traction. The flatter the sandmats can be placed the better and the less damage you will do to them. Drive on to the mats and try to get as much speed up as possible, do not stop until you are on to a firm surface again.

## Winching

Anchor points are the main factor when considering whether to winch yourself out of trouble or up steep slopes. There are two types of anchor point, natural and man-made. Natural anchors are anything that is strong enough to take the strain, ie: trees, rocks or posts. Man-made anchors are used only when nothing else is available and they usually require a lot of effort to construct.

One method of creating an anchor point is to bury a spare tyre or sandmats vertically in the ground, then attach an anchor strap using a bar behind the tyre or sandmats. The direction of pull needs to be as straight and as low to the ground as possible, so you will need to dig a trench for the strap to lie in.

A snatch block is a useful winching accessory. It is basically a heavy-duty, single-line pulley and can be used to double the pulling force by attaching it to an anchor point, then passing the winch cable through the snatch block and back to the vehicle. A snatch block can also be used to change the direction of pull when using another vehicle to winch you out.

Winches are potentially very dangerous. If the cable snaps or the anchor point fails, the cable can come whipping back very fast. One person should co-ordinate the recovery and operate the winch and everyone else should stay well back while the cable is under tension. A heavy mat or blanket can also be placed over the cable to help stop the cable if it snaps.

## High-lift jack

Always remember to put a jacking plate under the high-lift jack before jacking in soft ground conditions. This could be a sandmat, piece of wood or a spare tyre. Two useful methods for recovering a vehicle using a high-lift jack are 'jack and pack' and 'jack and push'.

In jack and pack, the high-lift jack is used to lift the wheels clear of the ground so that material such as rocks, wood, sandmats, etc can be packed under the wheels to increase traction. This method is useful when the vehicle is bogged up to its chassis in mud. The jack and push method involves jacking the vehicle from the front or rear, so that both the wheels are off the ground. The vehicle is then pushed sideways off the jack. This method is useful when the vehicle is stuck in deep muddy ruts or grounded on a central ridge.

The high-lift jack can also be used as a winch, but it is limited to a pull the length of the jack before the whole assembly has to be reset. With all high-lift jack operations it is important to remember to always leave the jack with the handle in the upright position when unattended.

## MAINTENANCE, BREAKDOWNS AND REPAIRS

The key phrase to remember here is 'regular maintenance prevents breakdowns and the need for expensive repairs.' This cannot be stressed enough. Dusty conditions, extreme temperatures, contaminated fuel and bad roads all take their toll.

Consult the manufacturer's handbook for service intervals as a start, then consider the conditions you are putting your vehicle through – often the intervals will have to be revised. For example, if you do a lot of desert driving, air and fuel filters will get clogged more quickly. If you do a lot of wading, gearbox and differential oils will get contaminated and you can pick up a tank of dirty fuel just about anywhere in Africa.

The tables overleaf are a guideline for maintenance and inspection intervals. It may seem like overkill to suggest checking something like the wheelnuts every day, but the heavy vibrations of corrugated roads means that they can loosen themselves at a frightening rate. We speak from experience!

### Regular maintenance

Servicing should be carried out more frequently than at home. In particular, keep all oil levels topped up. You should also get into the habit of a regular daily mechanical check. This shouldn't take long and it is just a matter of keeping an eye on things and looking out for advance warnings of potential problems.

It is also very important to familiarise yourself with every detail of your vehicle. Try to get into the habit of walking around it whenever you stop and lie under it for a few minutes every day. If you have a mental imprint of how your vehicle should look, you will be able to spot any potential problems far more quickly and easily. Keep an eye out for small leaks, cracks, chafing, loose nuts (put a spanner on all the vital steering and suspension nuts regularly) and fix any minor problems immediately. A stitch in time could save a hundred! Toilet stops or lunch breaks are a good time to have a quick walk-around and carry out the following checks:

• Feel hubs for abnormally high temperature – could indicate a worn bearing;

## INSPECTION SCHEDULE

| Daily inspection – check every day before starting the engine | Weekly inspection |
|---|---|
| Engine oil level | General inspection of undercarriage and engine |
| Radiator water level | Gearbox, transfer box and differential oil levels – change engine oil or differential oil if in extreme conditions |
| Battery level and corrosion of battery leads | Suspension – look for loose U-bolt nuts, signs of movement between spring leaves, cracks in coils or leaves, rubbing of main leaf against the hangers |
| Fanbelt tension | Battery acid levels |
| Spark plugs leads secure | Check for oil leaks |
| Tightness of wheelnuts | Loose drain plugs |
| Brake and clutch fluid levels | Engine mounts |
| Tyre pressure | Check for loose nuts |
| Water temperature | Check steering box oil |
| Oil pressure | Check swivel housing oil and grease level |
| Clean air-filter – dust-bowl or pre-filter if in dusty conditions | |
| Shock absorbers | |
| Steering damper | |
| Brake cylinders and brake hoses | |
| Exhaust system | |
| Check for leakage on the ground below vehicle | |

- Feel tyres for abnormally high temperature – could indicate too low tyre pressure;
- Visual check of hubs for signs of oil or brake fluid leakage;
- Check underneath for signs of leakage.

## Common problems
### Suspension
The poor state of the roads means that suspension problems are a constant threat – careful driving and constant vigilance are the only solutions. In order to reduce the chances of your springs breaking or cracking we would strongly recommend fitting new springs on older vehicles before you set out. Newer vehicles with coil springs are probably less trouble than those with leaf springs.

## MAINTENANCE SCHEDULE

| Item | Maintenance interval | Comments |
|---|---|---|
| Diesel engine oil | 5,000km (3,000 miles) | More frequently if doing a lot of low-range driving as mileage ceases to relate to engine hours |
| Petrol engine oil | 10,000km (6,000 miles) | |
| Diesel oil filters | 5,000km (3,000 miles) | |
| Petrol oil filters | 10,000km (6,000 miles) | |
| Gear box and transer oil | 15,000km (9,000 miles) | |
| Differential oil | 15,000km (9,000 miles) | |
| Set tappets | 10,000km (6,000 miles) | |
| Set timing | 10,000km (6,000 miles) | |
| Change spark plugs | 20,000km (12,000 miles) | |
| Air filters | 10,000km (6,000 miles) | Oil bath and reusable types, clean with every oil change |
| Diesel fuel filters | 10,000km (6,000 miles) | Loss of power can be due to clogged filter from bad fuel |
| Petrol fuel filters | 10,000km (6,000 miles) | Loss of power can be due to clogged filter from bad fuel |
| Greasing | Every two weeks or after every wade | |
| Sediment bowl (diesels) | 10,000km (6,000 miles) | Inspect regularly |

The chassis can also often break, particularly after wear and tear. There is no way of being certain this will not happen to any vehicle, but older ones are obviously more prone; make sure that the state of the chassis has been carefully checked before you buy a vehicle. If necessary you can get it strengthened.

Many suspension problems can be prevented by careful maintenance. Always keep your suspension nuts tight and in good condition. Loose U-bolts can lead to the leaf springs slipping against the axle and eventually a broken centre-bolt. When this happens the axle can then move fore or aft relative to the chassis and it is only a matter of time until the whole axle comes off completely. It is worth noting the ridiculously high number of trucks and buses that you will see 'going sideways' or 'crabbing' as a result of a skewed rear axle. Simply by keeping an eye on the tightness of their suspension parts, drivers could probably save countless deaths each year.

## INVENTIVE REPAIRS
Tim Larby

Africa is full of surprises; one of the great excitements of an overland trip through Africa is not knowing what's waiting round the next corner. Unfortunately, this element also seems to be adopted by vehicles venturing on to the continent! Sooner or later (probably sooner!) something is going to go wrong with your vehicle that no amount of spares, mechanical knowledge or workshop manuals is going to fix.

If you do not have the right spares and none are available, do not despair. African mechanics are among the most inventive in the world – they have to be. You will also need to become inventive yourself. Unless you are unlucky enough to have a catastrophic mechanical failure, it will usually be possible to fashion a repair that will get you to a place where the fault can be fixed properly.

One of the people to whom I owe a good deal of my mechanical knowledge had a golden rule for dealing with breakdowns. As soon as anything unexpected went wrong, he would walk 100 metres up the road, sit down and have a cigarette. Although this may have had more to do with his nicotine addiction than anything else, the philosophy is a good one. Stop, relax, assess the situation and take time in planning a solution. For non-smokers, brewing a pot of tea will probably do just as well!

The key to being able to carry out effective bush repairs lies in ingenuity, experience and having the right materials to hand. Ingenious solutions come from sitting down and thinking broadly about the problem until you come up with a good solution. This can take some time and your first idea will often not be the best. Ideas evolve, and once you have come up with a promising solution, think about it a bit more – you can probably make it even simpler.

Rather than trying to fix the immediate problem, it may be easier and simpler to implement a work-around of some sort. Say, for example, you have punctured your brake line on a rock. Rather than trying to repair the damage (which would be extremely difficult), it would be far easier and quicker just to cut the pipe back on the master cylinder side and crimp the end over. Rather than fix the immediate fault, you have worked around the problem and have a satisfactory solution that is going to get you to the next brake pipe shop.

Experience, they say, can only be learned. However, good training can be achieved by using those hours in the driving seat to think about imaginary breakdowns. 'What would I do if suddenly X happened?' or 'Have I got what I need to fix Y?'. Try to get into the habit of not delving into your spares box unless absolutely necessary and fixing minor problems where possible. Not only does this keep your spares stock up in case of emergency, but it also gives you good experience of 'bush techniques'.

Having the correct materials to hand relies on carrying a good stock of what we could call 'bush spares', including essentials such as miscellaneous nuts, bolts and washers, various bits of metal, wire, rubber and plastic, adhesives, cable ties, etc (see below for a list of suggested bush spares).

Bush repairs are usually required because you have experienced some unexpected or undocumented breakdown. As such, it is impossible to write a definitive 'Bush Repair Manual'. However, the following examples can hopefully provide some good ideas and starting points for similar problems.

## Broken propshaft or UJ
Remove the broken shaft and continue in 4WD. (Be very gentle as all the torque from the engine is now being transferred through one shaft that is not designed for it.)

## Broken throttle cable or pedal
Tie a piece of cord around the injector pump or carburettor arm and pass it through the window.

## Clutch not functioning
Start the engine in first gear and change gear by matching the engine and roads speeds.

## Broken main leaf or coil spring
Insert a wooden block or spare tyre between the axle and chassis.

## Radiator hole or cracked fuel tank
Soap, softened with a little water, will temporarily fix the leak.

## Diff or pinion
On some vehicles the front and rear differentials and pinions are interchangeable (you will need to check in your workshop manual whether this is possible or not with your specific vehicle). If they are interchangeable and your rear ones have gone, you can swap the rear with the front to maintain rear-wheel drive.

## Sticking thermostat
Remove the thermostat (let the engine warm up for longer).

## Hole in exhaust
Patch with an old food can and fencing wire.

## Suggested bush spares
- tub of mixed nuts, bolts and washers
- self-tapping screws
- duct tape and electrical tape
- cable ties in various sizes
- contact adhesive (spray-on contact is very quick and easy)
- Araldite or Permabond
- SuperGlue
- old bicycle/car inner tube
- coathanger wire or bicycle spokes
- thin gardening wire
- long piece of chain or steel cable
- plastic from oil tubs or similar containers
- pieces of sheet metal
- string or strong cord
- jubilee clips
- miscellaneous electrical wire

## Tyres

Punctures and tyre damage are also a constant threat in Africa and the expense of tyres makes caution in this area very worthwhile. Tyres are particularly vulnerable when running at low pressure. If you have to reduce your tyre pressures, eg; in soft sand, be extremely wary of buried rocks and sharp sticks and return the pressure to normal as soon as possible. Generally the sidewalls contain far fewer plies than the tread and are therefore more prone to punctures and tears. When running on low pressure, the tyre spreads and the weak sidewalls are in contact with the ground.

If you have to repair a tube, be very careful when re-fitting the tyre. Small stones, sand, grit or flakes of rust can puncture the tube very quickly if they are caught between the tyre and tube. A good dusting of talcum powder between the tube and tyre can help reduce the friction between the two and reduce the chances of a blow-out.

In general, look after your tyres with great care. Stay away from sharp rocks, sticks and acacia thorns; always keep them at the correct pressure; and carry a comprehensive selection of patches and repair material. It is also worth carrying tyre (rather than tube) patches to repair any large holes in the tyre itself.

## Fuel

The poor quality of some fuel means your fuel filter is likely to get blocked more often than normal. It is a good idea to rinse the fuel tank before leaving to get rid or any sludge that may be in the bottom, and flush the filter on the bottom of the pick-up (if fitted). This may not be necessary if your vehicle has been driven solely in countries with good fuel.

While on the road, clean out the sediment bowl regularly and try to filter your fuel through a fine gauze or cloth while filling the tank if you suspect the fuel might be dirty. Change your filter(s) at the first sign of spluttering or loss of power from the engine.

It is also a good idea to carry a short length of hose to blow through and clear any blockages. We had to use this method frequently in both Nigeria and Chad because of poor fuel.

## Extreme heat

If you need to heat any parts to a very high temperature (to flare a brake pipe, loosen a press-fitting, etc), a handy technique is to use the air-pump (a compressor if you are lucky enough to have air-brakes or a foot pump if necessary) to 'supercharge' your fire. Get a good charcoal fire burning on top of the end of a steel pipe (eg: a tent pole) and start pumping air down the pipe.

## De-greasing plastic tubes

A 50/50 mixture of diesel and washing-up liquid makes an excellent de-greaser for pre-cleaning very dirty areas – rinse off with water after several minutes.

## Tackling hidden problems

Sometimes, you may be faced with a problem of which the cause is not immediately obvious. An overheating engine is a typical example – there's an obvious symptom but the root cause may lie in a number of fairly complex problems. With a problem like this, it is often helpful to refer to a troubleshooting guide (found in most manuals) that matches mechanical symptoms against possible causes. However, the key to effective troubleshooting is a thorough understanding of how your vehicle works. You can then mentally follow through exactly what is happening and then, with a few tests, isolate the problem.

Here is an example of troubleshooting. Say the engine is overheating: it is only running for about half an hour before the water temperature light comes on you have to stop for 15 minutes to let the engine cool down. You need to understand what is happening so you can start eliminating possible causes:

- The engine is overheating so there must be either too much heat going in, or not enough leaving – or a combination of both;
- Heat goes into the engine through burning fuel and friction from moving parts;
- Heat leaves the engine from the radiator via the cooling water, exhaust, oil and airflow over the engine;
- Test each of these and eliminate possible causes;
- Burning too much fuel could be purely from the engine doing a lot of work, too much heat from friction could result from low oil – which then reduces the cooling ability of the oil;
- Reduced airflow over the engine could arise from a defective fan or a clogged radiator – or even the vehicle moving too slowly;
- Reduced cooling effect from the radiator could be due to many things (faulty thermostat, blocked radiator pipe, low coolant, faulty water-pump, etc).

A similar train of thought and analysis can be applied to most problems, but a troubleshooting list has been given as a starting point here.

## Troubleshooting list

The following information has been taken from the range of Haynes vehicle repair manuals (www.haynes.co.uk).

### Fault diagnosis

The vehicle owner who does his or her own maintenance according to the recommended schedules should not have to use this section of the manual very often. Modern component reliability is such that, provided those items subject to wear or deterioration are inspected or renewed at the specified intervals, sudden failure is comparatively rare. Faults do not usually just happen as a result of sudden failure, but develop over a period of time. Major mechanical failures in particular are usually preceded by characteristic symptoms over hundreds or even thousands of kilometres. Those components which do occasionally fail without warning are often small and easily carried in the vehicle.

With any fault finding, the first step is to decide where to begin investigating. Sometimes this is obvious, but on other occasions a little detective work will be necessary. The owner who makes half a dozen haphazard adjustments or replacements may be successful in curing a fault (or its symptoms), but he or she will be none the wiser if the fault recurs and may well have to spend more time and money than was necessary. A calm and logical approach will be found to be more satisfactory in the long run. Always take into account any warning signs or abnormalities that may have been noticed in the period preceding the fault – power loss, high or low gauge readings, unusual noise or smells, etc – and remember that failure of components such as fuses may only be pointers to some underlying fault. The pages which follow here are intended to help in cases of failure to start or of breaking down on the road. Whatever the fault, certain basic principles apply. These are as follows:

- **Verify the fault.** This is simply a matter of being sure that you know what the symptoms are before starting work. This is particularly important if you are investigating a fault for someone else who may not have described it very accurately.
- **Do not overlook the obvious.** For example, in cases where the vehicle won't start, is there fuel in the tank? If an electrical fault is indicated, look for loose or broken wires before digging out the test gear.
- **Cure the disease not the symptom.** Substituting a flat battery with a fully charged one will get you back on the road, but if the underlying cause is not attended to, the new battery will go the same way.

Do not take anything for granted. Particularly, don't forget that a 'new' component may in itself be defective (particularly if it's been rattling round in the boot for months), and do not leave components out of a fault diagnostic because they are recently fitted. When you do finally diagnose a fault, you'll probably realise it was there from the beginning.

### Electrical fault

Electrical faults can be more puzzling than straightforward mechanical failures, but they are no less susceptible to logical analysis if the basic principles of operation are understood. Vehicle electrical wiring exists in extremely unfavourable conditions – heat, vibration and chemical attack – and the first thing to look for are loose or corroded connections and broken or chafed wires, especially where the wires pass through holes in the bodywork or are subject to vibration.

All metal-bodied vehicles in current production have one pole of the battery 'earthed' and connected to the vehicle bodywork, and in nearly all modern vehicles it is the negative (-) terminal. The various electrical components – motors, bulb holders, etc – are also earthed, either by means of a lead or directly by their mountings. Electrical current flows through the component and back to the battery via the bodywork. If the component mounting is loose or corroded, or if a good path back to the battery is not available, the circuit will be incomplete and malfunction will result. The engine and/or gearbox are also earthed by means of flexible metal straps to the body or subframe – if these straps are loose or missing, starter motor, ignition or generator problems may result.

Assuming the earth return to be satisfactory, electrical faults will be due either to component malfunction or defects in the current supply. If the supply wires are broken or cracked internally, this results in an open circuit, and the easiest way to check for this is to bypass the suspect wire temporarily with a length of wire with a crocodile clip or suitable connector at each end. Alternatively, a 12V test lamp can be used to verify the presence of supply voltage at various points along the wire and the break can be isolated.

If the bare portion of a live wire touches the bodywork or other earthed metal parts, the electricity will take the low resistance path thus formed back to the battery; this is known as a short-circuit. Hopefully a short-circuit will blow a fuse, but it may cause burning of the insulation (and possible further short-circuiting), or even a fire. This is why it is inadvisable to bypass persistently blowing fuses with silver foil or wire.

## The engine will not start
### Engine fails to turn when starter operated
- Flat battery (recharge, use jump leads or push start)
- Battery terminals are loose or corroded
- Battery earth to body defective
- Engine earth straps loose or broken
- Starter motor (or solenoid) wiring loose or broken
- Ignition/starter switch faulty
- Major mechanical failure (seizure)
- Starter or solenoid internal fault

### Starter motor turns engine slowly
- Partially discharged battery (recharge, use jump leads or push start)
- Battery terminals loose or corroded
- Battery earth to body defective
- Engine earth strap loose
- Starter motor (or solenoid) wiring loose
- Starter motor internal fault

### Starter motor spins without turning engine
- Flat battery
- Starter motor pinion sticking or sleeve
- Flywheel gear teeth damaged or worn
- Starter motor mounting bolts loose

### Engine turns normally but fails to start
- No fuel in tank
- Other fuel system fault

- Poor compression
- Major mechanical failure

*Engine fires but will not run*
- Air leaks at inlet manifold
- Fuel starvation

### The engine cuts out and will not restart
*Engine misfires before cutting out – fuel fault*
- Fuel tank empty
- Fuel pump defective or filter blocked (check for delivery)
- Fuel tank filler vent blocked (suction will be evident on releasing cap)
- Other fuel system fault

*Engine cuts out – other causes*
- Serious overheating
- Major mechanical failure, eg: Camshaft drive

### The engine overheats
*Ignition (no-charge) warning light illuminated*
- Slack or broken drivebelt – re-tension or renew

*Ignition warning light not illuminated*
- Coolant loss due to internal or external leakage
- Thermostat defective
- Low oil level
- Brakes binding
- Radiator clogged externally or internally
- Engine waterways clogged

*Note:* Do not add cold water to an overheated engine as damage may result

### Low engine oil pressure
*Gauge reads low or warning light illuminated with engine running*
- Oil level low or incorrect grade
- Defective gauge or sender unit
- Wire to sender unit earthed
- Engine overheating
- Oil filter clogged or bypass valve defective
- Oil pressure failure valve defective
- Oil pressure relief valve defective
- Oil pick-up strainer clogged
- Oil pump worn or mounting loose
- Worn main or big end bearings

*Note:* Low oil pressure in a high-mileage engine on tickover is not necessarily a cause for concern. Sudden pressure loss at speed is far more significant. In any event, check the gauge or warning light sender before condemning the engine.

### Engine noises
#### Whistling or wheezing
- Leaking manifold gasket
- Blowing head gasket

#### Tapping or rattling
- Incorrect valve clearance
- Worn valve gear
- Worn timing chain
- Broken piston ring (ticking noise)

#### Knocking or thumping
- Unintentional mechanical contact (eg: fan blades)
- Worn drivebelt
- Peripheral component fault, ie: generator, water pump, etc.
- Worn big-end bearings (regular heavy knocking, perhaps less under load)
- Worn main bearings (rumbling and knocking, perhaps worsening under load)
- Piston slap (most noticeable when cold)

## MOTORBIKE DRIVING TECHNIQUES AND REPAIRS
*Alex Marr*
Once on the road, the two most important things are undoubtedly keeping your air-filter clean (in very dusty conditions this can be necessary every day) and performing regular oil changes (around every 2,000km/1,200 miles). Sponge air filters can be washed in petrol, dried, soaked in engine oil and the excess squeezed out.

Other frequent checks should include chain tension, spoke tension and tightness of nuts and bolts (nylock nuts help – lockwiring is impractical).

In dusty or sandy situations lubing the chain can have a detrimental effect. Gritty sand clings to the sticky lube and grinds away at the chain and sprockets. It is best to run the chain completely dry in these conditions.

## Security
Most theft in Africa is opportunistic. Keeping things packed away from sight and putting locks, no matter how superficial, on boxes and panniers, will go a long way to deterring potential petty thieves.

Almost every cheap hotel in Africa has some sort of courtyard or off-street area when you can park a bike at night. Many of them have security guards too, usually asleep but a deterrent nonetheless.

When bush-camping it is better to site yourself well away from the road. Even so you often attract some local interest, but it is usually of a friendly nature and problems rarely arise.

## Riding in difficult conditions
### Sand
Reducing tyre pressures considerably – as low as 8psi – increases the surface area of the tyre in contact with the sand and makes riding a lot easier. However, if the sand is in stretches alternating with rocky terrain, do not reduce tyre pressure too much as you risk a puncture on the rocks. In really deep sand which has been rutted by other vehicles, it can be easier to just move through at walking pace, paddling along with your feet until you feel in control enough to ride properly. If you feel the rear wheel getting bogged down, it is best to dismount immediately and push, simultaneously applying gentle engine power. If you do get completely bogged down, slowly start moving the bike from side to side until it is free enough to be lifted out of the hole. This may require removing the luggage and if it happens often, a sense of humour is very helpful!

### Mud
A real nightmare with a heavy bike, deep mud can mean you lose almost all grip and control over the bike. Stop before really bad sections and choose the best route – sometimes there is an easier way round the edges or side. Check the depth of water-filled sections before riding through.

### River crossings
The golden rule is to walk through first, checking the depth and the state of the bottom. Riding on large, rounded mossy rocks in deep water is going to have only one result!

In high-risk situations it is better to push the bike through, taking the luggage off first if necessary. If the bike is going to fall over in the water make sure you kill the engine first.

### Punctures
Everyone should know how to mend punctures. It is not difficult, but does require technique and practice – make sure you do the practising at home before you leave! Using heavy-duty inner tubes significantly reduces the chance of punctures.

## BICYCLE TROUBLESHOOTING
There are a few on-the-road problems that may arise for cyclists, including the possibility of numb hands. Should this happen, check the angle of the tilt on your seat or the direction of the bend of your handlebars and adjust as necessary.

Faced with unexpected noises, try the following:
- Click (only when pedalling) – make sure crank arms and pedals are screwed on tight. Make sure crank arms are not hitting derailleur cage, the wire on your derailleur, or kick stand.
- Click or rubbing sound (even when you don't pedal) – check for deformed rim hitting brake pad, broken spoke or broken axle.
- Rattle – check for loose screws all the way around on racks, waterbottle cages or other screw-on accessories.

# Bureaucracy

According to the Merriam-Webster Dictionary, bureaucracy means 'a system of administration marked by officials, red tape and proliferation'.

Without doubt you will have to deal with bureaucracy during your travels, and there are a few golden rules to remember: BE PATIENT, STAY CALM AND KEEP ON SMILING. There will be times when these golden rules are easier said than done, but remember that you do have time on your side and making a cup of tea for yourself and the officials indicates limited stress levels. This was one of our most successful *modus operandi* when we realised that a border post was going to be particularly sticky.

African red-tape is something that in time will drive you quite insane, but it is also the one aspect about Africa that you will probably most often talk about! If you are travelling with a vehicle or motorbike, you are more than likely going to have to deal with officialdom and sweet-talk your way through Africa. A friendly response to the ponderous pace of African bureaucracy will *always* pay dividends. It is true that some delays can seem pointless and almost designed to frustrate, but a positive attitude will ultimately help smooth the way and an aggressive manner can slow a snail's pace down to a dead stop.

## BORDERS AND POLICE CHECKS

Borders and police checks vary from country to country. Some border crossings will take hours, with an arduous amount of paperwork, while others have an easy and convenient system which takes a limited period of time. Never underestimate the systems of African border posts and always allow enough time to cross from one country into another.

It is worth seeking advice from other travellers who have recently crossed a specific border. Most border crossings will involve Immigration and Customs; vehicle or bike clearance; *carnet de passage*, international certificate for the vehicle and drivers' licence; vehicle insurance, which usually needs to be purchased; and a police or military check. Keeping on top of this can become a major occupation, but remember – BE PATIENT, STAY CALM AND KEEP ON SMILING.

Police or military checks are apparent at every border crossing, often on the outskirts of towns and sometimes in the middle of nowhere. This could take the form of just a glance over your vehicle or a demand to off-load every item. We met some bikers in southern Ethiopia who ended up at a border post for three days while every one of their items was meticulously searched – no amount of 'gifts' would speed up the process.

Since receipted administration fees are almost as common as 'dash' (palm greasing), the best advice we can give is to play it by ear. Normally, if you have to fill in a form and are given a receipt it is legitimate. A request for 'some money' means a bribe. It is up to you how to handle it. A custom we used on a regular basis when asked if we had anything was to indicate that 'a smile and handshake' were all we had! Unfortunately, some countries have an influx of tourists who bribe their way through Africa, throwing money and gifts around and setting a poor example for others. Some officials now expect that you will pay or give a gift. If you can get away with it, it's best not to hand anything over, except for that smile and a handshake!

A final point to remember is that often the police and military, especially in more remote areas, are not paid regularly by the government. Some of them also perform important services, for example restricting access to dangerous or remote areas, and are totally reliant on donations from tourists as well as the local community, so don't always dismiss requests for money out of hand; assess the situation and be fair.

## VISAS AND MONEY

Whenever you arrive in a large African town, particularly capital cities, you will probably have a huge list of things that need doing – like mending the vehicle, getting spares, changing money, getting visas, making phone calls, sending and receiving emails, collecting post, adding to depleted food supplies, etc. Whatever priorities you have listed, don't expect to get through them in a day!

Visa applications can be a waiting game, taking from 24 hours up to three days (the exception is Sudan – it took us three months!). Visiting a bank can take a whole day, if not longer. Of the five things you wanted to get done on a particular day, you'll probably get through two. Relax and get into the pace of Africa.

### Visas

There always seems to be an initial panic about trying to get all your visas before leaving home. Depending on the route you take and the time you intend to spend in Africa, more often than not your visa will have expired by the time you have arrived in the designated country.

It is also not necessarily a good idea to get every visa sorted before you leave, as the political shifts within Africa are forever changing and by the time you intend to visit that specific country, it might not be safe or convenient. Obviously if you are cycling, travelling will take a lot longer than in a vehicle, making visa validity and timing even more important. It is advisable to get a visa for the first few countries you'll be visiting at the start of your trip and any visas that are difficult to obtain in Africa. Libya, Sudan and Nigeria are notoriously difficult to get and well worth getting before you leave. Even if they run out before you arrive, at least you have something in your passport and that may just make the difference!

Once in Africa you are dependent on capital cities and the embassies represented therein. As a rule of thumb, try to have at least one onward visa before entering a new country. Not every country has an embassy in every

## KEEPING LEFT
*Tim Larby*

Driving from Lusaka up to the South Luangwa Park, with end of day near, we arrived at the bridge that crosses the Luangwa River. I pulled up at the line that was marked on the tarmac and a guard came up to the window.

His first comment to me was, 'Did you go to school?'

'Yes,' I answered.

He then motioned for me to come with him while hauling his rifle back over his shoulder.

And while we ambled back up the road he asked me how long I had attended school and what subjects I had studied.

'So,' he asked, 'you can read English?'

'Well, um, yes!' I replied, a little puzzled.

With almost rehearsed precision, he stopped walking, turned around and pointed at a sign that was now directly in front of us.

'What does that say?'

'Keep left,' I replied, still puzzled as to where this conversation was going.

The situation suddenly became clear when he pointed back to the strip beside the road where I had stopped the vehicle.

'Why have you not kept to the left?' he shouted. He was, of course, referring to the fact that I had parked the vehicle on the left-hand side and not pulled off onto the dirt which was clearly further left!

The debate began and he opened his bidding with, 'the crime carries a penalty of one hundred dollars,' and then added smugly after a dramatic pause, 'to be paid to my boss at the Department of Traffic in Lusaka.' Lusaka was about seven hours south of us.

After an exhausting hour and a tentative look inside the vehicle, particularly at our supplies, we were allowed to cross the bridge and be on our merry way, less some sugar and a box of Lipton tea.

African country, but with some foresight and planning, depending on where you want to go next, you'll be able to get your visa within a day or two. Some visas can take weeks, but that is in very unusual cases.

Filling out the forms for visas can be time consuming and involve loads of paperwork. Most embassies have specific opening times for visa applications, so check beforehand. Some embassies demand letters from your embassy, called 'Letter of Introduction'. It literally is a form of introduction from one embassy to another. These letters usually take 24 hours to process and vary in price, costing anything between US$20 to US$50, depending on the embassy.

Photographs *always* need to be attached to the visa application. Passport photos are not only useful for visa applications, but for other documentation that you might need for a specific country, such as photo permits.

When applying for a visa it is advisable to have some information with you about the country that you will be visiting. More often than not we were asked where we would be staying, and we often mentioned the Hilton or Sheraton, rather than 'camping'. It gives you a little more credibility and can make the difference between having your application accepted or rejected. Visa costs can vary from US$10 to $100 depending on your nationality and the country you are visiting.

Some guidebooks mention that EU nationals, New Zealanders and Australians need not pay for a visa application for a specific country. These requirements change regularly and should not be relied on. Some East African countries will issue visas at the border, but in the rest of Africa you need to obtain a visa before you arrive. If in doubt get a visa before you get to the border. British nationals are supposed to have a visa for Tanzania before entering, but this is ever-changing, so check beforehand with either your embassy or other travellers.

Visas for most francophone countries (ie: ex-French colonies) can be obtained from any French embassy. Check with your nearest French embassy or consulate for the current list of countries for which they issue visas, as it seems to change frequently. The following countries are relevant: Benin, Burkina Faso, Cameroon, Central African Republic (CAR), Chad, Congo, Ivory Coast, Equatorial Guinea, Gabon, Mali, Niger, Senegal and Togo.

Some border guards will ask to see a receipt for the visa. This is not a formal requirement, but is an excellent excuse to extract some cash from you. Try to get a receipt from the embassy or ask them to write the amount paid for the visa in your passport with an official stamp next to it.

## Money

> Finance is the art of passing currency from hand to hand until it
> finally disappears.
>
> Robert W Sarnoff

We mostly carried dollars in cash and travellers' cheques, divided into small and large denominations. Any kind of hard currency, US dollars or pounds sterling, will do. It is also advisable to get some French francs if you will be travelling in the French-speaking countries. We carried francs in cash and once again divided it into small and large denominations. For more information on suggested amounts and types of currency to take see *Chapter 4*, Money.

Finding a bank or somebody to change hard currency is never difficult, but like most travellers, we mostly carried travellers' cheques. These can be changed in banks or bureaux de change. Some campsites and backpackers will also change travellers' cheques for you and sometimes even accept travellers' cheques as payment.

Changing money, like visa applications, can be time consuming and filled with paperwork. Some banks are computerised and changing money is a simple process, while others need to go through all sorts of red tape before you see the cash. Always check opening and closing times of banks and leave plenty of time to change money, particularly in Arab countries where bank opening times vary between 08.30 and 09.00 – like in the Sudan – or 09.00 and 10.00. Though guidebooks might state that banks are open between 09.00 and 11.00, we found it best to go at 09.00, often having to wait half an hour while the bank attendant first had tea and said good morning to everyone. Remember that Friday is a holy day in Arab countries.

Rates and commissions vary widely from bank to bank, so it is worth shopping around to ensure you get a good rate. It is also advisable to check where your next bank will be and change enough money accordingly.

Most banks in Africa will charge a commission for changing travellers' cheques and this can vary from 1 to 10%. Trade sanctions by the United States against Sudan and Libya mean that it is not possible to change US dollar travellers' cheques, although it is possible to change US dollars cash.

It is always advisable to have smaller denominations as well as larger, particularly if you are travelling by motorbike or bicycle, as most people only have change for this. Large denominations can often cause problems. If you are in a vehicle, however, remember that you will probably spend US$100 just filling up with fuel, so here large denomination notes are useful.

Credit cards can be convenient in southern Africa and parts of East Africa, but generally the process is time consuming as it can take up to 48 hours to clear, sometimes as long as 12 days. Some countries have no facilities for credit cards at all.

## POST AND TELECOMMUNICATIONS

Throughout Africa, if there are people, there is a post office and a telephone. The only question is whether the phone is working. Some systems are so old you wonder how they manage to get a line! Even more surprising is that each capital city in Africa has at least one internet café, sometimes not on-line, sometimes very slow, sometimes expensive but always a good means of communication.

### Post

In every capital city and larger towns there is a post office with postal, telephone, fax, poste restante and courier services.

#### Poste restante

Poste restante is a postal service available at the main post office of almost every capital city. It is a general address where family and friends can send post to. Letters and parcels are kept for up to four weeks, and some form of identification will be needed for collection. You may also have to pay to collect it. All post is kept in alphabetical order. Make sure that your name is marked clearly in bold, black capital letters, underlining either the first letter of your surname or first name. This will make it a lot easier to collect. For example: Illya Bracht, c/o Poste Restante, Central Post Office, Accra (town as required), Ghana (country as required). Note that for all French-speaking countries you need to write 'PIT' instead of 'Poste Restante'.

## THE LOST RECEIPT AND FURTHER MISCHIEF IN NIGERIA

With all visa applications, one automatically presumes that the visa stamp within a passport is proof of payment and receipt. We learned the hard way when arriving at the border of Nigeria, Mubi, and also learned many other lessons that day!

On arrival at the border we could see two tin shacks, surrounded by wire fencing, no signs, and three men lounging under a tree. Unsure as to where to proceed first we yelled out the window to the three men, asking 'Where to?' The response: a shrug of the shoulders.

Without further ado, we took the left-hand tin shack, which had some available parking space, collected all appropriate paperwork, and walked up the stairs into the office directly in front of us, still unsure of what office we were actually stepping into it.

A very large officer came in behind us and started asking for all vehicle documentation, which we happily gave him, not realising that we had actually arrived at the Customs Office. Our first mistake.

All documentation was looked over and we were then asked to proceed to the vehicle for a thorough search. While in our vehicle and searching, one of the three men that had been lounging under the tree came running up to us, and, in Hausa, started shouting something at the other officer that had joined us at the vehicle.

In the same breath he turned to us and asked whether we had actually been to immigration yet. 'Of course not,' we replied, looking at the other man, and explained that when we had asked where to go we got a shrug of the shoulders and thought it best to go where there was safe parking.

He then started shouting, literally jumping up and down, and said, 'In what country do you not go to immigration first?' (Well, in Sudan for one, but logic is not something you attempt in Africa!)

Feeling a little intimidated we now rushed over to the right-hand tin shack, with three very irate men looking at us.

Passports were duly demanded and as every page was scrutinised (by now we had visited over 15 countries in Africa) he asked for the receipt for the Nigerian visa.

We knew we didn't have one, but to procrastinate and hopefully calm everyone down, we pretended to look for the receipt, turning the vehicle upside down.

On return we obviously had no receipt. The officer just shrugged his shoulders, leaned back in his chair and said, 'I can't let you proceed to

The success rate of actually receiving a poste-restante letter or parcel depends on the individual country, and do remember that it can take between two to three weeks for a letter to get to its final destination.

If you are collecting a parcel, it usually needs to go through an arduous customs check. It is advisable to indicate that the parcel contains old clothes and

Nigeria. You have to go back to Chad, N'Djamena, and get proof of receipt.' N'Djamena was about two days' drive away.

The negotiations began with Charlie stating that he had lived in Nigeria and this had never been a problem before, and what a beautiful country it is and we really would like to see this magnificent country and experience all it has to offer, but if we had to return to N'Djamena then he didn't think we would return to Nigeria, etc.

'Well,' the officer said, 'there is a form you can fill out, but I then need to send it to head office in Abuja and that will cost you postage.'

'How much postage will that cost me, do you think?' asked Charlie. I, at this stage, am staying quietly out of the negotiations. Unfortunately, in most of Africa, women are seen as inferior and have no say in such matters, and I thought we were already in enough trouble.

'Whatever you can afford,' the officer said.

We ended up giving him US$5 for postal services rendered, our passports were stamped and we rushed back to customs. Two hours had gone by.

Our very fat officer was not to be found, but instead a young gentleman was now sitting in his chair. The *carnet* was once again scrutinised, every page looked at, including the back where all countries you intend to visit are listed. Of course, Nigeria wasn't. Another set of negotiations began, but I think at this stage we were so exhausted, we just looked at him and again tried to formulate some type of 'other paperwork' that might be available to us.

In the interim, I was outside with the drug squad checking all medication, officers were doing a general search over the vehicle, and, pleased with all we had, asked me to return to the office with all our vaccination certificates.

Charlie was still in deep negotiation and eventually received a form, looking exactly like a carnet, that we had to drop off at the next town at the Customs office. To the boss, I might add. Our vaccination certificates were approved by the medical officers and we were allowed to leave.

Having arrived at the border post at 10.00, we made it out at 16.00, with not even a cup of tea! We also, conveniently, never found the next town and after arriving in Kano and asking some locals there about the form we had received, were met with a deep-throated chuckle, 'No way man, no such paper is needed in Nigeria!'

We had to presume that the officer wanted us to go to the Customs office in the next town, meet 'the boss', and share whatever loot they were able to get out of us. You live and learn!

food, rather than new goods, for which you may have to pay duty. But paying for a parcel is never really an issue, particularly if you've been on the road for a while.

It is also advisable when sending letters home to ask the cashier to frank all appropriate stamps in front of you as there are plenty of stories about stamps being removed from letters and never reaching their destination.

## Alternative postal services

A good and relatively safe alternative to post offices is that offered by American Express offices. Anyone carrying an Amex card or travellers' cheques is entitled to use the company's offices world-wide as a mailing address. This service is free. A booklet is available from American Express (Amex House, Edward Street, Brighton BN2 1YL; tel: 01273 693555) giving a complete list of its offices' addresses around the world.

## Telecommunications

Fax, telephone and email facilities are much more available than you might think. All capital cities and most larger towns will have public fax and telephone facilities and internet cafés are on the increase, so there is no excuse not to keep in touch!

All these facilities are obviously reliant on the individual country's telecommunications network, the quality of which varies greatly from country to country. It is often easier to call overseas than to a neighbouring town, as overseas calls are routed via satellites.

Telephone calls and faxes to Europe typically cost US$3 to $10 per minute, which is the same as an hour on the internet. So it is well worth setting up an internet email account, such as 'hotmail' or 'yahoo', before you leave. Some internet cafés will also let you work off-line at a reduced rate.

The French cultural centres in francophone countries and the British Council often have email facilities open to the public, but they can be more expensive than the local internet cafés. One important thing to remember is that computer viruses are much more of a problem when using public facilities, so be sure to warn the recipients to virus-check all the mail you send them.

## OVERLAND CAMPING SAFARIS

**Travelling as a group in a truck cooking on open fires in Africa and the Middle East. Trips from 3 to 10 weeks from £350.**

ON ALL TRIPS KITTY AND FLIGHT ARE EXTRA

## AFRICAN TRAILS

Tel: +44 (0)208 742 7724 Email: aftrails@globalnet.co.uk

## THE COMPLETE OUTDOORS

Suppliers of lightweight backpacking, camping & outdoor leisure equipment
10 mins from M25. Parking for 40 cards.
**Shop online at www.completeoutdoors.co.uk**
LONDON ROAD, BOURNE END, HEMEL HEMPSTEAD, HERTS HP1 2RS  TEL: 01442 873133

# Day-to-Day Issues

## WHERE TO STAY

Throughout your travels you will always be able to find a place to stay, whether it be with the local community, a hotel, bed & breakfast, pension, mission, youth hostel, backpackers' hostel, campsite, or just sleeping in the bush.

One of the more enticing reasons for driving, cycling or biking through Africa is the fascination of meeting other cultures and tribes in the context of Africa, its open spaces, beautiful scenery and often complete isolation from the outside world. Opportunities will arise for you to bush sleep, something that you may come to love, giving you freedom to move as you please. Even if you have prepared well in advance and are able to carry an adequate amount of water and food with you, there will come a time when you will need to depend on a village for water and basic supplies. The general rule which applies is RESPECT THE CULTURE AND LEAVE NOTHING BEHIND BUT YOUR FOOTPRINTS.

If bush sleeping is not your cup of tea, more conventional accommodation is available throughout the continent. In some parts of Africa, such as the east coast, there is plenty of lodging along the coast, while in central Africa you will need to find your own accommodation for the night. Along the west coast, some countries accommodate campers while others offer nothing but hotels.

Outside major cities in places like the Congo and Central African Republic, you are unlikely to find any type of accommodation unless you are lucky enough to come across a mission.

## Hotels

Hotels are plentiful in most parts of Africa. In some places they are run by the local community with no star structure at all, while in southern Africa, the east coast, parts of the west coast and parts of north Africa, there is one- to five-star accommodation. In many African countries, and particularly in the capitals, you will more than likely find a Hilton or Sheraton, a little of the first world within a third-world environment. Such places make great stopovers when you have been on the road for a while and usually offer all sorts of amenities, but expect to pay European rates.

'Hotels' in African terms can often just be the bare minimum, so always ask to see the room and negotiate the rate before booking yourself in. If you have your own vehicle, make sure that the hotel has a parking area with security; some hotels will allow guests to keep motorbikes in their rooms.

In many of the French-speaking countries along the west coast, you will struggle to find campsites or hostels, particularly in the larger towns, and you may have to depend on the kindness of a hotel manager to let you stay in his parking lot and use the hotel facilities. But don't try this with the Hilton or the Sheraton.

## Bed and breakfast

B&Bs are mostly found in southern Africa and along the east coast. Often quaint and family run, they offer a wonderful opportunity to relax and get information on what to do – or not to do – in that specific town or country. Most B&Bs belong to the National Hotel Association and/or are accredited by the tourist board, Automobile Association or various guidebooks. They are usually reasonably priced, around US$15 to US$25 for a double room.

Tourist information offices will be able to supply you with a list of B&Bs in the area and relevant prices.

## Pensions

Pensions are similar to B&Bs but are specific to the French-speaking countries such as Chad, Ivory Coast, Mali and Niger and are often run by a family; they are abundant in Morocco. Most of the pensions we experienced were economical, clean and well run. They are often also a wonderful introduction to the local community, usually offering an abundance of information about the town and surrounding areas. Most pensions cost between US$8 to US$15 for a double room.

## Missions

Throughout Africa missions, hospitals and aid organisations will often let you camp in their grounds or even offer you a room. Some will expect a small fee, others a hefty one – either way, a donation based on current camping rates is always welcome.

Although missions can be found in every country in Africa, unfortunately some travellers have abused their hospitality and now travellers are not always welcome. You won't find yourself being turned away by every mission, but we did find it more and more difficult to depend on them. Most missionaries adhere to strict rules and regulations in terms of curfews, shower time, kitchen and leisure time. If you feel that you cannot keep to such rules, find alternative accommodation; others are following in your footsteps and might like to use the opportunity, even if you don't.

## Youth hostels

Youth hostels are located in most capital cities and other larger cities. They are often the most convenient and cheapest places for a lone traveller, but two people travelling together can usually get a double room for the same price (US$18) – and greater privacy – elsewhere. Some are spartan with night-time curfews, daytime closing and no cooking facilities, often lacking in privacy and overrun by school groups. Others, however, are conveniently located and hassle free, affording a wonderful opportunity to meet other travellers.

## Backpackers' hostels

Backpackers' hostels are mostly found in southern Africa and along the east coast, with an occasional one dotted along the west coast and in north Africa. They are economical, ranging from US$8 to US$15 for a single room, with a huge variety of information on what to do around town, and a good place to meet up with other travellers.

Note that most travellers we met who were either cycling or driving through Africa did not particularly like backpackers' hostels. There seemed to be a silent war going on between independent travellers (those driving or cycling) and those backpacking in Africa. More often than not it was to do with space. Backpackers' hostels are specifically for 'backpackers', rather than those whose bulky vehicles or bikes clutter up the driveway.

## Campsites

You will often find that your day revolves around finding a good spot to stay for the evening, if not for a day or two. Along the main Africa overland route, there are campsites at fairly regular intervals, and major towns and out-of-the-way places will often have a site, but if you're intending to do a loop around West Africa, you might struggle to find any at all. Sites vary from one- to five-star ratings, and prices will usually vary from US$3 to $8.

Most campsites are visited on the recommendation of other travellers. They also give you the opportunity to catch up with other travellers, do some maintenance and repairs on your vehicle and catch up on all the other odd jobs that you might have been neglecting. Campsites are often a great source of information regarding vehicle repairs – where to go and who to see. Sometimes they even have their own individual mechanic, a sort of 'I-can-fix-it-all' person and usually an ex-driver for one of the tour companies.

Information on some of the main campsites is included in *Chapter 8*.

## Bush sleeping

Not to be missed! But make sure that you respect the bush, and be aware of the environment around you. If the surrounding area is particularly dry and there is a gale, do not light a fire. Leave only your footprints in the sand, bury biodegradable products and/or pack away tinned goods and all else that might cause damage to the environment. Do not, however, bury any goods in national parks as animals usually dig them up and can cause major damage to themselves, if not the environment. It is really better to carry all your rubbish with you until you find an appropriate place to discard it.

In the Congo or any other tropical rainforest area, bush sleeping can be very difficult, with solid vegetation right up to the sides of the road. The only two options are to find a village and ask for permission to camp or to find one of the 'gravel pits' which have been dug out for material to build the road. Such pits are few and far between and may often have large pools of water, making mosquito nets absolutely essential. You are also almost guaranteed to have visitors as gravel pits are frequently sited close to a village. It can also be hard to find a spot for bush camping in either southern Africa, Botswana, Namibia or Zimbabwe as almost all land is fenced off. In north Africa you can generally camp in *palmiers* (palm groves), but as these are privately owned you should ask permission if possible.

It is all too easy to forget that we are guests in the communities through which we are driving. The less visible you are from the road, the better, although trying to steer away from prying eyes can often prove difficult. Find a spot earlier rather than later as problems tend to multiply once it gets dark. Having spotted an area try to make sure that there are no other cars passing or people watching when you turn off. This is easier said than done, as villages tend to develop alongside a country's communication network; where there are a few roads and tracks, the population is likely to be concentrated along them. In this case, try and find the head of the village and ask permission to camp and light a fire. A small gift of appreciation such as a bottle of Coke, a chicken or cigarettes is often welcomed. Villagers are by nature curious, as we are of them, and you might feel a little intimidated by ogling adults and children. A sense of humour, a little magic, being able to play a musical instrument, drawing or just communicating usually helps to ease the situation, and is one of the better ways of getting to know a particular tribe, culture or village.

## FOOD AND DRINK
### Let's go local
Going local is an inexpensive exercise and one we suggest wholeheartedly. All of Africa's countries have their own unique meals and local brews. Some can be an acquired taste, others will be something you want to eat over and over again and a few you will hope never to taste again. For the local flavour of the day go to the markets, street vendors, restaurants or local cafes.

Each African country has its own beer, often brewed and bottled locally. In addition to this are fermented ricewater, honey beer, millet beer and all sorts of other local delicacies brewed up 24 hours a day. In some Muslim countries, alcohol is prohibited, but with a little bit of investigation, a local shebeen can usually be found – just be careful who you ask!

As in most African cultures, people eat with their hands. If you are invited into somebody's home, they will often offer you their one spoon or any other cutlery that might be available. If this does not happen, there is just one golden rule you need to remember; always eat with your right hand. The left hand is used for all other dirty business.

---

### LE GOUT DE BONHEUR
*Le goût de bonheur* means 'the taste of happiness'. In Chad it is Gala, the local brew, made by the most notorious brewery in Africa, the Gala Brewery. It is the only brewery that has stayed open and continued with its production of beer no matter what state the country is in – whether there be war or famine. This titbit was given to us by Fadoul, the brother of the Sultan in Abéché, Chad.

### FRESH CHICKEN, SIR!

We were somewhere in northern Morocco, and we needed some chicken. We asked the owner of a little café if he knew where we could get some. 'Follow me!' he said. After passing a butcher on the way, our friend indicated, 'Not fresh enough.' We kept on walking, a little baffled. A few metres further down the road was a door. A flat? A house? The shop?

We knocked and the door was opened. The first thing that assailed our senses was the smell and sound of chickens.

'Fresh chicken, sir?'

'Yes please.'

The chicken was weighed, alive and kicking, and we were charged accordingly. The chicken was then whisked behind the counter, the owner smiled a toothless grin, ducked under the counter with his head still sticking up and voilà – a dead chicken. It was plucked in the plucking machine, feet and head cut off and the rest wrapped in paper and into a plastic bag.

'Sir, fresh chicken!'

If you are unsure about how to react to a specific situation, watch what others do. In some cultures, they will only begin eating once you start. Usually, ask to wash your hands before a meal, then help yourself. Often your insecurity and mishap in eating with your hands can break the ice: learn to laugh at yourself!

## Local produce

Throughout Africa you'll have no problem finding local produce at markets or from street vendors. Onions, garlic and tomatoes are always available. Goat, mutton and chicken are also readily available, and fish is plentiful near rivers and on the coast. Many other fruits and vegetables can be found according to the country's economy and the season.

It can be great fun haggling and bartering your way through smiling vendors, each protesting that their produce is the freshest, nicest and cheapest. Visit a couple of stalls, ask around so you can get a feel for prices and always keep in mind the average local income. Sometimes you will be ripped off but if you are happy to pay the price offered, pay it! Most supermarkets have local produce, but at an increased rate as many of the products are imported from neighbouring countries, or even from Europe.

## Supermarkets

Most capital cities in Africa have an array of supermarkets, from well stocked to nearly empty. Local shops, often only a hole in the wall or a table set up on the pavement, have basic goods like toothpaste, toilet paper, margarine and other odds and ends.

## SOME LOCAL DELICACIES – TO TRY OR NOT TO TRY!

### Egypt

Stella (local beer)

*Alwa turki* Turkish-style coffee and a great energy booster, particularly with large amounts of sugar

*Molokhiyya* A soup made by stewing leafy vegetables with rice, garlic and chicken or beef broth. Do not be put off by its appearance.

*Grilled samak* (fish) Served by the kilogram and chosen by you. Usually includes salad, bread and dips like *tahina* (sesame spread with olive oil, garlic and lemon) and *baba ghanoug* (a mix of aubergine and *tahina*).

*Gibna beyda* (white cheese like *feta*) or *gibna rumi* (hard, sharp yellow-white cheese)

### Ethiopia

*Tej* A very potent honey beer that you will either hate or love!

Coffee ceremony A must; be ready to experience a caffeine overdrive!

*Shiro wot* Vegetable stew, great for vegetarians, and eaten by Ethiopians during religious fasting

*Doro wot* Hot chicken stew served on the famous injera bread

*Injera* Flatbread, generally made to cover a table. Food is placed on top for communal meals. Not to everyone's taste; can be quite sour.

*Kitfo* Raw meat with yellow pepper (*mitmita*)

Coffee shops serve fresh coffee, fruit juice and cakes.

### Ghana

*Apateche* Traditional firewater found everywhere. Try it!

Star (local beer)

*Shitor din* Traditional dark chilli sambal

*Palava* sauce 'Palava' means 'trouble'; this is a variation of vegetable and meat stew

### Ivory Coast

*Attiéké* Grated manioc served with fish and pepper sauce

*Maquis* Chicken with onion and tomatoes

Rice and offal balls A great delicacy

### Kenya

Tusker (local beer)

*Irio* Corn mash and maize which most Kenyans think is dull, but it's worth a try

*N'Dizi* Swahili for bananas, wrapped in groundnut. Crunchy n'dizi is self-explanatory.

### Morocco

Green tea Very sweet, served with fresh peppermint leaves

*Tagine* with chicken and prunes Astew cooked in the traditional *tagine* bowl and said to be one of the oldest recipes in Africa

## Niger

Green tea Traditionally brewed up by Tuaregs over an open fire and in very small teapots

Fresh camels' milk – like a warm milkshake and not to everyone's taste

Goat's cheese – a Tuareg delicacy and delicious if you're a lover of cheese; should be accompanied by dried prunes

Tuareg bread – baked in the sand

## Nigeria

Lager Star (local beer)

Gari foto Based on the root vegetable of the African diet

Gari Like rice, the base for many dishes

Okra soup – looks like slime but never say no to a new experience!

Kyimkying – West African kebabs and great street food, but not recommended by the local ex-pat community

## Southern Africa

Castle (local beer)

Red wines from Cape Town

Amarula A liquor made up from the amarula tree, which bears a fruit that elephants particularly like to eat

Biltong Dried game, not to everyone's taste

Bobotie A Malay dish served in southern Africa

Boerewors A type of sausage, delicious grilled over an open fire

## Sudan

Guava juice A must if you like guavas, freshly squeezed, served out of enormous cooler boxes

Fuul Fava beans with oil, lemon, salt, meat, eggs and onions

Ta'amiyya Deep-fried ground chick peas – very 'moreish'!

## Tanzania

Amstel (local beer)

Chapati ya n'dizi tamu Banana fritters, common throughout Africa

Chilled banana cream Good, depending on its freshness

Mboga ya maboga Pumpkin leaves and flowers in cream

Plantain or banana chips

## Tunisia

Brik A thin, crisp, pastry envelope filled with egg, cheese or meat. If you choose egg, bite carefully – the yolk may spurt out!

## Zimbabwe

Black Label (local beer)

Nhopi dovi Like pumpkin

Sadza Like the West African banku, the East African ugali, Zambian ntsima or South African 'mealie-meal', sadza is a stiff, steamed dumpling made from white maize flour. It is regarded as Zimbabwe's national dish.

For more luxurious items such as fresh cheese and chocolate, you will need to shop in large supermarket chains, like the Nakromat in Nairobi, which are found in most East African countries. If you have a favourite brand, take enough to last your entire trip, although this is only possible if you have your own vehicle.

## International restaurants

There will come a time when you are tired of eating locally or cooking for yourself, or a special occasion is on the horizon. Cuisine from all over the world can be found throughout Africa, particularly in the capitals, from Chinese to Italian, Indian to Lebanese, pizzas to hamburgers. The restaurants cater to every need and every pocket. Some are based on European prices while others are more affordable. Ask other travellers or wherever you are staying for advice on restaurants in the area. Most campsites and backpackers' hostels also offer basic international meals.

## Water

There is a saying in Agadez, Niger, that once you have tasted the water you will always want to return! In Agadez, the artesian wells are thousands of years old and the water is pure, coming deep out of the ground. This is not always the case but, throughout our trip, we were surprised by the availability of clean water, especially as it is one of the most important commodities in Africa. You will quickly recognise the gracefully slow walk of African women, and sometimes children, carrying enormous weights of water on their heads, often for great distances.

You must be prepared to respect local water sources. It is a very valuable commodity. Never do anything to a well that might contaminate it, such as throwing anything into it, or washing yourself or your clothes close by. This is particularly important in Arab countries where water is also used for prayer.

Obtaining water and the amount you need to carry depends on the time of year you are travelling, where you are and how dedicated you are to washing – both yourself and your clothes. In the desert at the hottest time of year you should allow six to eight litres a day intake per person, and even in January or February you will easily get through two or three. It is absolutely vital to drink as much as you need as you could run into serious problems if you do not. If your urine becomes concentrated in colour you could be heading for trouble. A good guide is that you should urinate often and it should be clear.

Cyclists will face the greatest difficulties in terms of how much they can carry, and bikers will also be restricted by weight. It is best to stick to the more major desert routes where water is more likely to be available from other travellers. Cyclists will need a good filter because they are less able to carry supplies of good water and will be more likely to rely on poorer sources. If water is not clear in any way, filter before purifying. We either drank straight from the source, filtered or used Chloromyn T. For more information see *Chapter 2*, Vehicle Equipment.

## AN ODE TO COCA-COLA

Coca-Cola is not only a great thirst quencher, but you will find it wherever you go. In the middle of nowhere, desolate and isolated, without a doubt a hut will appear that is selling Coca-Cola! It's not only good for tummy upsets or dehydration, but also great for cooking. If you have a very tough piece of meat, boil it up in Coca-Cola for an hour or so and you are guaranteed to have a tender piece of meat. Coca-Cola is indeed the real thing!

In general, wherever there is a village you will find a source of water. Open bodies of water, streams, lakes, etc are probably going to be contaminated and should be treated with caution. If you take water from an open source always purify it. Water from the tap can vary in quality; the best advice is to ask the locals if they drink it straight. If they do but you have a sensitive stomach, purify it. When faced with a village well, use some common sense. If people are washing nearby or the toilets are close then don't trust it, but if you are at a remote desert well which is well maintained and covered you should be OK.

## Soft drinks, beer and spirits

We all dream about sipping a G&T under a fading African sky. Except in north Africa, beer and local spirits are generally easy to find. Imported spirits can be found in most capital cities at European prices. In Arab countries, where alcohol is often banned, be prepared for the consequences if you intend to smuggle some in. It will mean at least a hefty bribe or possible fine or imprisonment or prohibition of entry into the country if you get caught.

Soft drinks can be found everywhere and Coke or Pepsi are always available. Beer is generally also available, except in strict Arab countries. Local beers range from excellent to unpleasant, but either way, try them – especially at local prices.

## HEALTH

with Dr Felicity Nicholson

This is one area where it can be difficult to strike the right balance between justified concern and outright paranoia. A lot of common problems can be avoided by being sensible about hygiene. There will, of course, be times when you are more or less dependent on local standards of hygiene. Some health guides for travellers visiting out of the way places will frighten you half to death. Basically you will find your own levels of hygiene and personal care – and even then your standards will vary according to the different conditions you find yourself in. Most of the time all you need is common sense.

Do not hesitate to see a doctor or take advantage of medical insurance cover if you think there is something really wrong with you. Some countries have

## TREATING TRAVELLERS' DIARRHOEA

It is dehydration which makes you feel awful during a bout of diarrhoea and the most important part of treatment is drinking lots of clear fluids. Sachets of oral rehydration salts give the perfect biochemical mix to replace all that is pouring out of your bottom, but unfortunatey they don't taste nice. Any dilute mixture of sugar and salt in water will do you good, so if you like Coke or squash, drink that with a three-finger pinch of salt added to each glass. Otherwise make a solution of a four-finger scoop of sugar with a three-finger pinch of salt in a glass of water. Or add eight level teaspoons of sugar (18g) and one level teaspoon of salt (3g) to one litre (five cups) of safe water. A squeeze of lemon or orange juice improves the taste and adds potassium, which is also lost during diarrhoea.

Drink two large glasses after every bowel movement, more if you are thirsty. If you are not eating properly (or at all) you need to drink three litres of water a day plus whatever is departing from you. If you feel like eating, have a bland, high carbohydrate diet. Heavy greasy foods will probably give you stomach cramps. If the diarrhoea is bad, or you are passing blood or slime, or if you have a fever, you will probably need antibiotics in addition to fluid replacement. Wherever possible seek medical advice before starting antibiotics. If this is not possible then a three-day course of ciprofloxacin (50mg twice a day) or norfloxacin is appropriate.

If the diarrhoea is greasy and bulky and is accompanied by eggy burps the likely cause is giardia (see opposite).

perfectly adequate hospitals and health clinics; some facilities are so basic they will make you cringe. Trust your judgement, but do not assume that health care will be bad just because it is African – after all, the doctors there are far more accustomed to tropical diseases than those at home. See also pages 97–102.

## Common medical problems
### Travellers' diarrhoea

At least half of those travelling to the tropics or the developing world will suffer from a bout of travellers' diarrhoea. The newer you are to exotic travel, the more likely you will be to suffer. By taking precautions against travellers' diarrhoea you will also avoid typhoid, cholera, hepatitis, dysentery, worms, etc.

Travellers' diarrhoea and the other faecal-oral diseases come from getting other peoples' faeces in your mouth. This most often happens from cooks not washing their hands after a trip to the toilet, but even if the restaurant cook does not understand basic hygiene, you will be safe if your food has been properly cooked and arrives piping hot. The maxim to remind you what you can safely eat is: PEEL IT, BOIL IT, COOK IT OR FORGET IT. This means that fruit you have washed and peeled yourself and hot food should be safe but raw food, cold cooked food, salad and fruit which have been prepared by others, ice-cream and ice are all risky. Foods kept lukewarm in hotel buffets are usually time-bombs waiting to go off!

## Giardia

Giardia is a type of diarrhoea or intestinal disorder caused by a parasite present in contaminated water. The symptoms are stomach cramps, nausea, bloated stomach, watery, foul-smelling diarrhoea and frequent wind. Giardia can occur a few weeks after you have been exposed to the parasite and symptoms can disappear for a few days and then return – this can go on for a few weeks. Giardia is basically a form of amoebic dysentery and is best treated with tinidazole (2g in one dose repeated seven days later if symptoms persist).

## Water sterilisation

It is relatively rare to get ill from drinking contaminated water, but it can happen, so try to drink from safe sources. Water should have been brought to the boil (even at altitude), or passed through a good bacteriological filter or purified with iodine. Chlorine tablets (eg: Puritabs) are also adequate, although theoretically less effective and they taste nastier.

Note that mineral water has been found to be contaminated in many developing countries and may be no safer than tap water.

## Malaria

Whether or not you are taking anti-malaria tablets, it is important to protect yourself from mosquito bites, so keep your repellent stick or roll-on to hand at all times. Some travellers carry a course of malaria treatment with them. Self treatment is not without risks and diagnosing malaria is not necessarily easy which is why consulting a doctor is the best option. If you are going somewhere remote in an area which is high risk for malaria you probably have to assume that any high fever for more than a few hours is due to malaria. Presently, quinine and Fansidar is the favoured regime, but check for up-to-date advice. Current experts differ on the costs and benefits of self-treatment, but agree that it may lead to people taking drugs they do not need. Discuss your trip with a specialist to determine your particular needs and risks.

Be aware that no prophylactic is 100% protective, but those on prophylactics who are unlucky enough to catch malaria are less likely to get rapidly into serious trouble. See also page 99.

## Avoiding insect bites

### Mosquitoes

It is crucial to avoid mosquito bites between dusk and dawn. As the sun is going down, put on long clothes and apply repellent on any exposed flesh. This will protect you from malaria, elephantiasis and a range of nasty insect-borne viruses. Malaria mosquitoes are voracious and hunt at ankle-level, so it is worth applying repellent under socks too. Sleep under a permethrin-treated

## QUICK TICK REMOVAL

African ticks are not the prolific disease transmitters they are in the Americas, but they may occasionally spread disease. Lyme disease has now been recorded in Africa, and tick-bite fever also occurs. This is a mild, flu-like illness, but still worth avoiding. If you get the tick off whole and promptly the chances of disease transmission are reduced to a minimum.

Manoeuvre your finger and thumb so that you can pinch the tick's mouthparts, as close to your skin as possible, and slowly and steadily pull away at right angles to your skin. This often hurts. Jerking or twisting will increase the chances of damaging the tick, which in turn increases the chances of disease transmission, as well as leaving the mouthparts behind. Once the tick is off, dowse the little wound with alcohol (local spirit, whisky or similar are excellent) or iodine. An area of spreading redness around the bite site, or a rash or fever coming on a few days or more after the bite, should stimulate a trip to a doctor.

bednet or in an air-conditioned room. During the day it is wise to wear long, loose (preferably 100% cotton) clothes if you are going through scrubby country; this will keep ticks off and also tsetse and day-biting *Aedes* mosquitoes which may spread dengue and yellow fever.

### Tsetse fly
Tsetse flies hurt when they bite and are attracted to the colour blue. Locals will advise on where they are a problem and where they transmit sleeping sickness.

### Blackfly
Minute pestilential biting blackflies spread river blindness in some parts of Africa between map co-ordinates 190°N and 170°S. The disease is caught close to fast-flowing rivers as flies breed there and the larvae live in rapids. The flies bite during the day but long trousers tucked into socks will help keep them off. Citronella-based natural repellents do not work against them.

### Tumbu flies or putsi
Tumbu flies or putsi are a problem in areas of East, West and southern Africa where the climate is hot and humid. The adult fly lays her eggs on the soil or on drying laundry and when the eggs come into contact with human flesh (when you put on clothes or lie on a bed) they hatch and bury themselves under the skin. Here they form a crop of 'boils', each of which hatches a grub after about eight days, when the inflammation will settle down. In putsi areas either dry your clothes and sheets within a screened house, or dry them in direct sunshine until they are crisp, or iron them.

## AVOIDING BILHARZIA

- If you are bathing, swimming, paddling or wading in freshwater which you think may carry a bilharzia risk, try get out of the water within ten minutes.
- Dry off thoroughly with a towel; rub vigorously.
- Avoid bathing or paddling on shores within 200m of villages or places where people use the water a great deal, especially reedy shores or where there is lots of water weed.
- Covering yourself with DEET insect repellent before swimming will protect you.
- If your bathing water comes from a risky source try to ensure that the water is taken from the lake in the early morning and stored snail-free, otherwise it should be filtered, or Dettol or Cresol added.
- Bathing early in the morning is safer than bathing in the last half of the day.
- If you think that you have been exposed to bilharzia parasites, arrange a screening blood test (your GP can do this) *more* than six weeks after your last possible contact with suspect water.

### Jiggers or sandfleas

Jiggers or sandfleas are another kind of flesh-feaster. They latch on if you walk barefoot in contaminated places, and set up home under the skin of the foot, usually at the side of a toenail where they cause a painful, boil-like swelling. These need picking out by a local expert; if the distended flea bursts during eviction the wound should be dowsed in spirit, alcohol or kerosene, otherwise more jiggers will infest you.

### Bilharzia or schistosomiasis

*With thanks to Dr Vaughan Southgate of the Natural History Museum, London*
Bilharzia or schistosomiasis is a disease which commonly afflicts the rural poor of the tropics who repeatedly acquire more and more of these nasty little worm-lodgers. Infected travellers and expatriates generally suffer fewer problems because symptoms will encourage them to seek prompt treatment and they are also exposed to fewer parasites. However, it is still an unpleasant problem that is worth avoiding.

The parasites digest their way through your skin when you wade, bathe or even shower in infested fresh water. Unfortunately many African lakes, including Lake Malawi, and also rivers and irrigation canals, carry a risk of bilharzia. In 1995, two-thirds of expatriates living in Malawi had evidence on blood testing of having encountered bilharzia, and 75% of a group of people scuba-diving off Cape Maclear in Lake Malawi for only about a week acquired the disease. The most risky shores will be close to places where infected people use water, where they wash clothes, etc. Winds disperse the cercariae, though, so they can be blown some distance, perhaps up to 200m from where they entered the water.

Scuba-diving off a boat into deep offshore water should be a low-risk activity, but showering in lake water or paddling along a reedy lakeshore near a village carries a high risk of acquiring bilharzia. Although absence of early symptoms does not necessarily mean there is no infection, infected people usually notice symptoms two or more weeks after penetration. Travellers and expatriates will probably experience a fever and often a wheezy cough; local residents do not usually have symptoms. There is now a very good blood test which if done six weeks or more after likely exposure will determine whether or not parasites are going to cause problems and the infection can be treated. While treatment generally remains effective, there are treatment failures for reasons that are not yet fully understood; retreatment seems to work fine and it is not known if some drug resistance is developing.

Since bilharzia can be a nasty illness, prevention is better than cure, and it is wise to avoid bathing in high-risk areas.

## Skin infections

Any mosquito bite or small nick in the skin gives an opportunity for bacteria to foil the body's usually excellent defences; it will surprise many travellers how quickly skin infections start in warm humid climates and it is essential to clean and cover even the slightest wound. Creams are not as effective as a good drying antiseptic such as dilute iodine, potassium permanganate (a few crystals in half a cup of water), or crystal (or gentian) violet. At least one of these should be available in most towns.

If the wound starts to throb or becomes red and the redness starts to spread, or the wound oozes, and especially if you develop a fever, antibiotics will probably be needed; flucloxacillin (250mg four times a day) or cloxacillin (500mg four times a day). For those allergic to penicillin erythromycin (500mg twice a day) for five days should help. See a doctor if the symptoms do not start to improve in 48 hours.

Fungal infections also get a hold easily in hot, moist climates, so wear 100% cotton socks and underwear and shower frequently. An itchy rash in the groin or flaking between the toes is likely to be a fungal infection. This needs treatment with an antifungal cream such as Canesten (clotrimazole); if this is not available try Whitfield's ointment (compound benzoic acid ointment) or crystal violet (although this will turn you purple!).

### Prickly heat

A fine pimply rash on the trunk is likely to be heat rash; cool showers, dabbing (not rubbing) dry, and talc will help; if it's bad you may need to check into an air-conditioned hotel room for a while. Slowing down to a relaxed schedule, wearing only loose, baggy 100% cotton clothes and sleeping naked under a fan will reduce the problem.

### Protection from the sun

The incidence of skin cancer is rocketing as Caucasians are travelling more and spending more time exposing themselves to the sun. Keep out of the sun during the middle of the day and if you must expose yourself to it, build up gradually from 20 minutes per day. Be especially careful of sun reflecting off water and wear a T-shirt and lots of waterproof SPF 15 or higher suncream when swimming; snorkelling often leads to scorched backs of the thighs, so wear bermuda shorts. Sun exposure ages the skin and makes people prematurely wrinkly; cover up with long loose clothes and wear a hat whenever you can.

## Foot protection

If you wear old plimsolls or jellies on the beach you will avoid getting coral, urchin spines or venomous fish spines in your feet. If you do tread on a venomous fish, soak the foot in hot (but not scalding) water until some time after the pain subsides; this may mean 20–30 minutes' submersion in all. Take the foot out of the water to top it up, otherwise you may also scald the injured foot. If the pain returns re-immerse the foot. Once the venom has been heat-inactivated, get a doctor to check and remove any bits of fish spines in the wound.

## Meningitis

This is a particularly nasty disease as it can kill within hours of the first symptoms appearing. Usually it starts as a thumping headache and high fever; there may be a blotchy rash too. Immunisation protects against meningococcal A and C strains of bacteria, which cause the serious form of meningitis. It is recommended for most of sub-Saharan Africa, but specific advice should be sought. Other forms of meningitis exist (usually viral), but there are no vaccines available for these. Local papers normally report localised outbreaks. If you have a severe headache and fever go to a doctor immediately.

## Animal attacks

If you are venturing into the bush remember that it is inhabited by some threatening wildlife. The most dangerous species are the big primates and wild buffalo. Hippos can also be dangerous if you happen to frighten them and you are between them and the safety of their waterhole or river.

**Rabies** may be carried by all mammals (beware the village dogs and small monkeys that are used to being fed in the parks) and is passed on to humans through a bite, or a lick of an open wound. You must always assume that any animal is rabid (unless personally known to you) and medical help should be sought as soon as is practicably possible. In the interim, scrub the wound thoroughly with soap and bottled/boiled water for five minutes, then pour on a strong iodine or alcohol solution. This can help to prevent the rabies virus from entering the body and will guard against wound infections, including tetanus. The decision whether or not to have the highly effective rabies vaccine will depend on the nature of your trip. It is definitely advised if you intend to handle animals, or you are likely to be more than 24 hours away from medical help.

Ideally three pre-exposure doses should be taken over a four-week period and can be given in two ways. The full dose (given intramuscularly) is used if

## SNAKES

Snakes rarely attack unless provoked, and bites are unusual among travellers. You are less likely to get bitten if you wear stout shoes and long trousers when in the bush. Most snakes are harmless and even venomous species will only dispense venom in about half of their bites. If bitten, therefore, you are unlikely to have received venom; keeping this fact in mind may help you to stay calm!

Many so-called 'first-aid' techniques do more harm than good: cutting into the wound is harmful; tourniquets are dangerous; suction and electrical inactivation devices do not work. The only treatment is anti-venom.

If you think you have been bitten by a venomous snake, follow this advice:

- Try to keep calm – it is likely that no venom has been dispensed
- Prevent movement of the bitten limb by applying a splint
- Keep the bitten limb BELOW heart height to slow the spread of any venom
- If you have a crepe bandage, bind up as much of the bitten limb as you can, but release the bandage every half hour
- Evacuate to a hospital which has anti-venom.

Here's what NOT to do:

- NEVER give aspirin; paracetamol is safe
- NEVER cut or suck the wound
- DO NOT apply ice-packs
- DO NOT apply potassium permanganate

If the offending snake can be captured without risk of someone else being bitten, take it to show the doctor – but beware since even a decapitated head is able to dispense venom in a reflex bite.

you are likely to be handling animals or are currently taking anti-malaria tablets. Otherwise a smaller, less expensive dose of vaccine, which is almost as effective, may be administered via an injection under the skin. If you are bitten by any animal, treatment should be given as soon as possible. At least two post-bite rabies injections are needed, even by immunised people. Those who have not been immunised will need a full course of injections together with rabies immunoglobulin (RIG), but this product is expensive (around US$800) and may be hard to come by. This is another reason why pre-exposure vaccination should be encouraged in travellers who are planning to visit more remote areas. Treatment should be given as soon as possible, but it is never too late to seek help as the incubation period for rabies can be very long. Bites closer to the brain are always more serious. Remember if you contract rabies, mortality is 100% and death from rabies is probably one of the worst ways to go!

## Further reading
Self-prescribing has its hazards, so if you are going anywhere very remote consider taking a health guidebook. Here are some we recommend:

*Bugs, Bites & Bowels* by Jane Wilson-Howarth (Cadogan, 1999). For adult health matters.

*Your Child's Health Abroad: A manual for travelling parents* by Jane Wilson-Howarth and Matthew Ellis (Bradt Publications, 1998). For those travelling with children.

*Where there is no doctor – a village health care handbook* by David Werner, Carol Truman and Jane Maxwell (Macmillan Heinemann, 1993).

## Day-to-day health issues
### Hygiene
One of the main problems you will face is being able to keep clean with only a limited amount of water after a hard days' driving with sweat, dust and sand clinging to every part of your body. Following the advice below will also help prevent dysentery.

- Carry a small, compact flannel with you and use a minimal amount of water, but still wipe the day's activities from your body
- Disinfectant soap, like Dettol, can be found throughout Africa
- Always wash your hands after visiting the local market and handling raw meat and vegetables
- When using a cutting board or any other surface to cut meat or vegetables, always use one side for meat and the other for vegetables
- Wash any vegetables you want to eat raw in potassium permanganate or Milton, and always peel fruit before eating
- When there is plenty of water available, give all your cutlery a good wash in hot water just to sterilise everything. This is a general rule in terms of clothing, too, but often not possible, unless you are intending to boil loads of water.

### Weight loss and gain
Travelling independently can cause weight loss and while some lose weight, others gain it. Constipation is a common problem among women, particularly on organised tours. You are much less likely to lose weight on an organised truck tour. In fact, the high quality of the three square meals per day, as well as the lack of activity, sitting and driving all day, mean you are more likely to put on the pounds rather than lose them. Remember to bring some laxatives with you.

If you find yourself losing weight, three square meals, if at all possible, should keep the weight loss under control and a multi-vitamin supplement will ensure your body gets any vitamins missing from your diet.

### Dental care
Make sure you have a dental check before you leave home. Toothpaste and toothbrushes are available in cities, but err on the side of caution and take

everything you are likely to need. When you see some of the African versions of toothbrushes you'll be glad you did! Oil of cloves is good for numbing toothache, though of course it will not solve any real problems.

## Contraceptives
### Safe sex
Travel is a time when we may enjoy sexual adventures, especially when alcohol reduces inhibitions. Remember the risks of sexually transmitted infection are high, whether you have sexual intercourse with fellow travellers or locals. About 40% of HIV infections in British heterosexuals are acquired abroad. Use condoms or femidoms. If you notice any genital ulcers or discharge get treatment promptly.

Condoms are usually extremely difficult to get hold of in Africa, though there is reputed to be a black market stall in Abidjan that sells nothing else. Generally you would be advised to bring what you are likely to need – and more. In the more remote areas thorough searches at border posts which concentrate on your washbags and medical box do so for a reason. Presumably the opportunity to relieve travellers of the odd three-pack of condoms is regarded as one of the perks of the job.

### Other contraceptives
If you are only having sexual intercourse with your regular partner, condoms are not your only choice of contraception. If you are taking the pill, you should refer to the guidance set out on the packet for storage (normally in a cool, dry place) and follow it carefully. This may rule it out for some travellers. A coil will get round this difficulty, but you must have it fitted at least six weeks before you leave to check you are not at risk from infection or expulsion. Some women experience heavy and painful periods with a coil. You can also use a cap, which can be sterilised easily in a mug with an ordinary water purifying tablet. But you should think about the number of times you will be using communal toilet facilities or washing in the open air before making a decision to rely only on your cap while you are away. One other possibility is to have an injectable contraceptive (Depo-Provera) which will last for two or more months. Side-effects can include irregular periods, or no periods at all – not necessarily a disadvantage on the road. Fertility can also be delayed for a year after the last injection. Another disadvantage could be needing another injection when you are miles away from anywhere. If you are thinking of changing your normal method of contraception talk this over in plenty of time with your doctor.

### Tampons and sanitary towels
You will be able to buy tampons and sanitary towels in most big towns in West Africa and more easily in East and southern Africa. Problem areas are north Africa, desert and other remote areas like the Congo and Central African Republic. Take enough supplies to get you through early problem areas and you will be able to stock up later on. If you have a definite brand preference and lots of spare space it's not a bad idea to bring extra supplies.

Previous page Orange River Gorge below Augrabies Falls, Northern Cape, South Africa

Above Driving in the Kalahari Desert, South Africa

Below The road from Amboseli to Loitokitok, with Mount Kilimanjaro looming, Kenya

Below right Overlooking Mier salt pan, Northern Cape, South Africa

Bottom right Truck in the Chalbi Desert, between Marsabit and Lake Turkana, northern Kenya

*Above Taxi-brousse*, the main form of public transport in West Africa, in St Louis, Senegal

*Below* Donkey cart, Riemvasmaak, South Africa

*Below right* Likoma Island, Lake Malawi

*Bottom right Matutu* at Soni, Usambara Mountains, Tanzania

*Above* Mountain gorilla, Parc National des Volcans, Rwanda

*Above right* Black-backed jackal, Hwange National Park, Zimbabwe

*Right* The African elephant is the world's largest terrestrial mammal

*Below* Forest buffalo, Senegal

*Bottom right* Senegal parrot, one of almost 2,000 birds recorded in Africa

*Bottom left* Lions are the largest African predators and common in most major game reserves

It might also be worth considering a reusable menstrual sponge, though if you have not used one before make sure you practise before you leave so you know exactly what is involved.

## Treating local people

You may be asked to provide medical help. Aspirin is particularly useful as it is unlikely to harm anyone and is often seen as a cure for everything. Vitamin pills also enjoy a legendary status. NEVER hand out antibiotics as you risk making someone seriously ill if you give them an inadequate dose or they fail to complete a course. Take care, too, when administering eye-drops or bandaging sores as infection is very easily passed on. Mostly we found it was more appropriate to send a person with these sorts of ailments to the local doctor, indicating that we had no medical experience whatsoever. In these cases, the reaction was disbelief. We still haven't quite figured out why many Africans, particularly in the remoter areas, believe that every white man is a doctor. We guess that it has to do with the amount of medication most travellers carry with them. News of this would most likely travel quickly through a village, and the inhabitants would automatically assume that you have some medical background.

## Health checks on your return

If you suspect you may have caught bilharzia, for example, you should certainly see a doctor when you return to your own country. This also obviously applies if you contracted malaria on your trip, or if you fall ill after you have come home.

## SECURITY

With day-to-day security issues you will need to make your own judgement on the situation and act accordingly, using common sense. Africa is generally a safe place to travel and, more often than not, you will be surprised by the kindness and hospitality of the African people; respect it. If in any way you do feel threatened by a situation, drive away or find the nearest local police station or security guard. As always, dress respectfully and do not boast your wares. Flashing money, cameras and jewellery around, when people in Africa have so little, will not help your security situation.

As you travel and meet other travellers you will undoubtedly hear horror stories of oranges filled with nails being flung under your car, ripped tyres, hostage situations – put it all into perspective as these are usually isolated incidents. Realise that there are hundreds of thousands of visitors to Africa every year and a small percentage may have had a bad experience. Realistically, that person might very well have had the same experience at home or put themselves in needless danger.

When walking around towns or cities, always know where you are going and stick to busy roads rather than isolated alleyways. It's common sense to lock everything up at night. Some travellers even have chains and locks which they wrap around possessions, which negates the need to have to pack the vehicle up every evening.

Locking yourself in your vehicle at night is generally not necessary but judge each situation for yourself. Always lock and put everything away before leaving your vehicle. If you are biking or cycling, many campsites and backpackers' hostels have secure areas for you to lock your valuables. We did not carry our passports or other important documents on us all the time, only when we left the vehicle unattended. Moneybelts that hug your body are the best way to carry cash and other valuables when away from your vehicle.

## WOMEN'S ISSUES

> Within this enclosed women's world, so to say, behind the walls and fortifications of it, I felt the presence of a great ideal, without which the garrison would not have carried on so gallantly; the ideal of a Millennium when women were to reign supreme in the world. The old mother at such times would take on a new shape, and sit enthroned as a massive dark symbol of that mighty female deity who had existed in old ages, before the time of the prophet's God. Of her they never lost sight, but they were, before all, practical people with an eye on the needs of the moment and with infinite readiness of resource.
>
> Karen Blixen, *Out of Africa*

We didn't often come across women, or for that matter men, travelling on their own. A lot of single women were either backpacking in loose groups or joining organised tours. I am sure that there are hundreds of travellers who have done Africa on their own, but we did find that those who had started out on their own would hitch up with other travellers on a variety of transport. This was often the case where a country, particularly certain borders or specific routes, had a dodgy reputation. We did meet a mother and daughter who were driving the African continent and had successfully completed most of Africa without any hitches. It did help that the daughter was a professional auto-mechanic!

### Knowing your vehicle

An important difference for women travellers is in weight distribution on the vehicle. Rather than carrying 20-litre jerry cans, it is a good idea to carry 10-litre cans, which are easier to lift off the vehicle. Tool boxes should be smaller and sparingly distributed, once again making them easier to lift. Tyres could be kept under the seat in the vehicle, rather than on top of the vehicle, so they are easier to access.

For women travellers everything else we have discussed regarding driving, biking or cycling through Africa is the same. One concern might be mechanical knowledge of your choice of transport, but then most men who drive the African continent have not much knowledge before departure either. After only a few months on the road, everyone will begin to learn very quickly the ins and outs of their vehicle, bike or bicycle. A helping hand is never far away in Africa and, although in more isolated areas you could run into problems, someone will always appear.

It would be a good idea to do a 4x4 course and drive the vehicle or bike as often as possible. Even with a team of man and woman, it is best to learn, listen and get involved as much as you can. Your male counterpart might fall ill and be completely dependent on your skills to get you from A to B.

## Attitudes to women

If you are a woman travelling on your own, your only other concern is going to be the mentality of the African people. Women are seen as having a specific role within the community, and in our eyes this may seem inferior. Remember that this has been part of their culture for centuries. Although not strictly true for every country you visit in Africa, most border posts, banks and embassies are usually run and staffed entirely by men. If you are travelling with a male, it is best to let the man do most of the talking. Obviously, if you are a woman travelling on your own, you have no choice but to communicate with whoever might be there. Be prepared that progress might be a little slower and their attitude a little nonchalant.

When travelling through more isolated areas of Africa you will often see men lounging under the acacia trees, enjoying the shade, while the women are collecting water, reaping the fields, cooking, looking after the children and generally running around making sure home and family are looked after. Men are supposedly the financial providers within the community.

Most African women (or at least those who initially had the opportunity to attend school) never complete school and start to help around the house as soon as they are able. It is also very rare to see children playing. Girls in particular have to start helping around the house at a very young age. We were delighted whenever we came across children just playing with sticks and stones, swimming and splashing around.

Through their indoctrination into helping the community at such a young age, women are usually very isolated within this community and will only speak the local tongue, even when their male counterparts speak either French or English. Thus you will find that you will mostly communicate with men.

A very good friend of ours, Kirsten Larby, who had lived in an isolated village in The Gambia for over three months, found herself with a male interpreter, and after some months managed to befriend the women – a slow process but a very fulfilling one. It just takes time.

If you have been invited to somebody's home, the women will often provide the meal and then disappear, eating with the family in the kitchen. In my frustration in wanting to meet women I would try to help with cooking the meal, cleaning up the dishes or clearing glasses and ashtrays, but more often than not I was treated with disdain. The women were offended, thinking I was not comfortable in their home and not enjoying myself. It took some time to explain our differences in culture, with the men interpreting, but I would still end up mostly with the men.

Women are also often shy in communicating with an outsider and are not used to being asked for an opinion, their lives revolving around their day-to-day responsibilities and survival. Their attitude often came across as – 'a European woman, what does she know? She is barren, no children, not married, driving this car, no home ...' This attitude is quite common and you should certainly not take offence. If time permits and you have the opportunity, it can make entertaining conversation between yourself and the local women. We can only learn from one another.

The greatest fun and the most enlightening experience I had with African women was at markets. In some Arab countries it is the men who trade but often it is a woman's world. Sometimes having walked for miles with their wares on their backs and heads, they transform a dust bowl into a riot of colour, smells and sounds. Children trace your every footstep, shouts offer you the local brew, food, cloth or even a sheep for sale ... you'll need plenty of patience and time to barter for whatever you might want to buy.

Sometimes you'll experience African life as just a rest under the awning of a stall, laughing and shouting with the women, as your hand, arm or back is slapped with delight as you make another foolish European comment. It was the closest I ever got to really learning about African women, their joys and fears, laughter and tears; I enjoyed every moment.

## How to dress

The way women dress is a very important aspect to be considered. I would sometimes watch young girls coming off organised tours in their shorts and tight little tank tops, then see the reaction of the women – one would often hear the tittering behind closed palms – and men, usually of disgust.

This does not mean that you cannot ever wear shorts, tank tops, bikinis or swimming costumes, just be very aware of your environment and what the other women are wearing. The most common dress for women in Africa is a wraparound skirt, T-shirt and headband. I found that, unless staying at a campsite or enclosed area where I was protected from prying eyes, I lived in skirts or loose cotton trousers and a T-shirt.

Much of southern Africa is pretty relaxed when it comes to clothing, but again this is dependent on the area you are visiting. Most of the rest of Africa, however, is conservative and should be respected accordingly.

Dressing down, as we could call it, also goes a long way to avoiding sexual harassment by African men, particularly in Muslim countries. Again, this is dependent on the area you are travelling in and can take many forms – you may be followed, laughed at, constantly touched, hissed or whistled at – usually innocently, but it can become uncomfortable and annoying.

If you are a woman travelling on your own, and you find that a particular town, city or even country is becoming a little overbearing regarding the attention of the opposite sex, you could either find other travelling companions, or use a guide (you'll have to shop around) who will often keep the masses at bay, or to leave town. No travel is worth getting hurt. We have heard that Egypt is particularly intensive regarding sexual harassment. Morocco can also be intensive, though I did not ever feel threatened, just irritated by the constant banter of touts wanting to sell their wares.

## Avoiding harassment

Sexual harassment is not isolated to single women. Even if travelling with a male companion, he could be asked by an Arab man whether he can perform liberties with her. It is unfortunate that Arab men, particularly Muslims, tend to think that Western women are promiscuous and ready to jump into bed with any man at the drop of a hat. It is best just to try and ignore such a situation and state a firm 'no'.

There are certain things you can do to minimise sexual harassment:

- Dress is the most obvious – do not flaunt your wares and dress conservatively. Your own personal experience in Africa will be so much more fulfilling, with both men and women.
- A wedding band is often helpful in Africa. If you are being hassled, refer to your husband as often as you can, even if you don't have one!
- Avoid eye contact and ignore all rude comments. If you are feeling threatened in any way, walk to the nearest public café and ask the owner for his or her help in getting a taxi home.
- Always know where you are and stick to busy roads rather than isolated alleyways.

At last! A guidebook to sustainable, ethical holidays

from TOURISM**CONCERN**

Visit some of the most beautiful places on earth on genuine holidays that also benefit local people and help fund grassroots development projects

**The Community Tourism Guide**
by Mark Mann for Tourism Concern (Earthscan £9.99) available in bookshops now or visit our website at **w w w . t o u r i s m c o n c e r n . o r g . u k**

exciting holidays for responsible travellers
the COMMUNITY tourism guide

Tourism Concern is a charity that raises awareness of the impact of tourism on local people and environments

EARTHSCAN w w w . e a r t h s c a n . c o . u k

156

# SWALA SAFARIS
**PO Box 207, Arusha, Tanzania**
Moderately priced safaris to Serengeti, Ngorongoro, Oldoinyo L'Engai
and Lake Victoria.
See www.safaris-tz.com or email swala@habari.co.tz

## Discover the beauty of Mt. Kilimanjaro with

**Shah TOURS**

PO Box 1821, Moshi – Tanzania
Tel: +255-27-2752370/2752998
Fax: +255-27-2751449
E-Mail: kilimanjaro@eoltz.com
Web: www.kilimanjaro-shah.com

# KILIMANJARO

Forty years experience of Kilimanjaro climbs. All routes arranged

Relax by the pool set in extensive tropical gardens

Safe and attractive campsite with all amenities

Exciting game park safaris also arranged

## MARANGU HOTEL
...the traditional choice

P.O. Box 40
Moshi, Tanzania

Tel: +255 27 2756594
Fax: +255 27 2756591
E-Mail: marangu@africaonline.co.ke

# Part Three

## Africa

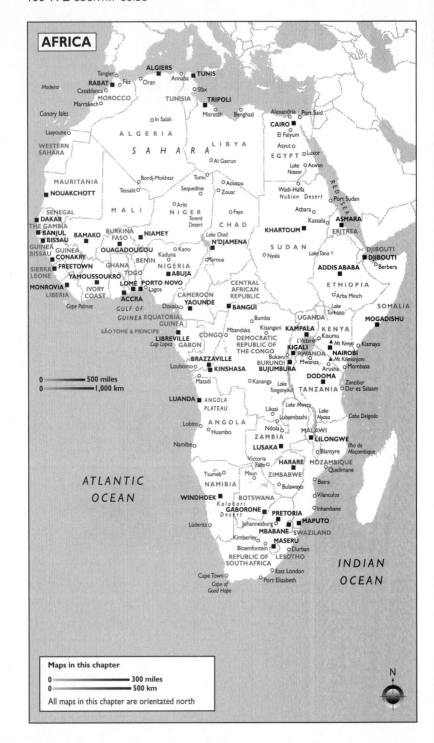

# AFRICA

Madeira

Tangier ○
Fès ○
ALGIERS ■
Annaba ○
TUNIS ■
Oran ○

Casablanca ○
MOROCCO
TUNISIA
Sfax ○

Marrakech ○
In Salah ○
TRIPOLI ■
Misratah ○
Benghazi ○
Alexandria ○ Port Said

Canary Isles
CAIRO ○
El Faiyum ○

Laayoune ○
A L G E R I A
L I B Y A
Asyut ○
E G Y P T
Luxor ○

WESTERN
SAHARA
S A H A R A
Al Gatrun ○
Lake
Nasser
Aswan ○

MAURITANIA
Bordj-Mokhtar ○
Tumu ○
Aouzou ○
Wadi-Halfa ○
Port Sudan ■

NOUAKCHOTT ■
Tessalit ○
Sequedine ○
Zouar ○
Nubian Desert

SENEGAL
M A L I
N I G E R
Arlit ○
Faya ○
Atbara ○
Kassala ○
ASMARA ■

DAKAR ■
Teneré
Desert
C H A D
KHARTOUM ■
ERITREA

THE GAMBIA
BANJUL ■
BAMAKO ■
BURKINA
FASO
NIAMEY ■
Lake Chad
N'DJAMENA ■
S U D A N
Lake Tana
DJIBOUTI ■

BISSAU ■
GUINEA
BISSAU
CONAKRY ■
OUAGADOUGOU ■
BENIN
Kano ○
Kaduna ○
Nyala ○
Berbera ○

SIERRA
LEONE
FREETOWN ■
GHANA
TOGO
NIGERIA
Maroua ○
ADDIS ABABA ■

YAMOUSSOUKRO ■
LOMÉ
PORTO NOVO ■
ABUJA ■
CAMEROON
CENTRAL
AFRICAN
REPUBLIC
E T H I O P I A

MONROVIA ■
LIBERIA
IVORY
COAST
ACCRA ■
Lagos ○
YAOUNDE ■
BANGUI ■
Arba Minch ○

Cape Palmas
GULF OF
GUINEA
Bumba ○
UGANDA
Lake
Turkana
SOMALIA

EQUATORIAL
GUINEA
Mbandaka ○
Kisangani ○
KAMPALA ■
K E N Y A
MOGADISHU ■

SÃO TOMÉ & PRÍNCIPE
LIBREVILLE ■
CONGO
DEMOCRATIC
REPUBLIC OF
THE CONGO
L Victoria
KIGALI ■
Mt Kenya ▲
Kismayu ○

Cap Lopez
GABON
BRAZZAVILLE ■
Bukavu ○
RWANDA
NAIROBI ■
Mt Kilimanjaro ▲

Loubomo ○
KINSHASA ■
BURUNDI
BUJUMBURA ■
Mwanza ○
Arusha ○
Mombasa ○

Matadi ○
DODOMA ■
Zanzibar
Kananga ○
Lake
Tanganyika
T A N Z A N I A
Dar es Salaam ○

LUANDA ■
ANGOLA
PLATEAU
Lake Mweru
Lake
Nyasa
Cabo Delgado

Likasi ○
MALAWI

Lobito ○
Huambo ○
Ndola ○
Lubumbashi ○
LILONGWE ■

Namibe ○
ZAMBIA
Blantyre ○
Ilha do
Moçambique

LUSAKA ■
MOZAMBIQUE
Quelimane ○

Victoria
Falls
HARARE ■
Beira ○

Tsumeb ○
Maun ○
ZIMBABWE
Bulawayo ○

N A M I B I A
Vilanculos ○

WINDHOEK ■
BOTSWANA
Inhambane ○

Kalahari
Desert
GABORONE ■
PRETORIA ■
MAPUTO ■

Lüderitz ○
Johannesburg ○
MBABANE ■
SWAZILAND

Kimberley ○
MASERU ■

Bloemfontein ○
Durban ○

REPUBLIC OF
SOUTH AFRICA
LESOTHO
East London ○

Cape Town ○
Port Elizabeth ○

Cape of
Good Hope

ATLANTIC
OCEAN

INDIAN
OCEAN

R E D
S E A

GULF OF
GUINEA

0 ━━━ 500 miles
0 ━━━ 1,000 km

**Maps in this chapter**

0 ━━━ 300 miles
0 ━━━ 500 km

All maps in this chapter are orientated north

N

# A–Z Country Guide

Your road is everything that a road ought to be ... and yet you will not
stay in it half a mile, for the reason that little, seductive, mysterious
roads are always branching out from it on either hand, and as these
curve sharply also and hide what is beyond, [you] cannot resist the
temptation to desert your own chosen road and explore them.

Mark Twain (1835–1910)

This section includes a guide to visa requirements, an indication of fuel costs
and a general overview of each country in Africa – particularly some of the red
tape you might have to go through. We have not tried to write a detailed guide
to each country; for that you should buy the relevant Bradt travel guide or
similar for the specific countries you intend to visit.

## RED TAPE

If most African travel guides are to be believed, you would think that the
average tourist to Africa is forced to plough through a minefield of bribery
and corruption. This is not the case. To put things into perspective, during
our one-year journey through Africa we were not once asked for a bribe.
Payment of a postal stamp and two speeding fines were all we suffered. There
are also no more than a handful of incidences of unbridled bureaucratic
stupidity, against which one must balance perhaps ten times as many
incidences when bureaucrats have gone out of their way to help. You are
more than likely going to come up against a certain amount of inefficiency,
but more often than not you will encounter a level of friendliness and
helpfulness from government employees which is no longer found in the
developed world. Some travellers seem to hit interminable problems with
bureaucrats, but many of these problems stem from the travellers themselves
and their attitude. In almost all of Africa you will usually be pushed to the
front of the queue and treated with the utmost respect.

## WHICH COUNTRY?

This section also includes a brief overview of the highlights of each country.
Many African countries are currently at war or there are border disputes or
tribal warfare, so be prepared that some of the information will be out of date.

There are numerous guidebooks available for each individual country
which provide information on public holidays, opening and closing times,

KEY
- Capital city ■
- Town ○
- Main road (not necessarily sealed) ▬▬▬
- Other road (track) ═════
- East-west routes (identified pages 12–17) EW1
- Trans-Sahara routes (identified pages 8–12) S2
- International boundary ▬·▬·▬

Strait of Gibraltar

MEDI

ALGIERS Bejaia
Annaba

Tangier Ceuta
Melilla Oran
RABAT
Casablanca Meknès Fès
Oujda
Constantine

MOROCCO MTS
ATLAS
HIGH

Madeira
ATLANTIC
OCEAN
Marrakech
Agadez Ouarzazate
Canary Isles S1
Tenerife Lanzarote
ANTI ATLAS MTS
Gran Canaria
Laayoune

Adrar
S2
In Salah

Reggane

ALGERIA

WESTERN SAHARA
S1

SA HA
HOGGAR
MOUNTAINS
Assekrem
Tamanrasset
Bordj-Mokhtar
S3
S2
Atar
MAURITANIA
Tessalit
Assamakka

MALI

Arlit
AIR M

Kiffa
S1
Nema
Timbuktu
Niger
Gao
Tegguidda-nTessoum
Agadez

Nioro
Nara
Mopti Bandiagara
Tahoua
NIG

Senegal
Kayes
Djenné
BURKINA FASO
NIAMEY
Birnin-konni
Zinder

BAMAKO
OUAGADOUGOU
Kano

Fouta Djalon Plateau
Zaria
Kaduna

GUINEA
Kankan
Bobo Dioulasso
BENIN
Niger
Jos

SIERRA LEONE
Korhogo
Tamale
NIGERIA
ABUJA

IVORY COAST
GHANA
TOGO
Benue

LIBERIA
YAMOUSSOUKRO
Bouaké
Lake Volta
Abomey
Kumasi
LOMÉ
PORTO NOVO

MONROVIA
Abidjan
Takoradi
Cape Coast
ACCRA
Lagos
Port Harcourt
Mt Cameroon 4070m

Cape Palmas
GULF OF GUINEA
Douala

Senegal

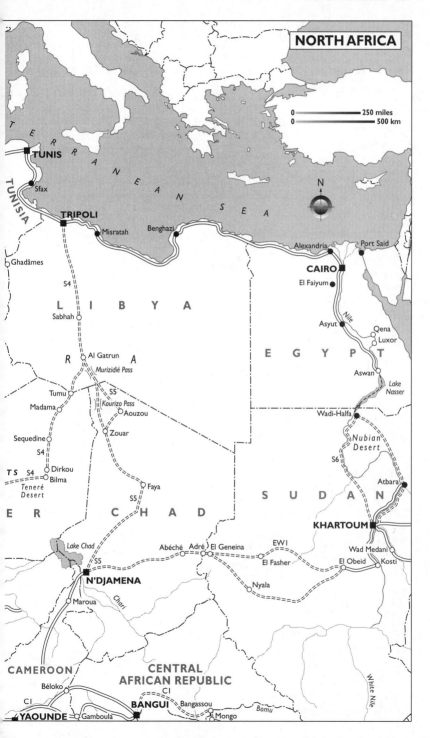

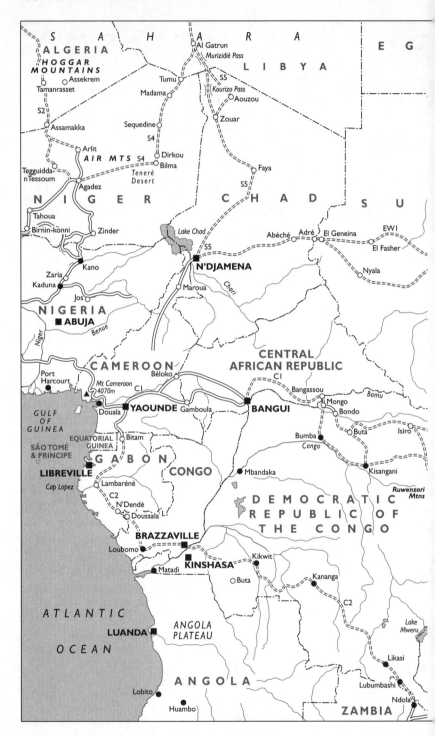

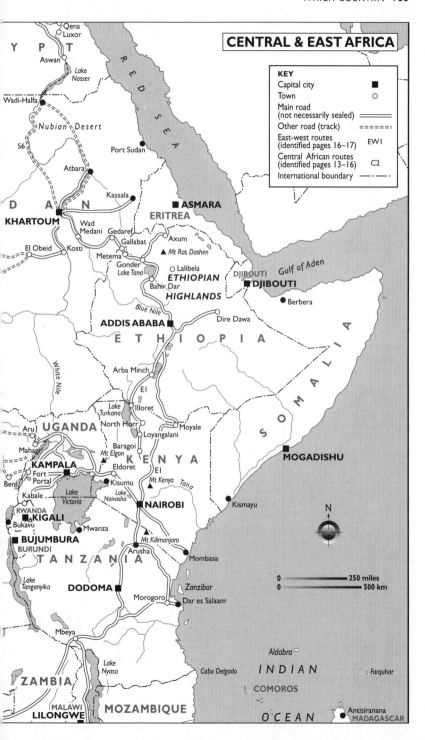

# CENTRAL & EAST AFRICA

**KEY**

| | |
|---|---|
| Capital city | ■ |
| Town | ○ |
| Main road (not necessarily sealed) | ═══ |
| Other road (track) | ══════ |
| East-west routes (identified pages 16–17) | EW1 |
| Central African routes (identified pages 13–16) | C2 |
| International boundary | ─ ·· ─ ·· ─ |

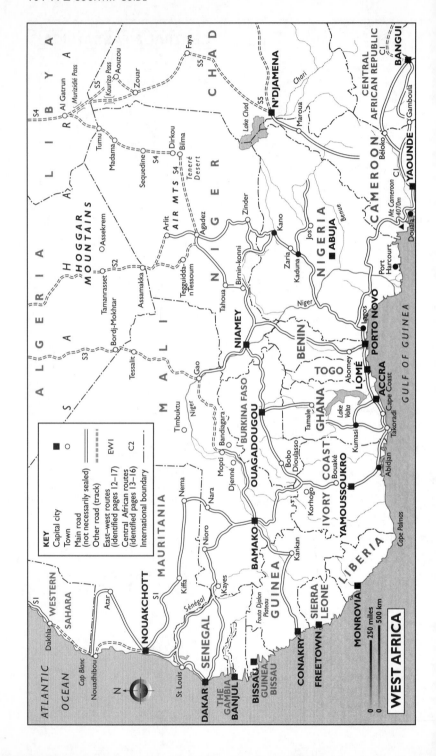

WEST AFRICA

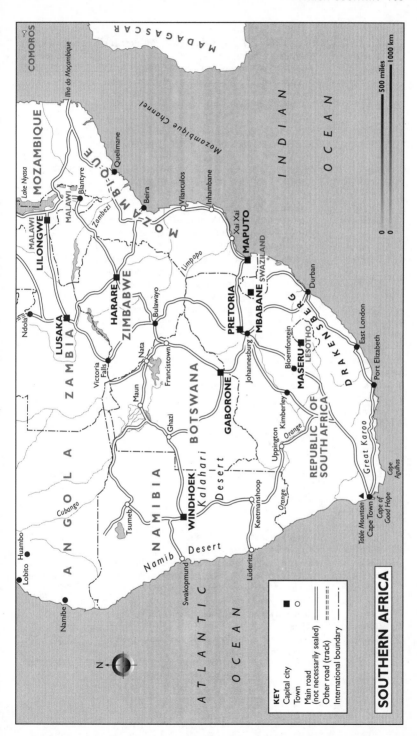

SOUTHERN AFRICA

KEY

■  Capital city
○  Town
———  Main road (not necessarily sealed)
=====  Other road (track)
—·—·—  International boundary

## VISA REQUIREMENTS AT A GLANCE (for details see country entries)

| Country | Visa requirements | Approx cost |
|---|---|---|
| Algeria | Required for all except nationals of other Arabic countries; if you have a stamp from Israel, South Africa, Malawi or Taiwan in your passport the visa application will be rejected; 30-day tourist visas are available | US$55–100 |
| Angola | Required for all nationals; visa applications are referred to Direçao de Emigraçao e Fronteiras (DEFA) in Luanda and will take about two weeks to issue. | US$80 |
| Benin | Required for all except nationals of the Economic Community of West African States (ECOWAS); 48-hour entry visas are available and can be extended in Cotonou | US$10–20 |
| Botswana | Visas not required for nationals of USA, UK, Germany, Netherlands and most Commonwealth countries | US$10–15 |
| Burkina Faso | Required for all except for nationals of the ECOWAS | US$60–100 |
| Burundi | Required for all nationals             Transit visa<br>One-month tourist visa | US$12<br>US$25 |
| Cameroon | Required for all except nationals of Germany<br>9-day multiple entry visa (cost depends on nationality) | US$25–70 |
| Central African Republic (CAR) | Required for all; nationals of France, Australia, New Zealand and the Republic of Ireland need to get permission from Bangui before entry | US$70–90 |
| Chad | Required for all except French and German citizens (valid up to three months). | US$25–40 |
| Congo (People's Republic) | Required for all except nationals of France<br>Two-week visa | US$70–90 |
| Democratic Republic of the Congo (DRC) | Required for all | US$50–100 |
| Djibouti | Required for all except for nationals of France | US$25–35 |
| Egypt | Required for all except nationals of Arab countries and Malta | US$25 |
| Equatorial Guinea | Required for all | US$65–80 |
| Eritrea | Required for all | US$40–60 |
| Ethiopia | Required for all except Kenyan nationals | US$65 |
| Gabon | Required for all; all applications need to be referred to Libreville and can take up to two weeks to issue | US$80–100 |
| Gambia | Required for all except for nationals of Commonwealth countries | US$20 |
| Ghana | Required for all except nationals of ECOWAS | US$25 |
| Guinea | Required for all | US$25–50 |
| Guinea Bissau | Required for all except nationals of Cape Verde and Nigeria | US$10–25 |
| Ivory Coast (Côte d'Ivoire) | Required for all except nationals of ECOWAS; US passport holders don't need visas for stays up to 90 days | US$25–50 |

| Country | Visa requirements | Approx cost |
|---|---|---|
| Kenya | Required for all except nationals of Commonwealth countries | US$20–40 |
| Lesotho | Required for all except nationals of Commonwealth countries and South Africa | US$10–15 |
| Liberia | Required for all; entry and exit permits are also required | US$30–40 |
| Libya | Required for all; independent tourist visas are not issued to nationals of Australia, New Zealand, Great Britain, United States or Canada without the approval of the Libyan People's Bureau; all details of your passport must also be translated into Arabic; nationals of Israel are not permitted entry; an Israeli stamp in your passport will deny you entry | US$30 on average |
| Malawi | Not required for most nationals | |
| Mali | Required for all except nationals of France | US$20–50 |
| Mauritania | Required for all except nationals of France and Italy and Arab League countries | US$15–30 |
| Morocco | Not required for most nationals except Israel and South Africa    One-month visa    Three-month visa | US$25–30 US$35–40 |
| Mozambique | Required for all | US$15–30 |
| Namibia | Not required for most nationals | |
| Niger | Required for all except nationals of Belgium, France, Germany, Italy, Luxembourg, The Netherlands and Scandinavian countries | US$40–60 |
| Nigeria | Required for all except nationals of ECOWAS | US$25–50 |
| Rwanda | Required for all except nationals of the US | US$30–70 |
| Senegal | Required for all except nationals of Commonwealth countries | US$20–50 |
| Sierra Leone | Required for all | US$10–50 |
| Somalia | Required for all | No current costs available |
| South Africa | Not required for most nationals | |
| Sudan | Required for all | US$70–95 |
| Swaziland | Not required except for nationals of Germany and France | Free, issued at the border |
| Tanzania | Required for all except nationals of Commonwealth countries | US$10–50 |
| Togo | Required for all except for nationals of ECOWAS; 48-hour transit visas available at the border | US$10–20 |
| Tunisia | Not required for most nationals | US$5–15 |
| Uganda | Required for all except nationals of Commonwealth countries; nationals of New Zealand and India require visas | US$25–35 |
| Zambia | Required for all except nationals of Commonwealth countries; British and Irish nationals require visas | US$25–35 |
| Zimbabwe | Not required for most nationals | |

specific accommodation, which bank to use, the nearest post office, shopping, markets and what to see in a specific country or town.

Africa is so vast that at first you will ask yourself which countries to visit and which to leave out – but it's an impossible task. Each country has its own unique 'something'! And, of course, your choice is totally subjective. As discussed in *Chapter 1*, time and funds will ultimately rule your choice of route.

Your choice also depends on what you want to get out of the trip. Some people go for landscape; others go for wildlife – we would suggest sticking to southern and eastern Africa where there are the majority of large national parks – Kruger National Park (Eastern Transvaal – South Africa), Umfolozi (Natal – South Africa), Kalahari Gemsbok Park (border of Botswana and South Africa), the Okavango Delta (Botswana), South Luangwa (Zambia), Lake Kariba (Zimbabwe), Masai Mara (Kenya) and Serengeti National Park (Tanzania). Some go for culture and people, for example the Himba in Namibia, the San people in Botswana, the Masai in Kenya, the Turkana along the Jade Sea (or Lake Turkana), or the Omatic tribes of southern Ethiopia.

Obviously, a combination of landscape, national parks and culture is the ideal. We found that in our one-year trip it was the people who were enlightening; individuals made the trip truly memorable.

The countries listed are in alphabetical order. Please note that we have given approximate prices of visas as these depend on your nationality and where you apply for your visa – prices vary from country to country. Currency rates and fuel costs were correct at the time of writing, but of course are subject to change.

## ALGERIA

*Warning* Due to the ongoing conflict in Algeria the information listed might be out of date. Algeria did not allow any overland travel for many years, but is slowly starting to open its doors again. Seek sound travel advice if you do intend to visit.

### Capital
Algiers

### Language
Arabic is the official language
International telephone code +213

### Currency and rate
Algerian dinar (AD); US$1 = AD81

### Red tape
*Carnet* is not accepted and a *laissez passer* will be issued at the border. Currency declaration form must be completed on entry and surrendered on departure.

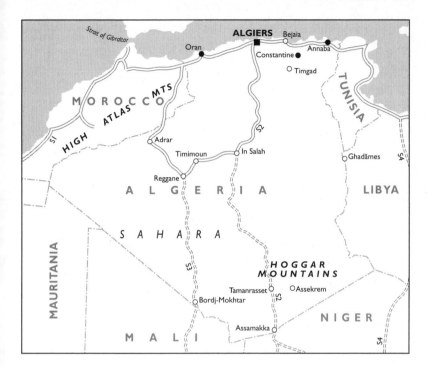

## Visas

Visas are required for all except nationals of other Arabic countries. Israelis, South Africans, Malawians and Taiwanese or any of these stamps in your passport will automatically mean that your visa application is rejected. Nationals of Germany, France and the United States can expect to pay steep fees for visas. Estimated visa costs can vary between US$55 (UK citizens) and $100 depending on the country of application. You will also need three photographs and an introduction from your embassy. Visas are not issued at the border. You may also be required to provide a copy of your hotel reservations confirming your stay in Algeria.

## Fuel costs

Diesel: US$0.16; petrol: US$0.31 per litre.

## Driving and roads

Drive on the right. Good surfaced roads throughout the north and most of the way down the central route to Tamanrasset. Desert pistes of varying quality.

## African embassies

**Angola** 14 Rue Curie El Biar, Algiers; tel 786772 / 797441; telex 936-61620
**Cameroon** PO Box 343 Algiers; tel 02/782864; telex 0480-52421
**Nigeria** 27 Bis Rue Blaise Pascal, PO Box 629, Agar Gare, Algiers; tel 02/60 6050
**Tunisia** 11 Rue du Bois de Boulogne, Mouradia, Algiers; tel 02/601388

The Gambia, Guinea, Libya, Mauritania, Morocco and Niger also have embassies in Algiers, but current addresses are unavailable.

## Climate
Desert temperatures are hottest in July and August.

## Highlights
Algiers is a highlight in itself. Along the eastern coast it's worth visiting Constantine, Djemila and the Kabylia Mountains. In the Sahara the highlights are Timgad (Cuicul) and Timimoun where there are some beautiful sand dunes. The Hoggar Mountains are a remarkable range of volcanic mountains in the centre of the Sahara.

## Where to stay
Bush sleeping is one option. Basic accommodation costs between US$5 and US$25 – depending on what you are after. With the lack of tourism in Algeria it is also said that the Algerians are extremely friendly and will go out of their way to help you, sometimes even offering accommodation.

## Other
On arrival in Algeria you must change the equivalent of AD1,000 at the official rate. Currency declaration forms also need to be filled out on arrival and will be checked on departure. Ensure that you get valid receipts when changing money at a bank, although the black market is thriving, particularly in French francs. Remember that your declaration form needs to tally with initial costs. It is easy enough to smuggle money in (or out) and border checks can be thorough. All other money found can be confiscated.

## Further information
*Morocco, Algeria and Tunisia*, Lonely Planet
http:/i-cias.com/m.s/algeria/index.htm – up-to-date information on Algeria with detailed information regarding places to see.

## ANGOLA

**Warning** Due to the ongoing civil war in Angola we strongly advise against any overland travel into Angola. Seek sound travel advice if you do intend to visit. Basic information is included.

## Capital
Luanda

## Language
Portuguese is the official language.
International telephone code +244

## Currency and rate
New Kwanza (Kw); US$1 = Kw 6.04

## Visas
Visas are required for all; applications are referred to the Direçao de Emigraçao e Fronteiras (DEFA) in Luanda and will take about two weeks. Visas cost US$80 and are valid for 15 or 30 days. Visas are not issued at the border.

## Fuel costs
Diesel: US$0.19; petrol: US$0.38 per litre.

## Further information
*Africa and Madagascar Total Eclipse 2001 and 2002*, Bradt Travel Guides
www.angola.org
http://lcweb2.loc.gov.frd/cs/aotoc.html

## BENIN

## Capital
Porto Novo

## Language
French is the official language.
International telephone code +229

## Currency and rate
West African CFA franc (CFA); US$1 = CFA 760

## Red tape
Of no huge significance in Benin.

## Visas
Visas are required for all except nationals of the Economic Community of West African States (ECOWAS). 48-hour entry visas are available at the border of Benin and Togo for US$10. Visa extensions are possible in Cotonou at US$15

per application and take three days to issue. You will need two passport photos. Vaccination certificates are also officially required but do not often get checked.

## Fuel costs

Diesel: US$0.31; petrol: US$0.39 per litre.

## Driving and roads

Drive on the right. Most roads in Benin are paved and even those that aren't are in good condition with only a few potholes.

## African embassies

**French Consulate** (issues visas for Burkina Faso, Ivory Coast and Togo) Av du Général de Gaulle, Cotonou; tel: 312638

**Ghana** Route de l'Aéroport, Cotonou; tel: 300746

**Niger** just off Av Clozel, one block behind PTT, Cotonou; tel: 315665

**Nigeria** Lot 21, Patte d'Oie district, Cotonou; tel: 301142

## Climate

Humid everywhere, with steady temperatures of 27°C. The dry seasons are from December to April and during August. Northern Benin, abutting the Sahel, is less humid but very hot during March and April. Its dry season lasts from November to May.

## Highlights

Ganvié, a village built on stilts in the middle of a lagoon and accessible only by dugout canoe. The palaces of Abomey and voodoo museums of Ouidah. Grand Popo and coastline. The impressive ancient site of Tingad (Thamagudi). Parcs Nationals du W.

## Where to stay

### Abomey

*Chez Monique*, a little way from the centre of town, has a shady tropical garden and straw roof restaurant. We camped at the back of the hotel in the courtyard for US$6. The staff are extremely helpful and will go out of their way to show you parts of Abomey, even a voodoo festival if one is in progress.

### Grand Popo

We stayed at *L'Auberge de Grand Popo* which has a hotel, restaurant and campsite with a view of the ocean. It is an extremely beautiful setting and we would also suggest that a meal at the restaurant, although a little expensive, is a must.

## Other

Taking of photographs is permitted but please be respectful when visiting fetish temples and shrines.

## Further information

*West Africa*, Rough Guides or Lonely Planet
www.sas.upenn.edu/African_Studies/Country_Specific/Benin.html

## BOTSWANA

### Capital
Gaborone

### Language
English and Satswana are the official languages.
International telephone code +267

### Currency and rate
Pula (P); US$1 = P5.26

### Red tape
The Botswana Defence Force (BDF) take their duties extremely seriously and can be aggressive. They are best avoided.

### Visas
Visas are not required for nationals of the USA, UK and most other Commonwealth countries, or western Europe (except for Spain and Portugal), as long as the stay does not exceed 90 days. Visas cost US$10–15. Entry permits for 30 days are issued at the border.

### Fuel costs
Diesel: US$0.29; petrol: US$0.31 per litre.

### Driving and roads
Drive on the left. There are some good surfaced main roads and the rest are tracks and pistes.

### African embassies
**Angola** 2715 Phala Crescent Gaborone; tel: 375089; CP Private bag 111; telex: 2361

**Namibia** BCC building, 1278 Lobatse Rd, Gaborone; tel: 314227

**Nigerian High Commission** Box 274, Gaborone; tel 2041

**Zambia** PO Box 362, Gaborone; tel: 351951; fax: 353952

**Zimbabwe** Orapa Close, Gaborone; tel: 314495

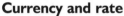

### Climate
It is hot throughout the year with the main rainy season from December to April.

# Highlights

The Okavango Delta, Moremi Wildlife Reserve and Chobe National Park all have an array of wildlife in various environments (Maun has various campsites and organisations that arrange tours into each of these national parks). The Kalahari Desert with its vast open spaces and Central Kalahari Game Reserve. The Makgadikgadi and Nxai Pans and Tsodilo Hills with ancient San paintings.

# Where to stay

## Maun

*Audi Camp*, *Crocodile Camp* and *Island Safari Lodge* all offer basic camping facilities at US$6 for camping. Each of these camps is a great stopover for planning excursions into the Delta and a safe spot for your vehicle.

## Okavango Delta

The cheapest option is *Oddball's Camp* which lies just across the channel from Chief's Island and Moremi Reserve. Camping costs US$10 per person. Camp meals are available and other camping equipment can be hired (there is a limit of 10kg luggage per person). Air transfers cost US$88 and can be booked through Okavango Tours and Safaris in Maun.

## Moremi Wildlife Reserve

South gate offers a developed campsite while most organised tours end up at the underdeveloped site of *Third Bridge*. Your will have to shop around and see what suits your needs the best.

## Chobe National Park

*Serondela* or *Buffalo Ridge Campsite* are both accessible and cost US$6 for camping. Savuti Camp is only accessible with a four-wheel drive, with high clearance, and is closed from January to March during the rainy season.

## Makgadikgadi and Nxai Pans and Tsodilo Hills

The pans can only be crossed with four-wheel drive and in the dry season, April to December. Only use well-marked tracks on the pan or your vehicle will sink. It is advisable to go with one other vehicle. Getting to the Tsodilo Hills is a nightmare and the road has the worst reputation in the whole of Africa, with deep Kalahari sand – the going is extremely slow. Once there, it's worth the effort. Bush sleeping is your only option in both the pans and the hills. There are various villages at the Tsodilo Hills where you will need to get permission to camp from the chief.

# Other

The importing of meat is prohibited and you will get checked regularly.

# Further information

*Botswana: The Bradt Travel Guide*, Chris McIntyre
www.botswananet.org
www.places.co.za/html/botswana_main.html

# BURKINA FASO

## Capital
Ouagadougou

## Language
French is the official language.
International telephone code +226

## Currency and rate
West African CFA franc (CFA); US$1
= 760 CFA

## Red tape
Police checks are numerous, every
10km (6 miles) or so as you cross
borders, and can be extremely time
consuming. Crime in major towns is
also on the increase.

## Visas
Visas are required for all except
nationals of the Economic
Community of West African States (ECOWAS). Visas cost US$60 to US$100
depending on country of application. Vaccination certificates for cholera and
yellow fever are checked. Visas are not issued at the border. In countries where
there is no representation, the French consulate usually handles Burkina Faso
visas.

## Fuel costs
Diesel: US$0.50; petrol: US$0.68 per litre.

## Driving and roads
Drive on the right. Good surfaced roads with occasional bursts of well-
maintained dirt roads.

## African embassies
**Algeria** close to the Place des Nations Unies, Ouagadougou; tel: 306401
**French Consulate** (issues visas for Central African Republic, Mauritania and Togo)
Boulevard de la Révolution, Ouagadougou; tel: 306774
**Ghana** Av Bassawarga, Ouagadougou; tel: 307635
**Ivory Coast** Av Raoul Follereau, opp American Embassy; tel: 306637
**Mali** 2569 Av Bassawarga, Ouagadougou; tel: 381922
**Nigeria** Av d'Oubritenga, Ouagadougou; tel: 306667
**Senegal** southern end of Av Yennenga, Ouagadougou; tel: 312811

## Climate

The cool dry season is from November to mid-February and the rainy season from March to April. The transitional period between November and February is the best time to go.

## Highlights

Ouagadougou is a food connoisseur's delight and known for its variety of restaurants ranging from African to European to American. Visit Banfora which is excellent for cycling, and the surrounding area. Bobo-Dioulasso and surrounding area. Gorom-Gorom's desert market is every Thursday starting at 11.00. Parc Nationals du W in the southeast.

## Where to stay

### Ouagadougou

*Camping Ouaga* (follow signs to Camping Ouaga for 1km on Avenue Bassawarga) charges US$5 per person for camping and is to be used for camping only.

### Banfora

The *Hôtel le Comoé*, on the southern edge of town, may allow you to camp in their courtyard for a minimal fee, or bush camping is an option on the outskirts of town.

### Bobo-Dioulasso

The biggest attractions are the *Bobo* (local tribe) houses, distinguished by their tall, conical roofs, in the surrounding countryside. *Casafrica* is the best camping option at US$5 for camping.

### Gorom-Gorom

*Le Campement Hôtelier* is the best option and camping costs US$6.

## Other

Photographic permits used to be a requirement but this is no longer the case. Just be aware of what you are photographing and remember that photos of government institutions are completely forbidden. Video permits are required and these are issued by the Ministère de l'Environnement et du Tourisme for US$6.

## Further information

*West Africa*, Rough Guides or Lonely Planet
http://africaonline.com/africaonline/countries/burkina.html
http://africanet.com/africanet/country/burkina
www.sas.upenn.edu/African_Studies/Country_Specific/Burkina.html

## BURUNDI

**Warning** Due to the ongoing political unrest in Burundi we strongly advise you to seek sound travel advice if you intend to visit. Basic information has been listed.

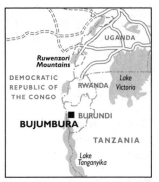

### Capital
Bujumbura

### Language
French and Kurundi are the official languages.
International telephone code +257

### Currency and rate
Burundi franc (BFr); US$1 = BFr741

### Visas
Visas are required for all visitors. Transit visas usually cost US$12 and a one-month tourist visa US$25 depending on place of issue. You will need two passport photos. Depending on place of issue, visas can be issued within 24 hours. Visas are not issued at the border.

### Fuel costs
Diesel: US$0.66; petrol: US$0.72 per litre.

### African embassies
**Rwanda** 24 Av de Zaire, Bujumbura; tel: 228755
**Tanzania** Av Patrice Lumumba, Bujumbura; tel: 24634

### Further information
*Africa on a Shoestring*, Lonely Planet
www.burunditoday.org

## CAMEROON

### Capital
Yaoundé

### Language
French and English are the official languages.
International telephone code +237

### Currency and rate
Central African franc (CFA); US$1 = 760CFA

## Visas

Visas are required for all except nationals of Germany. However, even with a German passport, a fee of US$25 was needed for a visitor's entry stamp. A multiple, 90-day entry visa costs US$65 and can be issued within 24 hours; you will need two photographs. Visas are not issued at the border. Usually, visas are only issued in your country of residence and must be activated within one month of issue.

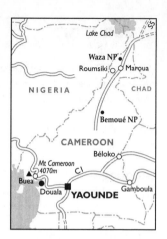

## Fuel costs

Diesel: US$0.48; petrol: US$0.64.

## Driving and roads

Drive on the right. Roads are fairly poor but there are a lot of new road projects so the situation is improving all the time.

## Red tape

You will continually be stopped for passport and vehicle checks. Never show the originals of documents; show photocopies only. If you are not carrying either then be prepared to pay a substantial bribe. Crime is on the increase, particularly in Yaoundé and Douala. Do not carry valuables with you at any time.

## African embassies

**Benin** (no current address available); tel: 22 3495
**Central African Republic** Rue 1810, Bastos, Yaoundé; tel: 20 5155
**Chad** Rue Mballa Eloumden, Bastos, Yaoundé; tel: 21 0624
**Congo** Rue 1816, Bastos, Yaoundé; tel: 21 2455
**Democratic Republic of the Congo** Bd de l'URSS, Bastos, Yaoundé; tel: 22 5103
**Equatorial Guinea** Rue 1872, Bastos, Yaoundé; tel: 22 4149
**French consulate** (issues visas for Burkina Faso and Togo) Rue Joseph Atemengué, Yaoundé; tel: 23 4013
**Gabon** Rue 1793, Bastos, Yaoundé; tel: 22 2966
**Ivory Coast** Bastos, PO Box 11357, Yaoundé; tel: 21 7459
**Niger** Tel: 21 3260
**Nigeria** Off Av Monseigneur Vogt, Centre Ville, Yaoundé; tel: 22 3455
**Senegal** Boulevard de l'USRR, Bastos, Yaoundé; tel: 22 0308

## Climate

The north is hot and dry with a long rainy season from May to October. The south is hot and humid with a long dry season from November to February, rains from March until June and then a heavy rainy season from July until October.

## Highlights

Climbing Mount Cameroon, which is West Africa's highest mountain. Waza and Bemoué national parks. The beaches at Kribi. Exploring the villages and markets around Maroua and in the Mandara Mountains, including Roumsiki. We have also heard that southern Cameroon is spectacular with the last of the Pygmy tribes left in the area. As it is extremely difficult to get to, however, you'll have to go on an organised expedition with a volunteer organisation in Yaoundé.

## Where to stay
### Buea
Buea is on the lowest slope of Mount Cameroon and is also the base camp. You must have a permit and guide; both are available in the main street in town. Climbing Mount Cameroon can take between three and four days. A good place to stay in Buea is the *Mountain Village*.

### Maroua
The best place to stay in Maroua is *Campement Bossou* at US$6. We stayed in Roumsiki at the only *Campement*, but at US$10 it is expensive.

## Other
Photographic permits are not required but many officials will tell you that they are. If hassles continue go to the Ministry of Information and Tourism and let them, for a small fee, write a letter stating as much.

## Further information
*West Africa*, Lonely Planet or Rough Guides
www.africaonline.com/africaonline/countries/cameroon.html
www.sas.upenn.edu/African_Studies/Country_Specific/cameroon.html
www.compufix.demon.co.uk/camweb (ie: personal encounter in Cameroon)

## CENTRAL AFRICAN REPUBLIC (CAR)

*Warning* Due to the ongoing civil disturbances in the Central African Republic the information listed might be out of date. We strongly advise no overland travel into the country. Seek sound travel advice if you do intend to visit.

## Capital
Bangui

## Language
French is the official language.
International telephone code +236

## Currency
Central African franc (CFA); US$1 = 760CFA

## Red tape

Avoid all military personnel and try not to stay longer than one day in one area.

## Visas

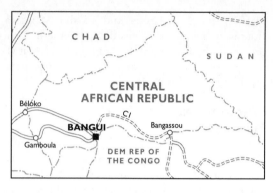

Visas (for up to 90 days) are required for all and can cost as much as US$90. Two photos, two application forms, a yellow fever certificate, a letter from your company stating that the applicant will resume work on returning and a return ticket are all required. Nationals of Australia, New Zealand, France and the Republic of Ireland need permission from Bangui before visa application is accepted. Visas are not issued at the border.

## Fuel costs

Diesel: US$0.65; petrol: US$0.81 per litre.

## Driving and roads

Drive on the right. Good roads have been built to the northeast and northwest of Bangui, but closer to the border of Cameroon, Chad and Sudan the roads are in very poor condition, particularly during the rainy season.

## African embassies

**Cameroon** Rue de Languedoc, Bangui; tel: 61 1687
**Chad** Av Valéry Giscard d'Estaing, Bangui; tel: 61 4677
**Congo** Av Boganda, Bangui; tel: 61 1877
**Democratic Republic of the Congo** Rue Gamal Abdel Nasser, Bangui; tel: 61 8240
**French Consulate** (issues visas for Burkina Faso, Gabon, Ivory Coast, Mauritania, Senegal and Togo) Bd Général de Gaulle, Bangui; tel: 61 3000
**Nigeria** Km3, Av Boganda, Bangui; tel: 61 0744
**Sudan** Av de la France, Bangui; tel: 61 3821

## Climate

Hot and humid in the south, drier in the north. Rainy season is from May to October, starting later and finishing earlier the further north you go.

## Highlights

The Chutes de Boali are spectacular during the rainy season.

## Where to stay

### Bangui

Our latest information is that *Centre d'Accueil Touristique Dalango* is still open and charges US$5 for camping. It is located in the African Quarter, on Avenue Boganda, 1.5km to the west on Km5.

## Other

We would suggest that your camera stays in its case as people in the Central African Republic are extremely sensitive about photography.

## Further information

*Africa on a Shoestring*, Lonely Planet
www.lonelyplanet.com/dest/afr/car.html
http://worldtravelguide.net/data/caf/caf.html

## CHAD

## Capital

N'Djamena

## Language

French and Arabic are the official languages.
International telephone code +235

## Currency and rate

Central African franc (CFA); US$1 = 760CFA

## Red tape

On entry from Sudan at the Adré border in Chad, we found the military and police to be extremely aggressive – and drunk. It also took up to four hours to clear all paperwork, which was not due to inefficiency, but with having to find the right person for the job who was having a game of cards with friends on the other side of town. Throughout Chad we found the military to be particularly aggressive – they are best avoided.

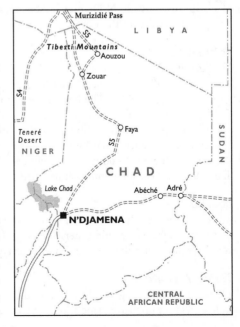

## Visas

Visas are required for all except nationals of Germany and France. Three application forms and three photos are required. Officially you also need a return air ticket. Visas are valid for three months. The estimated cost of a visa is US$25–40 depending on country of issue. Vaccination certificates will be checked on entry. Visas are not issued at the border.

## Fuel costs

Diesel: US$0.61; petrol: US$0.70 per litre.

## Driving and roads

Drive on the right. There are surfaced roads on either side of N'Djamena; the rest are either sandy desert tracks in the north or very bad mud roads in the south.

## African embassies

**Cameroon** Rue des Poids Lourds, N'Djamena; tel: 52 2894
**Central African Republic** Rue 1036, N'Djamena; tel: 52 3206
**Democratic Republic of the Congo** Av 26 de Août, N'Djamena; tel: 52 5935
**French Consulate** (issues visas for Burkina Faso, Gabon, Ivory Coast, Mauritania, Senegal and Togo) Rue de Lieutenant-Franjoux, off Av Félix Eboué, N'Djamena; tel: 52 2575
**Nigeria** Av Charles de Gaulle, N'Djamena; tel: 52 2498
**Sudan** off Rue de Gendarmerie, N'Djamena; tel: 52 5010

## Climate

The desert climate in the north is very hot and dry all year round. The heavy rains are from May or June to September in the south.

## Highlights

The bustling central market and Grand Marché in N'Djamena. The village of Gaoui just outside N'Djamena; Abéché, on the edge of the Sahel. The Tibesti Mountains in the north.

## Where to stay
### N'Djamena

The once-popular *Protestant Mission* has now closed its doors to all travellers (see *Chapter 7*, page 134). The best option is to ask permission at the *Novotel la Chadienne* who will allow you to camp in their grounds in return for eating at one of their restaurants – though neither are cheap. One word of advice: befriend the manager at the Novotel and you will be allowed to use the staff showers and the hotel's pool. Email facilities may also be available at no charge, depending on how long you wish to email for.

### Abéché

In Abéché we were lucky enough to meet the Sultan's brother (!) who put us up for the night. We would otherwise suggest bush camping. Abéché is not a very large town and the surrounding area is typical Sahel.

### Tibesti Mountains

There has been a long-standing border dispute between Chad and Libya, as well as fields of uncharted landmines – this tour of the Tibesti is definitely not for the faint-hearted. Your will need enough fuel, water and food supplies for approximately 1,000km (600 miles). Bush sleeping is the only option and a travel permit for the area is required, depending on which side you come in on. Obtaining permission to travel the area will be a slog and you will probably be rejected. It is best to avoid officialdom altogether.

## Other
A photographic permit is required but takes up to a week to issue so most travellers don't bother. The answer is – do not take any pictures. We were also told that the border between Sudan and Chad, Adré, was closed due to rebel activity in the area. In fact, the border was open; other than a lone camel herder, we did not see much else.

## Further information
*Africa on a Shoestring*, Lonely Planet
www.lonelyplanet.com/dest/afr/chad.html
www.sas.upenn.edu/African_Studies/Country_Specific/chad.html

## PEOPLE'S REPUBLIC OF THE CONGO

***Warning*** *Due to the ongoing civil war in the People's Republic of the Congo the information listed might be out of date. We also strongly advise no overland travel into the People's Republic of the Congo. Seek sound travel advice if you do intend to visit.*

## Capital
Brazzaville

## Language
French is the official language.
International telephone code +242

## Currency and rate
Central African franc (CFA); US$1 = 760CFA

## Red tape
As with most war-torn countries in Africa, avoid all military personnel. It has also been advised that all travel at night be avoided in the Congo.

## Visas
Visas are required for all except nationals of France. Two-week visas

are valid from the date of entry and will cost US$70–90 depending on country of application. Visas are not issued at the border.

## Fuel costs
US$0.46 per litre

## Driving and roads
Drive on the right. Roads are extremely poor.

## African embassies
**Cameroon** Rue Général Bayardelle, Brazzaville; tel: 81 3409
**Central African Republic** Rue Fourneau, Brazzaville; tel: 83 4014
**Chad** 22 Rue de Ecoles; Brazzaville tel: 83 2222
**Democratic Republic of the Congo** 130 Av de l'Indépendance, Brazzaville tel: 83 2938
**France** (issues visas for Burkina Faso, Ivory Coast and Togo) Av Alfassa, Brazzaville; tel: 83 1086
**Gabon** Av Monseigneur Augouard, Brazzaville tel: 83 0590
**Nigeria** 11 Boulevard du Maréchal Lyautey, Brazzaville; tel: 83 1316

## Climate
The dry season is from May to September and mid-December to mid-January.

## Highlights
The clean beaches along the coastline. Congolese music and food. Pointe-Noire. Parc National de Odzala for gorilla trekking.

## Where to stay
### Brazzaville
It seems that in Brazzaville, as in most West and central African countries, it is expensive and difficult to find camping accommodation. You could try either of the Catholic missions in town, *Eglise Sacré Coeur* (on Avenue Maréchal Foch behind the Méridien Hotel) or the *Eglise Kimbanguiste* (on Plateau de 15 Ans, near the Hotel Majoca).

### Pointe-Noire
You'll need to shop around, but most accommodation is along the Cité.

### Parc National de Odzala
Gorilla trekking needs to be booked through ECOFAC in Brazzaville (behind the hardware store Structor and known by most taxi drivers – the manager is Jean Marc Froment). The two-week trip including all transfer fees to and from Brazzaville, accommodation and meals, will set you back US$600. For further information try ECOFAC's website www.ecofac.com.

## Other

A photographic permit is not required but be extremely cautious when taking photos and stay clear of all government institutions.

## Further information

*Africa on a Shoestring*, Lonely Planet
www.geography.about.com/science/geography/library/maps/blcongo.html
www.countries.com/countries/chad
www.africaguide.com/country/congo
http://newafricaguide.com/country/congo

## DEMOCRATIC REPUBLIC OF THE CONGO (DRC)

*Warning* Due to the ongoing civil war in the Democratic Republic of the Congo the information listed might be out of date. We also strongly advise no overland travel into the country. Seek sound travel advice if you do intend to visit and, depending on the state of the country, travel in convoy.

## Capital

Kinshasa

## Language

French is the official language.
International telephone code +242

## Currency and rate

Nouveau Zaire (NZ); US$1 = 158,000NZ

## Red tape

Officials of the DRC are notoriously bad and known for their corruption and drunkenness – avoid at all times! Never stay in one place longer than a day and never walk or drive at night.

## Visas

Visas are required for all and costs vary depending on where you get the visa from. In Nairobi, Kenya, it costs US$100. Prices range from US$50 to $100 for a one-month visa. If you think you are going to stay longer than a month, which is very possible, get a three-month, multiple-entry visa which can range from US$150 to $200. You will also need three to four photographs and an introduction letter from your embassy. Vaccination certificates are obligatory. Visas are not issued at the border.

## Fuel costs

Diesel: US$0.50; petrol: US$0.50 per litre.

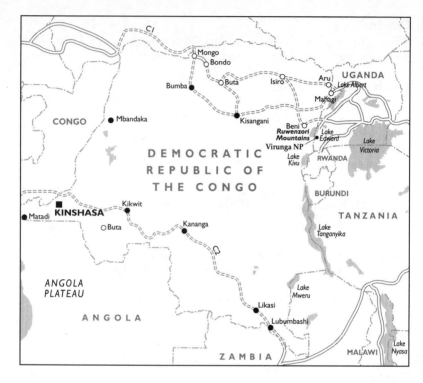

## Driving and roads

Drive on the right. There are not many stretches of road in the DRC that are good and they become a sea of mud during the rainy season.

## African embassies

**Benin** 3990 Av de Cliniques, Kinshasa; tel: 30 492
**Burundi** 4687 Av de la Gombe, Kinshasa; tel 33 353
**Cameroon** Bd du 30 Juin, Kinshasa; tel: 34 787
**Central African Republic** 11 Av Pumbu, Kinshasa; tel: 33 571
**Congo** Bd du 30 Juin, Kinshasa; tel: 34 028
**Gabon** Bd du 30 Juin, Kinshasa; tel: 50 206
**Kenya** 5002 Av de l'Ouganda, Kinshasa; tel: 33 205
**Nigeria** Bd du 30 Juin, Kinshasa; tel: 33 343
**Rwanda** 50 Av de la Justice, Kinshasa; tel 33 080
**Tanzania** BP 1612, 142 Bd 30 Juin, Kinshasa, tel 34 364
**Uganda** Av des Travailleurs, Kinshasa
**Zambia** 54 Av de l'Ecole, Kinshasa; tel: 21 802

## Climate

It is impossible to summarise the climate for the whole of the DRC as it is such a huge country. Along the northern route (the one taken by most travellers) the only time of year it is likely to be fairly dry is from December to February.

## Highlights
Parc National des Virunga for its gorilla trekking and volcanoes (although access has been affected by the civil war). The great lakes of Tanganyika, Kivu, Edward and Albert. And the music of the DRC.

## Where to stay
Bush sleeping will be the best option. Travellers used to stay at the various missions dotted around the country and this is one of the only reasons that certain roads are still driveable. The current state of the missions is uncertain.

### Parc National des Virunga
The park used to have basic camping facilities at the park headquarters. Permits for the national park are paid in hard currency and can be obtained from the headquarters. It is not known whether these facilities still exist. Travellers would stay on the Uganda side, getting individual guides to take them to see the gorillas on the DRC side – we would strongly advise against this, but it depends on the current situation of the country.

## Other
Photographic permits are required but only valid in the region of issue. Try any one of the tourist offices in Kinshasa, Kisangani and Lubumbashi. Cost is dependent on the official! There are also special requirements for travel in central DRC in the mining regions. These permits are only issued in Kinshasa and can take up to two weeks to get. Most travellers bribe their way through these areas.

## Further information
*Africa on a Shoestring*, Lonely Planet
www.africaguide.com/country/zaire
http://infoplease.com/ipa/A0198161.html

## DJIBOUTI

## Capital
Djibouti City

## Language
French and Arabic are the official languages.
International telephone code +253

## Currency and rate
Djibouti franc (DFr); US$1 = 174DFr

## Red tape
None of any significance.

## Visas

Visas are required for all except nationals of France. Visas are valid for month and cost US$25–35. Visas are not issued at the border.

## Fuel costs

Diesel: US$0.40; petrol US$0.91 per litre.

## Driving and roads

Drive on the right. Roads are generally good; desert tracks and piste outside the main routes.

## African embassies

**Eritrea** PO Box 1944; tel: 35 0381
**Ethiopia** Rue Clochette, Djibouti City; tel: 35 0718
**French Consulate** (issues visas for most African French-speaking countries) Av Maréchal Foch, Djibouti City; tel: 35 0325

## Climate

The climate is generally hot and humid with a cooler season from November to mid-April, and occasional rain during that period.

## Highlights

The L'Escale causeway in Djibouti City with a boat trip across the Gulf of Tadjoura. Lac Abbé for its birdlife. Enjoy the flamingos and natural chimneys formed by the escape of underground steam dotted along the foreshore.

## Where to stay
### Djibouti City

The *Auberge Sable Blanc*, a converted villa behind the post office on Boulevard de la République, may allow camping. In the African quarter there is loads of budget accommodation available – it's just a matter of finding secure parking.

### Gulf of Tadjoura

With superb coral reefs 10m from shore, this is a great place for a stopover. Bush sleeping outside the town is the only available option.

### Lac Abbé

Lac Abbé can only be reached by four-wheel drive and requires at least two days, including a guide. Bush sleeping is the only option.

## Other

No photographic permits are needed. Djibouti is an expensive country.

## Further information

*Africa on a Shoestring*, Lonely Planet
http://al.oueb.free.fr

http://ocuenat.free.fr (French only)
www.sas.upenn.edu/African_Studies/Country_Specific/djibouti.html

## EGYPT

### Capital
Cairo

### Language
Arabic is the official language.
International telephone code
+20

### Currency and rate
Egyptian pound (E£); US$1 =
3.70E£

### Red tape
The road south of Aswan has
been closed to all but the
military since the tourist
attacks and we suggest that you
get advice on routes if you are
intending to drive that way.
Egypt is also renowned for its
sexual harassment towards women.

### Visas
Visas are required for all except nationals of Malta and Arabic countries. Visas
cannot be obtained at the border. One month single-entry visas cost US$25.

### Fuel costs
Diesel: US$0.12; petrol: US$0.29 per litre.

### Driving and roads
Drive on the right. All the main routes are well surfaced. Outside the major
routes you will find road signs in Arabic only.

### African embassies
**Algeria** 14 Sharia Brazil, Zamalek, Cairo; tel: 341 8257
**Angola** 12 Midan Fouad Mohi El Dine, Mohandessin Cairo; tel: 707 021
**Burkina Faso** 9 Fawakeh St, Mohandessin, Cairo; tel: 360 8480
**Burundi** 22 El Nakhil St, Madint El Dobbat, Dokki, Cairo; tel: 337 8346, 337 3098
**Cameroon** 42 Rue Batel, Dokki; tel: 704622
**Central African Republic** 13 Sharia Mahmoud Azmi, Mohandiseen, Cairo; tel: 344
6873

**Chad** 12 Midan al-Rifai, Doqqi, Cairo; tel: 349 4461
**Democratic Republic of the Congo** 5 Sharia Al-Mansour, Mohammed, Zamalek, Cairo; tel: 341 1069
**Djibouti** 11 Sharia al-Gezira, Agouza, Cairo; tel: 345 6546
**Eritrea** 87 Sharia Shahab, Al Muhandesein, Cairo; tel: 303 0517
**Ethiopia** 6 Sharia Abdel Rahman Hussein, Midan El-Gomhouria, Dokki, Cairo; tel: 335 3696
**Kenya** 7 Sharia Mohandis Galal, Mohandiseen, Cairo; tel: 345 3907
**Libya** 7 Sharia As-Saleh Ayoub, Zamalek, Cairo; tel: 340 1864
**Morocco** 10 Sharia Salah ad-Din, Zamalek, Cairo; tel: 340 9849
**Somalia** 27 Sharia Somal, Doqqi, Cairo; tel: 337 4038
**South Africa** 21–23 Sharia al-Giza, Giza, Cairo; tel: 571 7234
**Sudan** 3 Sharia Ibrahimi, Garden City, Cairo; tel: 354 5043
**Tanzania** 9 Sharia Abdel Hamid Lotfi, Dokki,Cairo; tel 704 155
**Tunisia** 26 Sharia al-Gezira, Zamalek, Cairo; tel: 341 8962
**Uganda** 9 Midan al-Missah, Doqqi, Cairo; tel: 348 6070

## Climate
Most of the year, except for the winter months of December, January and February, Egypt is hot and dry.

## Highlights
The most obvious is one of the Seven Wonders of the World – the Pyramids of Giza. The Tutankhamun treasures in Cairo. The great temples of Karnak and Luxor in Luxor. Fantastic snorkelling and diving along the Sinai coast.

## Where to stay
### Cairo
Try the *Motel Salma*, just south of Giza. Camping will cost around US$5.

### Luxor
The *YMCA* or *Rezeiky Camp* are both very basic, charging US$5 for camping.

### Sinai
Try the *Pigeon House* in Na'ama Bay which has comfortable huts with fans, and serves breakfast. Accommodation costs around US$20.

## Other
*Baksheesh* (tipping) is widely expected, whether for somebody carrying your bags or opening a door or for a service. Haggling is an art form in Egypt and, whether it be for accommodation or curios, be aware of local prices, and never quote a price you are not prepared to pay.

## Further information
*Egypt*, Lonely Planet
www.tourism.egnet.net
wwwtouregypt.net

# REPUBLIC OF EQUATORIAL GUINEA

## Capital
Malabo

## Language
Spanish is the official language.
International telephone code +240

## Currency and rate
Central African franc (CFA); US$1 = CFA760

## Red tape
The police can be a little pushy but if all your paperwork is in order there shouldn't be a problem.

## Visas
Visas are required for all and one-month visas cost US$65–80. You will also need two photographs. Visas are not issued at the border.

## Fuel costs
Diesel: US$0.56; petrol: US$0.68 per litre.

## Driving and roads
Drive on the right. Roads are mostly very poor.

## African embassies
**Cameroon** 19 Calle de Rey Boncoro, Malabo; tel: 2263
**France** (issues visas for Burkina Faso, the Central African Republic, Chad, Ivory Coast and Togo) Carretera del Aeropuerto, Malabo; tel: 2005
**Gabon** Calle de Argelia, Malabo; tel: 2420
**Nigeria** 4 Paeso de los Cocoteros, Malabo; tel: 2386

## Climate
A tropical climate with rains occurring mainly between May and October.

## Highlights
Malabo with its old Spanish architecture and Luba's nightlife on Bioko Island. The rainforests of Bioko and Río Muni (the mainland).

## Where to stay
### *Bioko Island*
*Malabo*

Try the *Hostel Nely* where the owner speaks English. The rooms are clean with fan and shared bathroom facilities and will set you back around US$12.

### Luba

Luba is southwest of Malabo and known for its nightlife with beautiful beaches – a good spot to relax in for a few days. Accommodation is available at the *Hotel Jemaro* where the seafood is reputed to be excellent.

## Other

Photographic permits are essential and you will be asked for your permit on a regular basis. These can be obtained from the Ministry of Culture, Tourism and Francophone Relations. You will need to type up a request, preferably in Spanish on official stationary which will cost you US$60 and will be issued within 24 hours. Do not take pictures of any government organisations.

## Further information

*Africa on a Shoestring*, Lonely Planet
http://equatorialguinea.org

## ERITREA

**Warning** *The recent border disputes between Eritrea and Ethiopia have now been resolved, but seek advice before entering the country.*

## Capital

Asmara

## Language

Arabic and Tigrinya are the official languages.
International telephone code +291

## Currency and rate

Nakfa; US$1 = 7.38 Nakfa

## Red tape

None of any significance.

## Visas

Visas are required for all and should be applied for in your home country. Of course this is not always possible and the proof of visas from other countries, a letter of introduction from your embassy and two photographs will suffice. A one-month visa will cost US$40–60 and is valid from date of entry. Visas are not issued at the border.

## Fuel costs
Diesel: US$0.23; petrol: US$0.37 per litre.

## Driving and roads
Drive on the right. Roads are in good condition on most major routes, deteriorating as you get off the beaten track.

## African embassies
**Djibouti** Andinnet St, Asmara; tel: 354961
**Egypt** 5 Degiat Afwerk St, Asmara; tel: 123603
**Ethiopia** Franklin D Roosevelt Street, Asmara; tel: 116365

## Climate
Eritrea has a varied topography so the climate is different in each of the three main zones. In the highlands, the hottest month is usually May with highs of around 30°C. Winter is from December to February, with lows at night that can be near freezing point. Asmara's climate is pleasant all year round. Short rainy seasons are in March and April, the main rains from late June to early September. On the coast, travel is not recommended between June and September when daily temperatures range from 40 to 50°C (and considerably hotter in the Danakil Desert). In winter months the temperature ranges from 21 to 35°C. Rain is rare, and occurs only in winter. In the western lowlands the rainy seasons are the same as the highlands; the temperature pattern is the same as that of the coast.

## Highlights
The Danakil desert is an incredibly remote area sparsely populated by the Afar nomads. It is possible to drive through this area to Djibouti. However, with temperatures generally around 40°C, and with no facilities or main roads, it is really only for the seriously adventurous. Asmara and all it has to offer, the dusty alleys of Massawa across the first causeway on Taulud Island. Keren is a predominantly Muslim town and has a colourful daily market, renowned for its silversmiths' street, and the livestock market every Monday.

## Where to stay
There are few campsites but good-value accommodation is available and rooms are usually clean and well kept. It's just a matter of finding secure parking for the vehicle.

### Asmara
There are loads of *albergos* (inns) to be found along Liberation Avenue. For camping try the *Africa Pension,* which is an old converted villa. Good value.

### Keren
Try the *Eritrea Hotel* or the *Sicilia* with both boasting shady courtyards.

### Massawa

Massawa does not have any campsites but loads of accommodation on the mainland and on Taulud Island. You will need to shop around.

## Other

There are uncharted mines throughout Eritrea, so stay on main roads rather than off the beaten track, particularly after dark, and always ask the locals for route advice. In both Eritrea and Ethiopia the people are the kindest and most hospitable you will come across in the whole of Africa, going out of their way to help you. The *faranji* ('white man's') hysteria can get a bit much but wears off quickly.

## Further information

*Guide to Eritrea*, Edward Paice, Bradt Travel Guides
www.eritrea.org

---

## ETHIOPIA

'Ethiopians are completely bonkers. I knew, too, that I had to visit their country.'

Philip Briggs, from *Ethiopia: The Bradt Travel Guide*

## Capital
Addis Ababa

## Language
Amharic is the official language. International telephone code +251

## Currency and rate
Ethiopian birr (Birr); US$1 = 8.15Birr

## Red tape
None of any significance. Ethiopians are some of the most delightful people in all of Africa.

## Visas

Visas are required for all except nationals of Kenya. Visas are single entry only and cost US$65. You will also need to produce an onward visa for the next country and prove you have sufficient funds. Vaccination certificates are mandatory. Visas are not issued at the border.

## Fuel costs
Diesel: US$0.25; petrol: US$0.36 per litre.

## Driving and roads
Drive on the right. Roads are mostly poor with some tarred sections along the major routes.

## African embassies
Just about every African country has representation in Addis Ababa and the tourist board (near Maskal Square) issues a useful booklet listing all the embassies. Here are just a few:

**Djibouti** off Bole Rd, Addis Ababa; tel: 613006
**Egypt** Entonto Av, Addis Ababa; tel: 514302
**Eritrea** Ras Makonnen Av, Addis Ababa; tel: 512844
**French Consulate** (issues visas for most French-speaking African countries) Omedia St, Addis Ababa; tel: 550066
**Kenya** Fikre Maryam Aba Techan St, Addis Ababa; tel: 610033
**Sudan** off Roosevelt St, Addis Ababa; tel: 516477
**Tanzania** Bole Rd, Addis Ababa; tel: 448155/7

## Climate
The main rainy season is from June to September with lighter rains from February to April. In the lowlands it can get extremely hot from April to June while the colder season in the highlands can be very cold.

## Highlights
Southern Ethiopia and the Omo region. The northern historical route which includes Bahir Dar (near the source of the Blue Nile), Gonder, Axum and Lalibela. The Simien Mountains. Ethiopian cuisine and the elaborate coffee ceremony are a must, as well as the traditional music and dance.

## Where to stay
### Addis Ababa
Your options are limitless. We stayed at the *Bel Air* (head east from Arat Kilo roundabout and it's on the right), camping in the shady courtyard, for US$3 per person. The manager and his wife are delightful and will go out of their way to help.

### Bahir Dar
We camped up in the courtyard at the *Guna Terara Hotel* (east towards Gonder, opposite the Mobil garage) at US$3 per person. There are communal showers.

### Gonder

The *Terera Hotel* has a fine view of the Royal Enclosure – it is located just to the north. Camping costs US$3 per person. Gonder often has a shortage of water and getting a shower can be a little frenetic.

### Axum

At the time of writing a lot of travellers indicated that Axum was out of bounds due to fuel shortages as all fuel was being used for the border dispute between Eritrea and Ethiopia. But don't let this stop you – just carry adequate amounts of fuel with you. Try the *Axum Hotel*, east of town towards Adwa and government run, for camping.

### Lalibela

The government-run *Roha* to the west of town offers camping at US$6.

### The Omo region

The best bet here is to bush camp. If you decide to stay a night in Arba Minch, stay at *Rosa's Place* where camping is allowed in the courtyard and she makes the best fish cutlets in all of Ethiopia. It makes a great break from *injera* (a large pancake-shaped substance made of *tef,* a grain that is unique to Ethiopia).

## Other

Currency declaration forms are issued on arrival.

### The Julian Calendar and 12-hour clock

Ethiopians use the Julian Calendar, which means that their year falls seven or eight years behind the European calendar, and there are 13 months in the calendar of the Orthodox church. Ethiopian time is also measured in 12-hour cycles starting at 06.00 and 18.00. In other words, their 19.00 is our 13.00 and vice versa. Be very aware of this when booking a bus or flight and double check departure times. Most banks and other such institutions have both Western and Ethiopian calendars and times.

## Further information

*Ethiopia: The Bradt Travel Guide*, Philip Briggs
http://lcweb2.loc.gov/frd/cs/ettoc.html

## GABON

## Capital

Libreville

## Language

French is the official language.
International telephone code +241

## Currency and rate
Central African franc (CFA); US$1 = 760CFA

## Red tape
Police are suspicious of all foreigners so approach with care.

## Visas
Visas are required for all and can take as long as a week to be issued as all applications are telexed through to Libreville for approval. You will need a letter of introduction from your embassy, two photographs and US$80 for telex charges. Visas are not issued at the border.

## Fuel costs
Diesel: US$0.39; petrol: US$0.63.

## Driving and roads
Drive on the right. Roads are generally poor.

## African embassies
**Benin** Bd Léon Mba, Quartier Derrière Prison, Libreville; tel: 73 7692
**Cameroon** Bd Léon Mba, Quartier Derrière Prison, Libreville; tel: 73 2800
**Central African Republic** North of Voie Express; Libreville; tel: 73 7761
**Congo** Gué-Gué, off Bd Ouaban, Libreville; tel: 67 7078
**Democratic Republic of the Congo** Gué-Gué, off Bd Ouaban, Libreville; tel: 73 8141
**Equatorial Guinea** Bd Yves-Digo, Akébéville, Libreville; tel: 76 3051
**Ivory Coast** Immeuble Diamont, Bd de l'Indépendance, Libreville; tel: 72 0596
**Nigeria** Av du Président Léon Mba, Quartier de l'Université, Libreville; tel: 321 11

## Climate
The climate is hot and humid with the dry season from May to September and another short dry spell in mid-December.

## Highlights
Experiencing the various reserves in Gabon, with a stroll down to the beach at Cap Estérias and visiting the lake region of Lamberéné.

## Where to stay
### Libreville
The most popular place to stay is the *Maison Libermann* on Boulevard Bessieux, which is clean, quiet and offers hot showers. Camping facilities would need to be negotiated.

### Cap Estérias

Cap Estérias is just north of Libreville and very pleasant. Bush sleeping could be an option.

### Lambaréné

At *le Petit Auberge*, two blocks southeast of Bar Dancing Le Capitol, camping facilities would need to be negotiated.

### Réserve de la Lopez

Easiest national park to get to and with abundant wildlife. You will need your own vehicle but camping is not allowed inside the reserve. *Le Campement* just outside the main gates offers camping at US$5, but there's no restaurant so come well prepared.

## Other

Be wary of what you photograph as the Gabonese are quite touchy about photography and your camera could be confiscated.

## Further information

*Africa on a Shoestring*, Lonely Planet
www.sas.upenn.edu/African_Studies/Country_Specific/gabon.html
www.alderan.fr/presidence-gabon/a/data/soc

## THE GAMBIA

## Capital
Banjul

## Language
English is the official language.
International telephone code +220

## Currency and rate
Dalasi (D); US$1 = D15

## Red tape
Road blocks can be tiresome with officials surly at the best of times.

## Visas

Visas are required for all except nationals from the Commonwealth, for whom travel permits are issued at the border (usually for two weeks), and most EU nationals. Thirty-day visas for nationals of the United States,

Australia, New Zealand and South Africa cost US$20 and are *not* available at the border. Ensure that your passport is valid for six months or more. Vaccination certificates are obligatory.

## Fuel costs
Diesel: US$0.45; petrol US$0.59 per litre.

## Driving and roads
Drive on the right. Roads are generally poor.

## African embassies
**Guinea** 78 Wellington St (Liberation Av), Banjul; tel: 22 6862
**Guinea-Bissau** 16 Wellington St (Liberation Av), Banjul; tel: 22 8134
**Ivory Coast** Care of NPE, Bund Rd (Kankujeri St), Banjul; tel: 22 8771
**Mali Consulate** VM Company Ltd, Cotton St, Banjul; tel: 22 6947
**Mauritania** off Kairaba Av, Fajara; tel: 49 6518 or 4098
**Senegal** corner of Nelson Mandela and Buckle St, Banjul; tel: 22 7469
**Sierra Leone** 67 Hagan St (Daniel Goddard St), Banjul; tel: 22 8206

## Climate
Cool dry season from December to April followed by a warmer dry season and rains between June and October.

## Highlights
The mysterious Wassu Stone Circles, with a trip up the Gambia in a local boat. Enjoying the beaches along the Atlantic coast and market-day at Basse Santa Su. The birdlife of the river.

## Where to stay
### Banjul
For camping try the *Black Cow Cross Cultural Arts Centre* across the river in Bara, 300m from the ferry. You can also learn to dance and drum. Accommodation in traditional grass tents, including a traditional meal, will cost US$10.

### Bakau
Try the *Overlanders Rest* which is situated in a village near Serrekunda. Camping costs would need to be negotiated.

### Fajara
You will have to shop around, but most travellers end up staying at *The Mango Tree* where a double room will set you back US$16.

## Other
Crime is on the increase in Banjul so do not walk on your own at night along the beaches of Bakau and Fajara. There have also been many complaints about beach boys, known as 'bumsters' or 'bumsan', who offer you everything and anything. Ignore them unless you would like to use one or other of their services.

## Further information

*The Gambia: The Bradt Travel Guide*, Linda Barnett and Craig Emms
www.gambia.com
www.gambianews.com

## GHANA

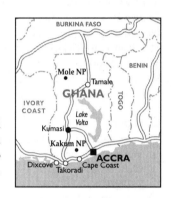

## Capital

Accra

## Language

English is the official language.
International telephone code +233

## Currency and rate

Cedi (C); US$1 = C6,718

## Red tape

There are occasional roadblocks with minimal
hassle – just ensure all your paperwork is in
order. Between the border of Ghana and Togo
the touts can be a nightmare – politely ignore.

## Visas

Visas are required for all except nationals of the Economic Community of
West African States (ECOWAS) and cost around US$25. (Commonwealth
citizens require an entry permit rather than a visa, but they are much the same
thing). Vaccination certificates are obligatory. Visas are not issued at the
border. On arrival you may be asked how long you intend to stay. Whatever
you say will be written in your passport and you won't be able to stay longer,
despite what your visa says – so always state the duration of your visa.

## Fuel costs

Diesel: US$0.30; petrol: US$0.32 per litre.

## Driving and roads

Drive on the right. The coastal roads are excellent but as you move further
north they get a little patchy.

## African embassies

**Benin** 19 Volta St, Accra; tel: 774860
**Burkina Faso** off 2nd Mango Tree Av, Accra; tel: 221988
**Guinea** 11 Osu Badu St, PO 5497; tel: 777921
**Ivory Coast** 18th Lane, Accra; tel: 774611
**Mali** 8 Agostino Neto Rd, Airport residential area; tel: 775160
**Niger** E 104/3 Independence Av (PO 2685); tel: 224962

**Nigeria** 5 Josef Tito Av; tel 776158
**Togo** Cantonments Rd, Accra; tel: 777950

## Climate
Hot and dry in the north and humid along the coast. The rains arrive in late
April or early May and last to September.

## Highlights
The coastline from Accra to Dixcove, with a tour of the various slave forts along
the coast. The ancient Ashanti capital, Kumasi. Kakum and Mole national parks.

## Where to stay
### Accra
In Accra try the rundown *Coco Beach Resort* which offers camping and is 7km
(4 miles) east of central Accra. Alternatively, head 30km (18 miles) west to
Kokrobite and *Wendy's Place*, also known as *Big Milly's Backyard*. Wendy
charges US$3 for camping. Meals are available and at Mike's Place, just
outside on the beach, you can get a fine toasted egg fry with a taste of the local
fire water, *apatechi*. Kokrobite is renowned for the Academy of African Music
and Arts Ltd (AAMAL) with live music, drumming and dancing every
weekend from 14.30 to 16.00.

### On the coast
There is plenty of camping along the coast. Our first night was spent at the
*Anomabu Beach Resort*, just east of Biriwa, on the beach under palm trees. US$6
per person but it's worth it. We then drove on to see Elmina Castle and Cape
Coast Castle, with an overnight stay at the *Drum and Dance Workshop* near
Ampenyi, also known as *Ko-Sa*, which is 25km (15 miles) from Cape Coast.
Turn right at the Ajensudo junction. The campsite is on the beach and costs
US$3 per person. A fortnight later we stayed at the local fort at Princes Town
(for a minimal fee). Meals and drinks can be obtained from the local shebeen
down the road. A wonderful place to stay for a few days.

### Kumasi
The only place you can camp is at the *Presbyterian Guesthouse* at US$5. It's a
beautiful place with huge shady trees, located close to the city centre.

## Other
If you own a Land Rover Accra is the place to get it fixed. Seek advice before
diving into the ocean as Ghana is plagued with dangerous currents.
Photographing people is not a problem but always ask beforehand and do not
photograph near government institutions.

## Further information
*Ghana: The Bradt Travel Guide*, Philip Briggs
www.ghanaweb.com
http://interknowledge.com/ghana/index/html

## GUINEA

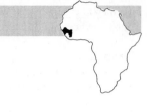

### Capital
Conakry

### Language
French is the official language.
International telephone code +224

### Currency and rate
Guinean franc (GFr); US$1 = GFr 1,750

### Red tape
The police in Guinea like to host roadblocks at night and hold your papers until you pay a bribe – in other words, don't drive at night. If you do get caught in one of these notorious roadblocks, you shouldn't pay more than US$5 as a bribe.

### Visas
Visas are required for all and cost US$25–50. Depending on which country you are in, the Guinea embassy may ask for a letter of accreditation from your own embassy. You will also need a photocopy of the identification pages of your passport. Those issued in Africa are normally issued for two weeks only but this depends on where you apply. Visas are not issued at the border.

### Fuel costs
Diesel: US$0.56; petrol: US$0.68 per litre.

### Driving and roads
Drive on the right. The roads are generally poor and those that are paved are usually potholed.

### African embassies
**France** (issues visas for Burkina Faso and Mauritania), Bd du Commerce, Conakry; tel: 41 1605

**Ghana** Place de Martyrs, Imm Kaloum, Av de la République, Conakry; tel: 44 1510

**Guinea-Bissau** Quartier Bellevue, Commune de Dixinn, Conakry; tel: 44 4398

**Ivory Coast** Com de Kaloum, Boulbinet Bd du Commerce; tel: 45 1082

**Mali,** Com De Matam, close to the Total station, Conakry; tel: 46 14 18

**Nigeria** Corniche Sud, Place du 8 Novembre, Conakry; tel: 41 4375 or 46 1341

**Senegal** Corniche Sud, just past the Nigerian embassy, Conakry; tel: 46 2834

**Sierra Leone** Route Donka, Commune de Dixinn; Conakry; tel: 44 5099

**Togo** Com de Matam, Conakry; tel: 46 2408

## Climate
Tropical climate with lengthy rainy season determined by altitude and location. Rainy season takes place between May and October.

## Highlights
The Fouta Djalon Plateau, the beaches on the Iles de Roume, Iles de Los and Iles de Kassa, where you may even get a spontaneous musical performance. Most can only be reached by *pirogue* but are worth the effort for a day's excursion. The picturesque towns of Dalaba and Pita.

## Where to stay
### Conakry
*Pension Doherty* on 5th Avenue between 8th and 9th Boulevards is an option, but camping costs would have to be negotiated.

### Fouta Djalon Plateau
This plateau with its rolling green hills and cooler climate is a must for any visitor to Guinea with some excellent hiking. Bush sleeping is a good option.

## Other
Guinea is a great country for outdoor enthusiasts – particularly cyclists and hikers. The Fouta Djalon is the most obvious option; remember to carry adequate water and food with you. There is also the great biking/hiking Pita to Télimélée route, which was part of the Paris to Dakar rally in 1995.

## Further information
*West Africa*, Rough Guides or Lonely Planet
www.boubah.com/guineanews/guineaFAQ.html

## GUINEA BISSAU

## Capital
Bissau

## Language
Portuguese is the official language.
International telephone code +245

## Currency and rate
West African franc (CFA); US$1 = CFA760

## Red tape
You might find intermittent roadblocks, but locals, including government personnel, are extremely friendly.

## Visas

Visas are required for all except citizens of Cape Verde and Nigeria. Visas cost between US$10 and US$25 and are valid for one month. Visas are not issued at the border.

## Fuel costs

US$0.44 per litre

## Driving and roads

Drive on the right. The roads are generally poor and those that are paved are usually potholed.

## African embassies

**French Consulate** (issues visas for Burkina Faso, Central African Republic, Chad, Ivory Coast and Togo) Bairro de Penha, Avenida de 14 Novembro, Bissau; tel: 25 1031

**Gambia** Av de 14 Novembro; Bissau

**Guinea** corner of Rua Ngouabi and Rua 12, Bissau; tel: 21 2681

**Mauritania** Av de 14 Novembro, Bissau

**Senegal** off Praça dos Heróis Nacionais, Bissau; tel: 21 2636

## Climate

The hottest months are April to May with the coolest months from December to January.

## Highlights

Losing yourself in the jumble of Portuguese colonial Bissau. Exploring the ruined fort at Cacheu and taking a boat ride to the Bijagos Islands.

## Where to stay

### Bissau

Your only option is to ask around at the bus depot on Avenida de 4 Novembre and hope that a local will be able to put you up for the night or that one of the many hotels offer camping accommodation.

### The Bijagos Archipelago

These are a group of islands off Guinea-Bissau. Your best bet is to pack an overnight bag, find parking space for the vehicle for a night or two and head over to one of the following islands which have loads of accommodation:

**Bolama Island** – the closest island to the mainland. The ferry leaves every Friday and returns on Sunday. There are no hotels but locals are happy to put you up for the night.
**Bubaque Island** – at the centre of the archipelago and one of the easiest to reach. The best part is Praia Bruce (Bruce Beach) on the southern end of the island. *Chez*

*Patricia* is a good place to stay, offering meal and a well, so water is never a problem. A double room costs US$10–15.

**Galinhas Island** – about 60km (40 miles) south of Bissau and not frequented by many visitors – sounds ideal!

### Cacheu
Try the *Hotel Baluarte* where camping accommodation will need to be negotiated.

### Other
Guinea-Bissau is one of the poorest countries in Africa and if you are invited by a local person always offer to pay for your accommodation and/or meal.

### Further information
*West Africa*, Rough Guides or Lonely Planet
www.sas.upenn.edu/African_Studies/Specific_Countries/G_Bissau.html

## IVORY COAST (COTE D'IVOIRE)

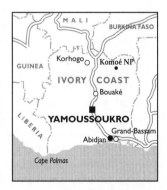

### Capital
Yamoussoukro is the official capital, though Abidjan remains the commercial and diplomatic centre.

### Language
French is the official language.
International telephone code +225

### Currency and rate
West African franc (CFA); US$1 = 760CFA

### Red tape
We had minimal hassles throughout the country, except for camping accommodation which was sometimes hard to find.

### Visas
Visas are required for all except nationals of the Economic Community of West African States (ECOWAS). Citizens of the United States do not need visas for stays of up to 90 days. Visas are valid for three months from the date of entry and cost US$25–50. Vaccination certificates are obligatory. Visas are not issued at the border.

## Fuel costs
Diesel: US$0.45; petrol: US$0.74 per litre.

## Driving and roads
Drive on the right. Good surfaced roads on main routes with mainly good dirt roads elsewhere.

## African embassies
**Algeria** 53 Bd Clozel, Plateau, Abidjan; tel: 212340
**Benin** Rue de Jardins, Deux Plateaux, Abidjan; tel: 414413
**Burkina Faso** 2 Av Terrason de Fougères, Plateau, Abidjan; tel: 211501
**France** (issues visas for Togo and Chad) Rue Lecour, Plateau, Abidjan; tel: 200504
**Ghana** Immeuble Corniche, Bd du Général de Gaulle, Plateau, Abidjan; tel: 331124
**Guinea** Immeuble Crosson Duplessis, Av Crosson Duplessis, Plateau, Abidjan; tel: 222520
**Liberia** 20 Av Delafosse, Plateau, Abidjan; tel: 331228
**Mali** Maison du Mali, Rue de Commerce, Plateau, Abidjan; tel: 323147
**Niger** 23 Bd Angoulvant, Marcory, Abidjan; tel: 262814
**Nigeria** Bd de la République, Plateau, Abidjan; tel: 211982
**Senegal** Immeuble Nabil, Av Général de Gaulle, Plateau, Abidjan; tel: 332876

## Climate
There are two climatic regions. In the south the temperature remains at a steady 30°C all year round and has heavy rainfall. There are four seasons – a long dry season from December to April, a long rainy season from May to July, a short dry season from August to September and a short rainy season from October to November.

The north has a broader temperature range, with a rainy season from June to October and a dry season November to May.

## Highlights
Grand-Bassam is a stretch of bustling beachfront entertainment. Abidjan offers contrasting affluence and poverty. It has some great supermarkets, a huge market for second-hand spares, and is a great place to stock up on all sorts of goodies. It was the one time we could not resist the French import of cheeses – costly but worth the taste sensation!

Yamoussoukro is one of the most fascinating cities in Africa and full of contrasts, with deserted streets, European concrete structures, eight-lane highways lined with over 10,000 lights ending abruptly in the jungle. A must-see is the Basilique de Notre Dame de la Paix, which bears a striking resemblance to St Peter's in Rome, the white elephant in Africa, built by President Houphouët-Boigney and costing a mere US$300 million to build. There is nothing else quite like it!

Korhogo is the capital of the Senoufo, famous for its wooden carvings and Korhogo cloth (mud-coloured designs painted on fabric). The best time to visit is in December when festivals occur on a regular basis. We found Korhogo to be a bustling and energetic place. You need to spend a little time there to delve into the areas that are less frequented by tourists – a definite visit should be to the pottery and blacksmith quarters, with temples for each of the separate crafts. Also visit Komoé National Park.

## Where to stay
### Abidjan
Though initially confusing, Abidjan is built on the banks of a lagoon and the more exclusive areas are divided as such. The city is generally divided into six sections – Plateau is the commercial hub; Treichville is a vibrant quarter and worth a visit, but not safe at night; Marcory is more intimate with loads of budget accommodation; Adjame is north of Plateau; Cocody is east of Plateau, an exclusive suburb which spreads northwards into the final area, Deux Plateau.

The only camping availability is *Camping Virdi* and *Camping Coppa-Cabana*. Both are on the beachfront, south of Abidjan, tiny properties surrounded by huge brick walls – US$5 for camping. It is the only option unless you want to stay in a hotel, of which there is an enormous selection from budget to top of the range.

### Grand-Bassam
Grand-Bassam is south of Abidjan and frequented mostly by ex-patriots during the weekend. We would suggest visiting only during the week. There isn't much regarding camping accommodation, although a few locals have set up very rustic campsites for a minimal fee. Just watch all your stuff as crime is rampant.

### Yamoussoukro
There is no camping in Yamoussoukro and you will have to beg one of the hotel managers to allow you to stay in their courtyard. We stayed at the *Hotel Agip* at no charge but had to eat in their restaurant. It's a family-run business and we found them extremely helpful regarding the surrounding area.

### Korhogo
There is no camping facility in Korhogo but loads of budget accommodation. It's just a matter of finding secure parking for the vehicle, which is a problem. We ended up staying with an ex-patriot from South Africa who was working for a mining company in the surrounding area.

## Other
A photographic permit is not required.

## Further information
*West Africa* Rough Guides or Lonely Planet
www.sas.upenn.edu/African_Studies/Country_Specific/Cote.html

## KENYA

### Capital
Nairobi

### Language
English and Swahili are the official languages.
International telephone code +254

### Currency and rate
Kenyan shilling (KSh); US$1 = KSh79.38

### Red tape
You will need to take the convoy from Isiolo to Moyale to get to Ethiopia or vice versa. See *Chapter 1*, Route Planning, for further details.

### Visas
Visas are required by all visitors except nationals of most Commonwealth countries (passport holders of Australia, New Zealand, Sri Lanka and UK *do* need visas), Denmark, Ethiopia, Germany, Ireland, Italy, Norway, Spain, Sweden, Turkey and Uruguay. Those who don't need visas are issued a visitors' pass on entry which is valid for up to six months. Visas are valid for three months from the date of issue and cost US$20–40 depending on country of application. Getting a visa for Kenya in Tanzania or Uganda is simple and hassle free. So long as your visa remains valid you can visit either Tanzania or Uganda and return without having to apply for another visa. This does not apply if you are visiting any other countries.

### Fuel costs
Diesel: US$0.54; petrol: US$0.70 per litre.

### Driving and roads
Drive on the left. Most of the roads in Kenya are excellent, it's just the driving skills of other vehicles, particularly buses, that one needs to avoid! The roads get worse the further north you go.

### African embassies
**Burundi** 14th floor, Development House, Moi Av, Nairobi; tel: 218458
**Democratic Republic of the Congo** Electricity House, Harambee Av, Nairobi; tel: 229771
**Djibouti** 2nd floor, Comcraft House, Haile Selassie Av, Nairobi; tel: 339633
**Egypt** Harambee Plaza, Haile Selassie Av, Nairobi; tel: 225991
**Eritrea** New Waumuni House, Westlands, Nairobi; tel: 443163
**Ethiopia** State House Av, Nairobi; tel: 723027
**French Consulate** (issues visas for most French-speaking African countries) Barclays Plaza, Loita St, Nairobi; tel: 339783

**Madagascar** Hilton Hotel, Mama Ngima St, Nairobi; tel: 225286
**Malawi** Waiyaki Way, Westlands, Nairobi; tel: 440569
**Mozambique** HFCK Building, Kenyatta Avenue, Kyuna, Nairobi; tel: 222446
**Rwanda** International House, Mama Ngina St, Nairobi; tel: 212345
**South Africa** Lonrho House, Standard St, Nairobi; tel: 228469
**Sudan** Minet-ICDC House, Mamlaka Rd, Nairobi; tel: 720883
**Tanzania** Continental Towers, corner of Uhuru Highway and Harambee Av, Nairobi; tel: 331056
**Uganda** Uganda House, Baring Arcade, Kenyatta Av, Nairobi; tel: 330801
**Zambia** Nyerere Av, Nairobi; tel: 718494
**Zimbabwe** Miner-ICDC Building, Mamlaka Rd, Nairobi; tel: 721049

## Climate
Coastal areas are tropical and hot but tempered by monsoon winds. The wettest months are April, May and November; the hottest are February and March; the coolest are June and July. The lowlands are hot and dry. Much of Kenya, however, stands at over 1,500m (4,500ft) and has a more temperate climate with four seasons. There is a warm and dry season from January to March; a rainy season from March to June; a cool, cloudy and dry season from June to October and a rainy season from November to December.

## Highlights
Visiting the Masai Mara and other numerous national parks throughout Kenya, climbing Mount Kenya and visiting Lake Turkana, which is Kenya's largest lake and also known for Leakey's famous Rift Valley digs. Enjoying the various tribes in Kenya – the Samburu, Turkana and Masai. There is a great ice-cream and cheese factory in Eldoret.

## Where to stay
### Nairobi
Most overlanders end up at either one of these camps – *Upperhill Campsite* on Menegari Road, just off Hospital Road, which is within walking distance of the city centre, camping costs US$3; or *Kumuka Castle* (15 Magadi Road, Langata) which is a little way out of town. Camping costs US$3. The bar is reported to be superb. An alternative is *Mrs Roche's*, located away from the city centre on 3rd Parklands Avenue. This is particularly popular with campers and people with their own vehicles.

### Eldoret
There is a great campsite just outside Eldoret called the *Naiberi River Campsite* with the most comfortable bar imaginable. Every visitor to the campsite has also drawn a poster of their visit to Kenya, which now makes an amusing art gallery. Unfortunately, on our second visit the campsite had burned down, but already a new bar was in progress and the first poster was already up! Camping costs US$6.

## Lake Naivasha

The lake makes a good break from the chaotic lifestyle in Nairobi. Try *Fisherman's Camp* which has huge acacia trees, an incredible amount of birdlife, loads of water activities and a great bar. Camping will cost about US$6.

## Mount Kenya

For all information on Mount Kenya go to the *Naro Moru River Lodge* (1.5km/3 miles off to the left on the main Nairobi to Nanyuki road) which also offers camping accommodation at US$4 per person.

## Maralal

Maralal is high up in the hills and above the Lerochi Plateau. The best place to stay is at the *Yare Club and Campsite*. Maralal is a good stopover on your way up to Lake Turkana. It is also famous for its Camel Derby which takes place every October.

## Up to Lake Turkana

Bush sleeping is the best option. The road up to Lake Turkana is made of volcanic outcrops, which means that there are lots of sharp stones which make it slow going. On Lake Turkana, in Loyangalani, there are two campsites. The first is *El-Molo Campsite* and the other is the *Oasis Lodge*. El-Molo charges a little less than the Oasis.

## Coastline

The options are endless but most people rave about *Tiwi Beach*. The only problem is finding safe parking facilities for your vehicle. Take a local ferry across and be self-sufficient from there. There are various beach bungalows offering accommodation and prices range from US$3 to US$25 per person, depending what you are after.

## National parks

Most of Kenya's national parks allow vehicles and have camping facilities. Be aware that the cost of taking a foreign-registered vehicle into most national parks is very high – it can cost you US$100 per day (US$27 per person park fee and US$40 per vehicle plus US$10 per person camping). The best option is to organise a tour in Nairobi for the various national parks and get a referral from either Upperhill Campsite or Kumuka Castle regarding the best and most economical tours available.

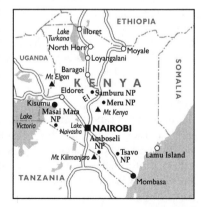

## Other
Nairobi has the worst reputation regarding crime and petty theft. Watch your back and find out from the locals which areas are being targeted.

## Further information
*East and Southern Africa: The Backpacker's Manual*, Philip Briggs, Bradt Travel Guides
www.kenyaweb.com
http://www.rcbowen.com/kenya
http://kenyalogy.com

## LESOTHO

## Capital
Masenu

## Currency
South African Loti but rand universally accepted. US$1 = LSL6.24

See also *South Africa*, page 237.

## LIBERIA

**Warning** *Due to the ongoing political troubles in Liberia we suggest no overland travel into Liberia. Basic information is listed but seek sound travel advice before going.*

## Capital
Monrovia

## Language
English is the official language.
International telephone code +231

## Currency and rate
Liberian dollar (L); US$1 = L$0.425

## Visas
Visas are required for all and cost US$30–40. Within 48 hours you also need to report to the first Bureau of Immigration that you find and they will issue you with a visitor's permit and will determine the length of your stay. Vaccination certificates are obligatory. Visas are not issued at the border.

## Further information
*West Africa*, Rough Guides or Lonely Planet
www.liberian-conection.com

## LIBYA

**Warning** Due to ongoing embargos with Libya and general mistrust of Westerners, it is best to research and get as much information as possible on the country before departure.

## Capital
Tripoli (administrative) and Benghazi (commercial centre)

## Language
Arabic is the official language.
International telephone code +218

## Currency and rate
Libyan dinar (LD); US$1 = LD0.54

## Red tape
If all your paperwork is in order you shouldn't experience any major hassles.

## Visas
Visas are required for all. Nationals of Israel or those with an Israeli stamp in their passport will not be admitted. All visitors also need permission from the

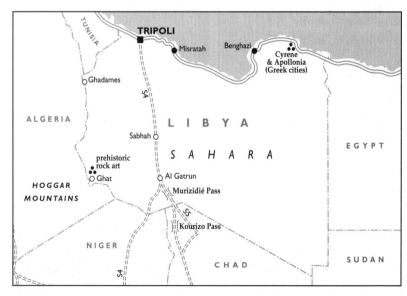

Libyan People's Bureau, ie: the embassy, which means that a tourist visa needs to be sponsored by a Libyan tour company, particularly for nationals from Australia, New Zealand, UK, USA and Canada. You will also need to have all the details of your passport translated into Arabic. Visas cost US$30 and are valid for one month. You will be required to register within 48 hours at the first police station you come across in Libya.

## Fuel costs
Libya has the cheapest fuel available in Africa. There are even reports of travellers who only topped up their tanks and weren't charged for the fuel!

## Driving and roads
Drive on the right. The roads on major routes are good and the rest are desert pistes and tracks.

## African embassies
**Egypt** Sharia Omar al-Mukhtar, Tripoli
**Tunisia** Sharia Bin' Ashur, Tripoli; tel: (021) 607 161

## Climate
The best time to visit is during the northern spring and autumn months from September to January, although you might come across the *ghibli,* which is a hot, dry and sand-laden wind that can raise the temperatures to 40+°C.

## Highlights
The Sahara. Ghat (for prehistoric rock art) in southwest. Roman ruins at Bulla Regia. Ancient Greek cities of Cyrene and Apollonia.

## Where to stay
Bush sleeping is the only option and throughout Libya this is not a problem. Just remember to carry adequate fuel and water when visiting the Sahara. Even in the larger towns it's best to park up for the day, do what needs to be done, and leave in the early afternoon to find a camping spot outside town. There are hotels in most major cities but prices are high and you'll be charged in foreign currency.

## Other
Libya is a strict Muslim country, so dress and act accordingly, and remember, no alcohol is allowed whatsoever. It is also advisable not to mention any personal political views or criticism of the country's leadership. Libyans are sensitive towards photography, so be careful what you photograph and never ever take pictures of women.

## Further information
*Africa on a Shoestring*, Lonely Planet
www.arab.net/libya/libya_content.html
http://www.geocities.com/Athens/8744/mylinks.html

## MALAWI

### Capital
Lilongwe

### Language
English and Chichewa are the official languages.
International telephone code +265

### Currency and rate
Malawi kwacha (MK); US$1 = MK47.49

### Red tape
None of any significance. There are occasional roadblocks which just check vehicle particulars and your travel itinerary.

### Visas
Visas are not required for nationals of Belgium, Commonwealth countries, Denmark, Finland, Germany, Iceland, Ireland, Luxembourg, the Netherlands, Norway, Portugal, Sweden and the USA. A visitor's stamp is issued at the border.

### Fuel costs
Diesel: US$0.45; petrol: US$0.51 per litre.

### Driving and roads
Drive on the left. Roads throughout Malawi are generally in good condition.

### African embassies
**Mozambique** Commercial Bank Building, African Unity Av, Lilongwe; tel: 784100
**South Africa** Impco Building, Lilongwe; tel: 783722
**Zambia** Convention Drive, Lilongwe; tel: 731911
**Zimbabwe** off Indépendance Drive, Lilongwe; tel: 784988

### Climate
The climate in Malawi is very pleasant and the rainy season is from November to March.

### Highlights
Zomba Plateau and the coastline of Lake Malawi, specifically Mangochi and Chitimba. Liwonde also has an array of wildlife.

# Where to stay
## Lilongwe
*The Gap*, a South African-run campsite on Beatrice Road, is a good spot to camp at US$3 per person. The Gap is also a good place to meet other travellers and get a feel for what to see in Malawi, with suggested campsites along the way. The campsite offers daily excursions to Cape Maclear.

## Blantyre
Though extremely full at the best of times, the *Wayfarers* (formerly known as Doogles) on Mulomba Place is a great place with a good atmosphere, bar, food and pool. Camping costs US$3 per person.

## Zomba Plateau
The Zomba Plateau is in the highlands and is a little cooler. There are great hiking opportunities available all along the Plateau. The campsite on the top of the Plateau is run by the local community and will cost you next to nothing, US$0.50, including a hot shower. At the time of writing a dam was being built in the area.

## Mangochi
Just north of Mangochi, 21km (13 miles) from town, there is a campsite called *Nanchengwa Lodge* (*nanchengwa* means hammerkop in Swahili, a local bird). It is a family-run business and all travellers are welcomed with open arms and eventually form part of the family! Camping is available under the shaded car-park or on the beach and costs US$3 per person. The lodge is right on Lake Malawi and boasts a stunning bar and all sorts of water activities.

## Cape Maclear
There is plenty of accommodation along the beachfront of Cape Maclear. The most popular are *The Gap*, *The Ritz* or *Steven's Place*. For a quieter alternative and particularly if you are bringing in a vehicle, try the *Golden Sands Beach Resort*. Camping costs US$3 per person and expect to party at Cape Maclear. Bilharzia and malaria are both rampant in this area, so dry off and cover up!

## Chitimba
Here you have two options – either at the bottom of Livingstonia where Adela, John and Gisela run a campsite on the beachfront (as you come into town you'll see the sign on the right – look out for Jack the pig!), or up at Livingstonia, a hell of a steep drive with parts of the road having been washed away, at the ecofriendly campsite on your right, just before town. At the time we visited it was still under construction but had the most incredible toilets ever, and a stunning view over Livingstonia.

## Liwonde National Park
The best place to stay is *Mvuu Camp* which has a restaurant and open-plan bar looking over the river. Camping will cost US$10 and they also arrange boat rides on the river.

## Other

In the past, under the Hastings Banda regime, if you were caught carrying the Lonely Planet guide it would have been confiscated at the border, or if you were a man with long hair it was sheared off there and then. We're glad to say that Malawi has calmed down considerably and is today a relaxed country to travel in.

The reason might be that Malawi is renowned for its good 'grass', known as 'Malawi Gold', which many travellers try at least once. Whatever happens, do not get caught. The police are clamping down on users and dealers. In many of the campsites you visit you will find notes on signboards saying 'Hi, I am from England and am currently in jail for carrying drugs. I really just need somebody to talk to.' You have been warned.

## Further information

*Malawi: The Bradt Travel Guide*, Philip Briggs
www.malawi-tourism.com
www.members.tripod.com/~malawi/

# MALI

## Capital

Bamako

## Language

French is the official language.
International telephone code +223

## Currency and rate

West African franc (CFA); US$1 = CFA760

## Red tape

It has been reported that there are secret police operating who may engage you in conversation, particularly regarding Mali politics, and then reveal their true identity and ask for a hefty fine regarding your response. Not once did we come across this and neither did any other travellers we came across, so it might just be an urban legend.

## Visas

Visas are required for all except French nationals. A one-month visitor's visa can cost US$20–50, depending on where you apply for it. Most guidebooks will tell you that you need to register with the police, but the only place we had to do this was in Djenné, so find out from other travellers what the current status is. Visas are not issued at the border. Inoculation certificates are obligatory.

## Fuel costs

Diesel: US$0.48; petrol: US$0.77 per litre.

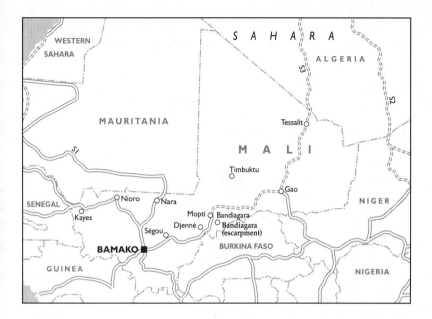

## Driving and roads

Drive on the right. Roads are generally poor. The desert piste to Timbuktu and the road from Bamako to Senegal are awful. There was some construction going on as we drove to Senegal.

## African embassies

**Algeria** Route de l'Aéroport in Daoudabugou, Bamako; tel: 205176
**Burkina Faso** Rue 224, off Route de Koulikoro, Bamako; tel: 22 3171
**Guinea** Av de Farako in Badalabougou, Bamako; tel: 22 2975
**Mauritania** Route de Koulikoro, Bagadaji (6km north of city), Bamako; tel: 22 4815
**Nigeria** Route de Ségou in Badalabougou, Bamako; tel: 22 5771
**Senegal** 341 Rue 287 (south of city, three blocks west of Av de Fleure); tel: 218274

## Climate

Mali spans desert, sahel and tropical areas, creating big differences across the country. The three main seasons are rainy season June to September/October; cool dry season October/November to February; hot dry season March to June.

## Highlights

Ségou, Djenné and Mopti, with their traditional architecture and mosques. The Bandiagara Escarpment in Dogon country. Timbuktu, for its location at the edge of the Sahara and its history.

## Where to stay
### Bamako

The only camping place in Bamako is the *Lebanese Mission,* near the centre of the city on Rue Poincaré, run by George. It's a rundown place but is within walking distance of everything. Camping costs US$3 per person.

### Ségou

You can try the *Office du Niger Campement* for camping, but when we tried it they had no running water and were charging US$10 for camping in the car park. We ended up staying with some peace corps volunteers we met a little later. You'll just have to try your luck.

### Djenné

The only place to stay is *Le Campement* near the Grand Mosque (which is a must-see). Your vehicle is safe in the car park and sleeping on the roof costs US$3.50 per person. It's a wonderful experience.

### Mopti

Mopti, other than being an impressive town, is the gateway to the Dogon country. For the Dogon country you'll need a guide and we would suggest hiking the area. We took our vehicle, but to really enjoy the whole area, hiking is the best bet. There are a few places to stay in Mopti – you'll have to look around. Try *Le Campement* (on right-hand side as you come into town from the main road); camping in the car park costs US$4.

### Dogon country

As you travel in Dogon country all fees, including accommodation, should be arranged with your guide beforehand. Meals are not included but costs are minimal at each of the villages you stop at. Accommodation is a mattress on the roof and once again, a wonderful experience as you hear the village sounds all around you. Take some time in choosing your guide and in negotiating the fees. You'll initially be hassled but once a guide has been chosen, the rest peter away.

### Timbuktu

Try *Le Campement*, also known as the *Hôtel Bouctou*, for camping. Once again your vehicle is secure in the parking area as you climb upon a roof to rest for the night.

### Other

There have been some reports of armed rebels in northern Mali, so find out from other travellers and locals what the latest status is. Crime is on the increase in Bamako, so watch your back. It is also one of the most frenetic towns in Africa with vendors, cars, people and animals using every part of the road and pavement. We found it best to walk everywhere rather than drive.

### Further information

*Mali: The Bradt Travel Guide*, Ross Velton
www.mailnet.ml/mali/pages/index/html (French)
www.sas.upenn.edu/African_Studies/Specific_Country/mali.html
www/geocoties.com/mali.html

# MAURITANIA

## Capital
Nouakchott

## Language
Arabic is the official language.
International telephone code +222

## Currency and rate
Ouguiya (UM); US$1 = UM252

## Red tape
You will probably have to buy insurance at the border even if you have a valid insurance for West Africa.

## Visas
Visas are required for all except nationals of Arab League countries and nationals of France and Italy. On application you will need to show your vaccination certificate and get a letter of introduction from your embassy. Three-month visas cost US$15–30. Visas are not issued at the border.

## Fuel costs
Diesel: US$0.31; petrol: US$0.59 per litre.

## Driving and roads
Drive on the right. Roads are generally in good condition on all major routes, except the road to Nama which has deteriorated badly. Watch out for sand drifts over the roads. The desert roads are typical Saharan pistes.

## African embassies
**Mali** Rue Abdalaye; tel: 540218
**Morocco** South of Rue de Abdalaye, Nouakchott; tel: 251411
**Senegal** Av du Général de Gaulle, Nouakchott; tel: 252106

## Climate
Mostly desert climate – very dry and extremely hot throughout the year.

## Highlights
Most travellers we met along the way were crossing through

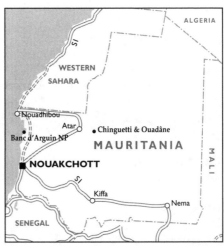

Mauritania from Mali to Morocco or vice versa. It is said that the Parc National de Banc d'Arguin has spectacular birdlife and that the Adrâr region of Atâr, Chinguetti and Ouadâne oases are supposedly beautiful. It is very rare that you'll find people touring Mauritania, though we have heard it's quite worth it – due to lack of tourism you are more likely to come across some interesting experiences.

## Where to stay
For most of Mauritania bush sleeping is the only option.

### Nouakchott
Try the central *Auberge Nomad*, just off Rue Abou Baker, which has hot showers and a pleasant bar and eating area. You can also stay at the *Auberge Central*, on Plot K opposite the Chinese Embassy, which comes highly recommended but isn't signposted. Once you know what you are looking for it's easy to find (a two-storey house with huge metal gates in Lot K, opposite the Chinese Embassy). Ask for Hamedine Ould El Hassam, who will also find you a guide – Ahmed Ould Mouhamed comes highly recommended. You'll pay about US$150 for one vehicle crossing from Nouakchott to the Moroccan border (see *Chapter 1*, Route Planning, for further information). Camping throughout Nouakchott will cost US$3 per person.

### Parc National du Banc d'Arguin
The best time to visit the park is during the nesting period from April to July and October to January. The park is quite hard to get to, but information can be obtained from the park's head office in Nouâdibou on 45085.

## Other
Alcohol is not permitted except at expensive European restaurants at expensive prices in Nouakchott.

## Further information
*West Africa*, Rough Guides or Lonely Planet
http://www.virtualmauritania.com
www.sas.upenn.edu/African_Studies/Country_Specific/mauritania.html

## MOROCCO

## Capital
Rabat

## Language
Arabic is the official language.
International telephone code +212

## Currency and rate
Dirham (Dr); US$1 = Dr11.02

## Red tape
We found the officials to be some of the nicest in Africa – extremely helpful and kind – but we can't guarantee that they are always like that.

When crossing the Sahara it is advisable to have several copies of the document in *Appendix 2*, plus copies of your passport and driving licence, as these are required at roadblocks in Morocco and Western Sahara.

## Visas
Most visitors to Morocco do not require visas and are granted leave to remain in Morocco for 90 days on entry. Exceptions to this rule include nationals of Israel, South Africa and Zimbabwe, who can apply for a one-month single-entry visa (US$25–30) or a three-month double-entry visa (US$35–40). These can take up to four weeks to issue. It you have just crossed from Mauritania, it will take up to 36 hours for you to get permission to enter Morocco and you will then proceed with an armed guard to Dakhla where all other paperwork is cleared.

## Fuel costs
Diesel: US$0.47; petrol: US$0.79 per litre.

## Driving and roads
Drive on the right. Roads are generally in good condition on all major routes, apart from more remote desert tracks.

## African embassies
**Algeria** 46 Boulevard Tariq ibn Zayid, Rabat; tel: 76 5092
**Mauritania** Souissi II Villa, No 226, OLM, Rabat; tel: 65 6678
**Senegal** 17 Rue Qadi Amadi, Rabat; tel; 75 4138
**Tunisia** 6 Av de Fès, Rabat; tel: 73 0576

## Climate
Morocco has a variety of climates – Mediterranean in the north, Atlantic in the west, continental in the interior and desert in the south.

## Highlights
The Atlas Mountains with their Berber villages and stunning landscape. The historical towns of Ouarzazate, Marrakech, Fès, Meknès and Chefchaoen. In Marrakech there is the famous Djemaa el-Fna, a huge fair in the square of the old city which comes to life in the early afternoon. The coastline, including Casablanca and Rabat. It is said that Casablanca is a European getaway, with private villas dotted all along the coastline. The art-deco buildings in Casablanca

are superb. Rabat is famous for its magnificent architecture and lack of tourists.

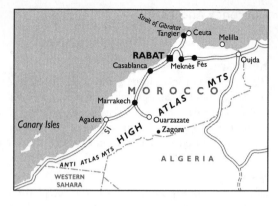

## Where to stay

In Morocco it is generally more convenient to stay in towns rather than on the outskirts. There are hundreds of *pensions* available in all major towns at minimal cost. A double will set you back US$6. Most serve breakfast.

### Rabat

*Camping de la Plage* at Salé Beach is the only camping option in Rabat. Camping costs US$4 per person.

### Casablanca

The only camping option is way out of town on the road to El-Jadida called *Camping de l'Oasis*.

### The Atlas Mountains

The best option is to bush sleep, but as you cross the Atlas Mountains you will find that most towns have campsites. In the Dadès Gorge, near Ait Oudinar, there is a wonderful campsite, very basic, called *Hotel Restaurant Camping du Peuplie,* which costs – wait for it – US$0.30! It is owned by Mohammed Eachaouichi, who is extremely helpful and has abundant knowledge on the surrounding area. A walk with him to one of the nearby Berber villages is worth your while.

### Marrakech

Marrakech does not really have any campsites. The most popular travellers' spot is the *Hotel Ali*, on the Djemaa el-Fna. Sleeping on the roof costs US$4 per person. They have mattresses and pillows and will let you park in the basement.

### Fès

Fès is the oldest imperial city in Morocco. There are two options regarding camping – *Camping Diamant Vert* and *Camping International*. The latter can get a little noisy as the local disco is held daily at the campsite.

### Meknès

There is a campsite with a very abstract pool just outside Meknès (watch out for camping signs) on the way to Volubilis, the old Roman ruins.

### Ouarzazate

There is a campsite just outside town, within walking distance, on the road to Tinerhir. Camping costs US$3 per vehicle. They also serve great meals.

### Chefchaouen

Not only famous for its supply of hashish, this town in the Rif Valley is a favourite among travellers. Wonder why?! The town has a Hispanic look of white-washed houses and tiled roofs. The only campsite is just a little out of town and signposted *Campsite and Youth Hostel*, just behind the *Hotel Asma*. Their green tea is great – you'll just need to ignore all the hashish touts who hang around.

## Other

To ease the hassle factor from the hashish touts it is best to dress conservatively and respect the culture, although you will see tourists running around with next to nothing on – the choice is yours. Hashish itself is the other problem. Though it's easy to get, do not get caught as the fines are heavy. Chefchaouen is renowned for its hashish sellers who cruise the major routes in black Mercedes and can cut you off for a sale. Wind up all windows, ensure your vehicle is in perfect working order and do not get caught out.

## Further information

*Morocco*, Barnaby Rogerson, Cadogan
http://marocnet.com
www.kingdomofmorocco.com
http://arab.net/morocco/morocco_contents.html
www.mincom.gov.mo/english/e-page.html

## MOZAMBIQUE

## Capital

Maputo

## Language

Portuguese is the official language.
International telephone code +258

## Currency and rate

Metical (Mt); US$1 = Mt16,540

## Red tape

There are various rumours regarding roadblocks in Mozambique. On arrival we were told that one could get fined for wearing sunglasses or having three rather than two triangles. This is no longer the case, and with the recent employment of a new Police Commissioner who actually pays his staff, most roadblocks now consist of a quick English lesson – 'Hello, how are you? 'Where are you going to?' and 'How do I say ...?'

## Visas

Visas are required for all and cost US$15–30. You also have to pay a border tax of US$10 and it is better to pay in South African rand if you are coming in that way as it is cheaper than paying in Metical. Visas are not issued at the border.

## Fuel costs

Diesel: US$0.41; petrol: US$0.55 per litre.

## Driving and roads

Drive on the left. Due to the floods in April 2000 we are not sure of the status of roads and a lot of the landmines have now been displaced. At the time of writing roads were in good condition, except those in the remoter areas. Ask locals and other travellers about routes in remote parts of Mozambique. When we were travelling there was a lot of construction work going on.

## African embassies

**France** (issues visas for most French-speaking countries in Africa) 1419 Av Julius Nyerere, Maputo; tel: 491461

**Malawi** 75 Av Kenneth Kaunda, Maputo; tel: 491468

**South Africa** 745 Av Julius Nyerere, Maputo; tel: 490059

**Swaziland** 608 Av do Zimbabwe, Maputo; tel: 492451

**Tanzania** 852 Av Martires de Machava, Maputo; tel: 490110

**Zambia** 1286 Av Kenneth Kaunda, Maputo; tel: 492452

**Zimbabwe** Av Martires da Machava, Maputo; tel: 490404

## Climate

The dry season is from April to September, when it is cool and pleasant. The wet season is from October to March when it is hot and humid.

## Highlights

The old colonial buildings in Maputo and its hectic nightlife. Beaches on the southern coast and beautiful islands and surrounding area of the Bazaruto Archipelago. The more remote and less inhabited northern beaches, Pemba and Ilha do Moçambique.

## Where to stay
### *Maputo*

The only place to stay in Maputo is at *Fatima's Place* on 1317 Mao Tse Tung Road. Two vehicles can be parked in the garage and there is a security guard at night. Fatima herself is the owner and full of news regarding Maputo and surrounding areas. A double chalet costs US$12. Meals and drinks are available.

## The south coast

All along the coastline there are various campsites, usually signposted along major routes. Camping will cost US$3–6 per person. A favourite spot for travellers is Vilanculos, where day excursions can be planned for the Bazaruto Archipelago, and diving is supposed to be excellent. *John's Place* is reputed to sell the best meals and a new campsite under the same name is currently under construction.

## The north
### Chocas

One of our highlights in Africa was an area called Chocas, 21km (13 miles) south of Ilha do

Moçambique, towards Mossaril. Camping on the beach is the only option. Water is available from wells in the village and fish is sold every morning, fresh from the ocean. You will be completely isolated except for the occasional curious villager and the ex-patriot community who enjoy Chocas at weekends.

### Ilha do Moçambique

It is possible to drive across to the island as there is a 3km (2-mile) bridge that joins the mainland to the island. There are no camping facilities on the island, so if you intend to stay the night, it is best to ask one of the restaurateurs or hoteliers to let you park in their yard.

### Pemba

North from Ilha do Moçambique is Pemba – you'll stay for days! There is a fantastic campsite just outside town along the coastline called *Pemba Magic*. It is a beautiful setting with huge, shady baobab trees. It is run by Margot and Russell, a South African and Australian partnership. Camping costs US$3 per person.

Further up from Pemba the roads become really bad and going is slow but the whole northern area is wild and untamed. Villagers are surprised to see you as not many travellers head north. It's a great adventure!

At the time of writing the bridge between Mwambo (Mozambique) and Mtwara (Tanzania) was reportedly being rebuilt. It is predicted that this will become another transit route heading north into Tanzania.

## Other

Do not photograph anything remotely resembling or near to a government institution.

## Further information

*Guide to Mozambique*, Philip Briggs, Bradt Travel Guides
www.mozambique.mz

# NAMIBIA

## Capital

Windhoek

## Language

English and Afrikaans are the official languages.
International telephone code +264

## Currency and rate

Namibian dollar (N);
US$1 = N7.43

## Red tape

Avoid the mining area around Lüderitz as the police who patrol this area can be a bit over-zealous. To visit a mining area a special permit needs to be arranged by the mining company in Windhoek, but it has been said that these are very hard to come by.

## Visas

No visas are required by nationals of Australia, Canada, Ireland, New Zealand, South Africa, the UK, the USA, and most other southern African and western European countries.

## Fuel costs

Diesel: US$0.36; petrol: US$0.38 per litre.

## Driving and roads

Drive on the left. The roads are in excellent condition except for parts of the Namib Desert, Kaokaland and Kuadom Reserve.

# African embassies

**Angola** Angola House, 3 Ausspann St, Windhoek; tel: 227535
**Egypt** 6 Stein St, Klein Windhoek; tel: 222408
**Kenya** Kenya House, Robert Mugabe Av, Windhoek; tel: 226836
**Nigeria** (High Commission) 4 Omuramba Rd, Eros, Windhoek; tel: 232103
**South Africa** RSA House, corner Jan Jonker Strasse and Nelson Mandela Drive,
Klein Windhoek, Windhoek; tel: 229765
**Zambia** 22 Sam Nujoma Drive, corner of Republic Rd, Windhoek; tel: 237610
**Zimbabwe** (High Commission) corner Independence Av and Grimm St, Windhoek;
tel: 228134

# Climate

Hot in summer (October to April). Most rainfall occurs throughout the summer
months. Winter is cool and the evenings can get quite cold. The coastal region of
the Namib desert is cool, damp and rainfree, with mist for much of the year.

# Highlights

The Namib Desert, with its dunes and coastal ghost towns. Kaokaland, with its
beautiful scenery and Himba people. The national parks, including Waterberg
Plateau, Etosha, the Skeleton Coast, Fish River Canyon, Kalahari Gemsbok and
Namib Naukluft, all teeming with wildlife.

# Where to stay

## Windhoek

A popular campsite is the *Daan Viljoen Game Park*, 18km (11 miles) west of
town. You can pre-book at the MET in Windhoek which handles all park
bookings, or you can just turn up. Camping costs US$5 per person.
Alternatively, the *Arebbush Travel Lodge* in Olympia, on the road south to
Reheboth, charges US$10 per person to camp.

## Lüderitz

Lüderitz is a surreal colonial relic – a Bavarian village set on the edge of the
Namib desert. The only place to stay is the windy *Shark Island Campground* (on
Shark Island, north of town) which costs US$8 per site.

## Swakopmund

Although not as ethereal as Lüderitz, Swakopmund is an attractive and
interesting town. The choice of campsites is limited; try the *Youth Hostel*, on
the corner of Bismarck and Lazareftstrasse, where camping costs US$3 per
person.

## National parks

*Etosha National Park* offers lodges and camps at Namutoni, Halali and Okaukuejo.
The park entry fee is US$6 per person and US$6 per vehicle. Camping costs
US$10 for a maximum of eight people. *Fish River Canyon National Park* has the
*Hobas* camping ground, costing US$10 for a site. You are not allowed to stay
overnight in the *Skeleton Coast National Park*, but along the coastline, south of the

park, there are various and very basic campsites at Mile 14, Jakkalsputlz, Henties Bay, Mile 72 and Mile 108. Campsites are cheaper along this route.

### Kaokaland

Bush sleeping is the only option as you head north towards Angola. At Epupa Falls you can sleep under the palm trees, or in the enclosed campsite. Due to the influx of tourists the Himba's lifestyle has been threatened. Do not give them alcohol or medication, which you will continually be asked for.

## Other

Do not photograph anything remotely close to a government institution. Crime is on the increase in larger towns, but campsites have also been targeted – lock your valuables away at night.

## Further information

*Namibia: The Bradt Travel Guide,* Chris McIntyre
www.namibiaweb.com

## NIGER

## Capital

Niamey

## Language

French is the official language.
International telephone code +227

## Currency and rate

West African franc (CFA); US$1 = CFA760

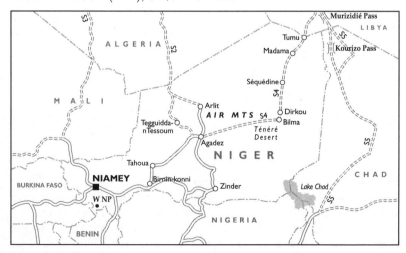

## Red tape

After some research and talking to various travellers we thought that borders and roadblocks would be fraught with problems, but it was one the friendliest and easiest countries we have travelled in.

## Visas

Visas are required for all except nationals of the countries of ECOWAS. One-month visas are issued within 48 hours and cost US$40–60. They are easily obtained from the countries bordering Niger (though not Mali). You'll need one to four photos for each application. Vaccination certificates are obligatory. Visas are not issued at the border.

## Fuel costs

Diesel: US$0.52; petrol: US$0.76 per litre.

## Driving and roads

Drive on the right. Roads are generally in good condition, particularly along major routes. Remoter routes are desert pistes and tracks.

## African embassies

**Algeria** north of Route de Tillabéri, Niamey; tel: 72 3583
**Benin** Rue des Dallois; Niamey; tel: 72 2860
**Chad** off Route de Tillabéri, Niamey; tel: 73 4464
**France** (issues visas for most African French-speaking countries) Corner of Av Mitterand and Bd de la République, Niamey; tel: 72 2722
**Mali** Boulevard de Mali Bero, Niamey; tel: 75 2410
**Nigeria** Rue Luebke, Niamey; tel: 73 2410

## Climate

The climate is hot and dry except for a brief rainy season in July and August. The coolest months are November to January when the *harmattan* blows the dust off the desert.

## Highlights

The Grande Marché in Niamey and market day in Zinder. An expedition into the remote areas of the Aïr Mountains and Ténéré Desert. The backstreets and Vieux Quartier of Agadez.

Getting into the Aïr Mountains or Ténéré Desert is quite a mission. It is obligatory to have a guide and a 'permit of transit' into the area from the tourist board. Guides are expensive but you can go in convoy and share the guide. It is worth every cent and is one of the most beautiful areas of Africa. It is also a wonderful introduction to the Tuaregs and their culture. Tuaregs are a nomadic tribe and famous for their salt caravans to Bilma oasis. They are also known as 'the blue men of the desert'.

Permits to the Ténéré Desert were not being issued at the time of writing, but all this could change in the future.

## Where to stay
### Niamey
There is only one campsite in Niamey and it is in shocking need of repair. There is no running water, toilet or shower facilities, but for one night it could be an option. We asked hoteliers whether we could park up for a night in their courtyard and through this met a young gentlemen who took us to a German NGO organisation that was offering accommodation at US$3 per person. You'll just have to shop around.

### Zinder
The only possible option is the *Hotel Central,* which is run down and frequented mostly by prostitutes. There was a new campsite under construction called *La Cafeteria* just north of town – ask locals for details.

### Agadez and surrounding areas
In Agadez you could try *Camping L'Escale,* a huge campsite 4km northwest of town with lots of shade and great toilet and shower facilities, costing US$10 per person. In the city, just north of the Sultan's Palace, is *Hotel Telden*, costing US$4 for camping. It's central and has all amenities close by, including a great bar.

### Other
Dress conservatively as dress is taken very seriously in this Muslim country. Always ask permission before taking photographs and stay clear of all government institutions. You'll need to register with the local police on entry to most towns in Niger – this is referred to as *vu au passage.*

### Further information
*West Africa* Lonely Planet or Rough Guides
www.txdirect.net/users/jmayer/fan.html
www.sas.upenn.edu/African_Studies/Country_Specific/niger.html

## NIGERIA

**Warning** *There have been recent violent clashes between Muslims and Christians. Seek sound travel advice before travelling into Nigeria.*

## Capital
Abuja

## Language
English is the official language.
International telephone code +234

## Currency and rate
Naira (N); US$1 = N108.7

## Red tape

Roadblocks are evident throughout Nigeria – sometimes within 5km (3 miles) of each other. We were told by the ex-patriot community that if a policeman asks if you have anything for him or her, in other words *dash*, it is sometimes good to give him a little 'gift' for services rendered as most of these government employees

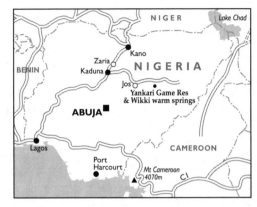

have not been paid in years and they are keeping you safe on the road. It is up to the individual.

## Visas

Visas are required for all except nationals of the Economic Community of West African States (ECOWAS). The cost of a visa depends on your nationality but visas can cost between US$25 and US$50. You will also need two to three photographs and a letter of introduction from your embassy. Vaccination certificates are obligatory. Visas are not issued at the border.

## Fuel costs

Diesel: US$0.10; petrol: US$0.13 per litre.

At the time of writing there was no fuel available. The only fuel you could get was on the black market at US$0.60 per litre. It's a bit crazy when you think that fuel is Nigeria's major income!

## Driving and roads

Drive on the right. Roads are generally in good condition.

## African embassies

**Algeria** 26 Maitama Sule St, Ikoyi Island, Lagos; tel: 68 3155

**Benin** 4 Abudu Smith St, Victoria Island, Lagos; tel: 61 4411

**Burkina Faso** 15 Norman William St, Ikoyi Island, Lagos; tel: 68 1001

**Cameroon** 5 Fermi Pearse St, Victoria Island, Lagos; tel: 61 2226

**Chad** 2 Goriola St, Victoria Island, Lagos; tel: 61 3116

**Democratic Republic of the Congo** 1A Kofo Abayomi St, Victoria Island, Lagos; tel: 61 0377

**French Consulate** (issues visas for most French-speaking African countries) 1 Oyinkan Abayomi Drive, Ikoyi Island, Lagos; tel: 269 3427

**Ghana** 21–23 King George V Rd, Lagos Island, Lagos; tel: 60 1450

**Ivory Coast** 3–5 Abudu St, Victoria Island, Lagos; tel: 61 0963

**Niger** 15 Adeola Odeku St, Victoria Island, Lagos; tel: 60 2300
**Togo** Plot 976, Oju Olobun Close, Victoria Island, Lagos; tel: 61 7449

## Climate

The south is hot and humid with a long rainy season from March to November. The north has far greater extremes of temperature, due to the Saharan influence, and the rains last from April to September.

## Highlights

Unless you need an onward visa there is no reason to go south, which is reputed for its hassles and crime. It's best to stick to the northern areas which are more hassle free. Highlights include Kano and Jos and Yankari Game Reserve. Jos Plateau is 1,200m (3,600ft) above sea level, has a relatively cool climate all year round, is green and shrubby and surrounded by rolling green hills. Kano is famed for its old city and thousands of narrow streets lined by the old city wall.

## Where to stay

### Lagos

Highly recommended is the *Onikirp Hotel* on 328 Borno Avenue in Yaba. It's clean and quiet, all rooms have air-conditioning, a fridge, TV and hot showers. Accommodation costs US$15 for a double. In Lagos it's worth it – all you need to do is organise secure parking for your vehicle. Lagos lacks trustworthy campsites, and you'll have to shop around for cheaper accommodation.

### Jos

Jos has no campsite so you'll have to ask at one of the larger hotels whether it is possible to park up for a night or two.

### Kano

The only campsite in Kano is the *Kano State Tourist Camp*, just off Bompai Road, which is friendly, secure and helpful. Camping costs US$2.50 per person.

## Other

To avoid any hassles in Nigeria ensure that all paperwork is in order and be patient – with a capital 'P'. Do not photograph any government institutions and dress conservatively, particularly in the north where there is more of a Muslim influence.

## Further information

*West Africa*, Rough Guides or Lonely Planet
http://motherlandnigeria.com
www.sas.upenn.edu/African_Studies/Country_Specific/nigeria.html
http://lcweb2.loc.gov/frd/ngtoc.html

## RWANDA

*Warning* Although travel within the country is currently safe, Rwanda is still recovering after many years of unrest and violence. The border with the DRC remains sensitive but access is possible via Uganda and Tanzania. Always heed local advice about possible trouble-spots and do not wander off the beaten track alone in unpopulated areas of the northwest, where landmines may be a danger.

### Capital
Kigali

### Language
Kinyarwanda, French and English are all official languages; English is not yet widespread outside Kigali.
International telephone code +250

### Currency and rate
Rwandan franc; US$1 = RFr386

### Red tape
Not a great deal. To change travellers' cheques you must have your sales advice note.

### Visas
Visas are required for all but US nationals and are not currently issued at the border. Visas usually cost US$30, but may be as much as US$70.

### Fuel costs
Diesel: US$0.72; petrol: US$0.72 per litre.

### Driving and roads
Drive on the right. Roads linking main cities and border points are generally good; some smaller roads are narrow and twisty, and may be muddy after rain.

### African embassies
**Burundi**, **Egypt** and **Tanzania** have embassues in Kigali. For up-to-date locations, contact ORTPN (see below).

### Climate
Not too hot as Rwanda is a high, hilly country. Rainy seasons are March/May and October/November. Hottest months are August and September.

## Highlights

The Parc des Volcans in the northwest for mountain gorillas; also Akagera Park (savannah) and Nyungwe Forest (primates). In Butare, the National Museum of Rwanda, with displays on Rwandan history and culture, is one of East Africa's best museums. Permits for visits to the Parc des Volcans and Akagera must be bought in advance (US$250 cash, for the Parc des Volcans) from the National Office for Tourism and National Parks (ORTPN) in Kigali (BP 905; tel: 76515; fax: 76512). It's located in the Avenue de l'Armée near its junction with Place de la Constitution.

## Where to stay

Currently camping is advisable only at authorised sites, which include those at the Parc des Volcans and Nyungwe Forest, but most main towns have a reasonable guesthouse/hotel. Details of accommodation throughout Rwanda are obtainable from the ORTPN (see above).

## Further information

*Rwanda: The Bradt Travel Guide* Philip Briggs and Janice Booth
www.rwandemb.org (website of the Rwandan Embassy in Washington)
www.rwanda.com

# SENEGAL

## Capital

Dakar

## Language

French is the official language.
International telephone code +221

## Currency and rate

West African franc (CFA); US$1 = CFA765

## Red tape

Roadblocks are frequent; the police are particularly zealous if you are in a vehicle or on a motorbike. Always adhere to all the rules and never hand over original documentation.

## Visas

US and EU citizens do not need a visa, nor do citizens of most Commonwealth countries. Australians and New Zealanders are among those who do, however; a visa costs US$20–50, depending on country of application. Visitor's entry permit is issued at the border. A yellow fever certificate is obligatory.

## Fuel costs
Diesel: US$0.48; petrol: US$0.71 per litre.

## Driving and roads
Drive on the right. Roads are generally in good condition.

## African embassies
**Cameroon** 157 Rue Josef Gomis; tel: 8232195
**French Consulate** (issues visas for most French-speaking African countries) 1 Rue Assane Ndoye, Dakar; tel: 823 4371
**Gambia** 11 Rue de Thiong, Ponty, Dakar; tel: 821 7230
**Guinea** Rue 7, Point E, Dakar; tel: 824 8606
**Guinea-Bissau** Rue 6, Point E, Dakar; tel: 25 5946
**Ivory Coast** 2 Av Albert Sarraut, Dakar; tel: 821 0163
**Mali** 46 Bd de la République, Dakar; tel: 823 4893
**Mauritius** 37 Bd Général de Gaulle, Dakar; tel: 821 4343
**Nigeria** Rue 1, Point E, Dakar; tel: 824 4397
**Sierra Leone** Clinique Bleu at 13 Rue da Castor, Dakar

## Climate
Dry from December to May; hot, humid and wet from May to June. The dry season is shorter in the south and east.

## Highlights
Lazy days and party nights in the city of Dakar. A boat trip to the historic Ile de Gorée. Hiking in the Casamance region and the beaches of the Siné-Saloum Delta. Parc National de Niokolo-Koba. Look out for the magnificent birdlife of the north in St Louis. Senegal is also famed for its musicians, such as Youssour n'Dour and Salif Kaita.

## Where to stay
### Dakar
There are two options – *Campement le Poulagou* and *Campement Adama Diop*, both near the airport on Yoff Village. They are next door to each other, a little out of town and close to the beach. Camping at either place costs US$3 per person.

### Ile de Gorée
Ferries leave from the wharf area in Dakar every one to two hours. The cost is US$4 per person.

### Siné-Saloum Delta
The delta is often overlooked by visitors and is a wild, beautiful area of mangrove swamps lagoons, forests, dunes and sand islands. Camping accommodation is available at *Campement Pointe du Sango-Mar*, on the western edge of the delta at the tip of a narrow split of land called Pointe de

Sangomar. From here you are able to hire *pirogues* to reach the beautiful islands of Guior and Guissanor.

### St Louis

As you head south, just outside of town there is a campsite nestling off the Parc National de la Langue de Barbarie, famed for its birdlife. The *Zebrabar* is pleasant with beautiful surroundings and run by a Swiss family. Camping costs US$6 for a site.

### The Casamance

The best bet for accommodation is to stay at one of the local campsites called *Campements Touristique Rurals Intégrés* (*CTRI*) where prices are standard at US$5 for a bed – camping costs would need to be negotiated. The beaches at Cap Skiring are some of the nicest, but can get a little hectic. This area is worth a week to two weeks visit, with loads of hiking opportunities.

### Further information

*West Africa*, Rough Guides or Lonely Planet
www.senegalonline.com
www.homeviewsenegal.com
www.earth2000.com

## SIERRA LEONE

**Warning** Due to ongoing civil war in Sierra Leone it is not advisable to travel overland. Basic information has been included.

### Capital

Freetown

### Language

English is the official language.
International telephone code +232

### Currency and rate

Leone (Le); US$1 = Le2,250

### Visas

Visas are required for all and cost between US$10 and US$50 depending on your nationality. Visas are not issued at the border.

### Further information

*West Africa*, Rough Guides or Lonely Planet
www.sierra-leona.org

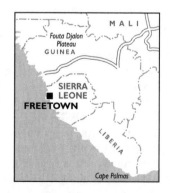

## SOMALIA

*Warning Due to ongoing civil war in Somalia it is not advisable to travel overland. Basic information has been included.*

### Capital
Mogadishu

### Language
Somali is the official language.

### Currency and rate (last updated in 1998)
Somali shilling (SSh); US$1 = SSh2620

### Visas
Visas are required for all, but with the current affairs of the country, anyone can enter without a visa – though it is not recommended!

### Further information
*Africa on a Shoestring*, Lonely Planet
www.ase.net

## SOUTH AFRICA (with LESOTHO and SWAZILAND)

### Capital
Pretoria (administrative) and Cape Town (legislative)

### Language
English and Afrikaans are the official languages, with another nine local official languages – those spoken most are Zulu, Xhosa and Sotho.
International telephone codes: *South Africa* +27, *Lesotho* +266, *Swaziland* +268

### Currency and rate
Rand (R); US$1= R7.48

### Red tape
If you are intending to sell your vehicle in South Africa, you have to discharge your *carnet* by officially importing the vehicle or bike. To do this, you need a

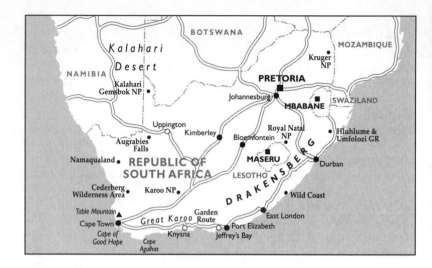

current valuation of your vehicle or bike based on which you will pay import duty. Passports must be valid for at least six months after your date of departure from South Africa.

## Visas

Visas are not required for most holiday visitors. You'll be issued with an entry permit on arrival. If you are applying for an extended stay or work visa, which are issued free, allow a couple of weeks for the process. Visas are not issued at the border. With overland travel you might have to convince the immigration officer that you have sufficient funds for your stay, but crossing borders is usually hassle free.

National of EU need a visa for **Swaziland**, issued free at the border. Visas for **Lesotho** cost US$5 (US$10 multiple entry) and are required by nationals of Australia, New Zealand, Ghana, Nigeria, India, Pakistan and Namibia. Applications at the border.

## Fuel costs

Diesel: US$0.39; petrol: US$0.43 per litre.

## Driving and roads

Drive on the left. Roads are in excellent condition.

## African embassies

**Angola** CPK Building, 153 Olivia St, Brooklyn, Pretoria; tel: (012) 46 6104
**Botswana** 2nd Floor, Futura Bank House, 122 De Korte St, Johannesburg; tel: (011) 403 3784
**Kenya** 302 Brooks St, Menlo Park, Pretoria; tel: (012) 342 5066
**Lesotho** 6th Floor, West Tower, Momentum Centre, 343 Pretorius St, Pretoria; tel: (012) 322 6090

**Malawi** 770 Government St, Arcadia, Pretoria; tel: (012) 342 0146
**Mali** Suite 106, Infotech Building, 1090 Arcadia St, Pretoria; tel (012) 3427464
**Mozambique** 7th Floor, Cape York House, 252 Jeppe St, Johannesburg; tel: (011) 336 1819
**Namibia** 209 Redroute, Carlton Centre, Johannesburg; tel: (011) 331 7055
**Nigeria** 138 Beckett St, Arcadia, Pretoria; tel: (012) 3432021
**Swaziland** 6th Floor, Braamfontein Centre, Johannesburg; tel: (011) 403 2036
**Tanzania** 845 Government Av, Arcadia, Pretoria; tel: (012) 342 4393
**Uganda** Suite 402, Infotech building, 1090 Arcadia St, Arcadia, Pretoria; tel: (012) 342 6031
**Zambia** 353 Sanlam Building, corner of Festival and Arcadia St, Hatfield, Pretoria; tel: (012) 342 1541
**Zimbabwe** 17th Floor, 20 Anderson St, Johannesburg; tel: (011) 838 5620

## Climate

The summer (wet season) is from September to April. Winters can be cold, particularly at night. In Cape Town the winter months are wet and it can be very windy along the coast. The best time to visit is August to October when the rains have just started. June and July are the best months for game viewing.

## Highlights

South Africa is such a vast country that months could be spent exploring it. Highlights would include the Kruger National Park and surrounding area, as well as Karoo National Park and Augrabies Falls. Cape Town, Table Mountain and all the vineyards in the surrounding area. The Garden Route and the surrounding area, including Knysna, when in flower at the beginning of summer and – for all surfers – Jeffrey's Bay, which is reputed to have some of the best waves in the world. The south and north coast of Natal, with its lush and green rolling hills and incredible beaches. The Drakensberg Mountains and Cedarberg Wilderness Area. Swaziland for its landscape beauty and people and Lesotho for its mountains – a must for hikers.

## Where to stay

The options are limitless and the country is well set up for camping. Facilities are excellent. Costs are US$3 to US$10 per person depending on the site.

### Swaziland and Lesotho

There are campsites and hotels dotted throughout these areas, but bush sleeping is another option.

## Other

Crime is on the increase in most major towns so watch your bag and always carry minimal valuables. Most accommodation places in South Africa offer to place all valuables in a safe. It is also not advisable for any white person to enter a black township unless with a guide or tour company.

## Further information

*East & Southern Africa: The Backpacker's Manual*, Philip Briggs, Bradt Travel Guides
*South Africa: The Bradt Budget Guide*, Paul Ash
www.southafrica.co.za
www.gov.co.za
http://sabtin.co.za
www.africa-insites.com/lesotho
www.sas.upenn.edu/African_Studies/Specific_Country/lesotho.html
www.sas.upern_swazi

## SUDAN

## Capital

Khartoum

## Language

Arabic is the official language.
International telephone code +249

## Currency and rate

Sudanese pound (S£); US$1 = S£25.87

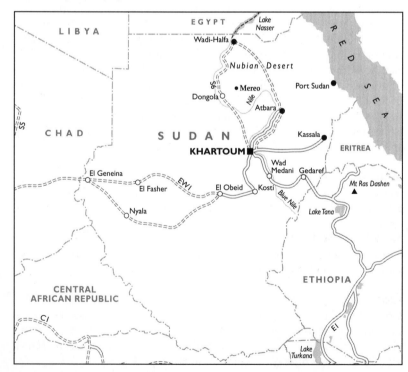

## Red tape

The bureaucracy in Sudan is onerous and obtaining the relevant permits is a time-consuming and frustrating task. However, you have little choice but to stick at it, get round all the offices and put your paperwork in order. If this is achieved, travelling round Sudan is a breeze, provided you stay within the restrictions of your permits. Your paperwork will be checked often on the road so make sure it's right. This is easier said than done as most of it is in Arabic, so paying someone to help you round the offices and translate for you can be a useful investment.

The most important paperwork you must get is an 'Aliens Movement permit'. This document is required for all travel within Sudan and states the towns you wish to visit and the route you intend to take. Any deviation from this can cause you a great deal of trouble, so make sure you know where you want to go and by which route before you apply. If you cross one of the land borders you will have to obtain your permit at the border (or the next major town, Gedaref if entering from Ethiopia). At the border you will inevitably be issued a permit to go to Khartoum only, where you will have to obtain another permit for onward travel. These permits should only cost about US$20. It is worth photocopying this permit along with your passport to hand out at all the police checks as it can save you some time and form-filling.

You will also need to obtain a currency declaration form at the border. All your money will be counted out in front of you and listed on the form. You cannot change any money at a bank without this form. On leaving the country your leftover money, change receipts and declaration form should all tie up – don't get caught out! Also remember you cannot change US$ travellers' cheques in Sudan due to the embargo, but US dollars in cash is no problem.

At every town in which you wish to stay the night you are supposed to check in with the local police. This can become tedious, especially as you usually stop in the late afternoon when all the offices are closed. It is better to camp in the bush and just stop briefly in the towns for supplies or sightseeing, then leave and camp outside town again.

## Visas

Visas are required for all and the process is lengthy as your application will first need to be approved by Khartoum. One-month entry visas cost US$70–95. Visas are not issued at the border.

## Fuel costs

Diesel: US$0.26; petrol: US$0.33 per litre (note that all fuel costs are charged in gallons in Sudan). The further north or west you go, the more expensive fuel becomes.

## Driving and roads

Drive on the right. All the major tarred roads are in good condition and all other roads are desert pistes and tracks.

## African embassies

**Chad** Sharia 17, New Extension, Khartoum; tel: 471084
**Democratic Republic of the Congo** Sharia 13, New Extension, Khartoum; tel: 471125
**Egypt** Sharia al-Gamhuriyya, Khartoum; tel: 772190
**Ethiopia** Khartoum 2, north west of the cemetery, Khartoum; tel: 471156
**French Consulate** (issues visas for most French-speaking African countries) Sharia 13, New Extension, Khartoum; tel: 471082
**Kenya** Sharia 3, New Extension, Khartoum; tel: 40386

## Climate

The summer months in Sudan are extremely hot and arid, reaching 45+°C. The best time to visit is during the winter months from December to mid-March when temperatures still reach 40°C but evenings are cool and pleasant.

## Highlights

Dinner at one of the restaurants along the Blue Nile; the pyramids – reputed to be the oldest in the world – of Mereo; and Port Sudan, with its excellent diving and fishing excursions.

## Where to stay

Throughout Sudan bush sleeping is the best option.

### Khartoum

The only place that offers camping is the *German Club*, opposite the airport. Vehicles are parked up in the car park and all other facilities can be used – showers, toilets and a huge pool. Camping costs US$6 per person.

## Other

Photography is a sensitive issue and photographic permits are needed for both a camera and a video camera. Don't take photos of anything with even the slightest military connection, including airports, government buildings, post offices, bridges, etc. An interesting little quirk of Khartoum is driving at night; if you cross the major bridge over the Nile at night you must turn off your headlights as you cross. Apparently this is so that the bridge cannot be targeted by American bombing missions. This may well be an urban legend, but it's worth bearing in mind if you choose to drive around Khartoum at night.

## Further information

*Africa on a Shoestring*, Lonely Planet
www.arab.net/sudan/sudan_content.html
www.theodora.com/wfb/sudan/sudan2.html
www.yasin.dirconco.uk/sudan
www.columbia.edu/~tm146/sudan.html

## SWAZILAND

### Capital
Mbabane

### Currency
Lilangeni (SZL), but South African rand universally accepted. US$1 = SZL7.23

See also *South Africa*, page 237.

## TANZANIA

### Capital
Dodoma

### Language
English and Swahili are the official languages.
International telephone code +225

### Currency and rate
Tanzanian shilling (TSh); US$1 = TSh801

### Red tape
Watch out for radars and hefty speeding fines.

### Visas
Visas are required for all except nationals of most Commonwealth countries. A visitor's pass for up to three months is issued at the border, costing US$10–50, depending on nationality: a German citizen will pay US$10; a British citizen up to US$50.

### Fuel costs
Diesel: US$0.57; petrol: US$0.63 per litre.

### Driving and roads
Drive on the left. Roads are in good condition.

### African embassies
**Burundi** Plot 1007, Lugalo Rd, Dar es Salaam; tel: 38608

**Democratic Republic of the Congo** 438 Malik Rd, Dar es Salaam; tel: 66010
**French Consulate** (issues visas for most French-speaking African countries) corner of Bagomoyo and Kulimani Rd, Dar es Salaam; tel: 66021
**Kenya** 14th Floor, NIC Building, Samora Av, Dar es Salaam; tel: 31502
**Malawi** IPS Building, 9th Floor, PO Box 7616, Dar es Salaam; tel: 113238/41
**Mozambique** 25 Garden Av, Dar es Salaam; tel: 113208
**Rwanda** 32 Upanga Rd, Dar es Salaam; tel: 117631
**South Africa** c/o Oysterbay Hotel, Touré Drive, Oyster Bay; tel: 68062
**Sudan** 64 Ali Mwinyi Rd, Dar es Salaam; tel: 46509
**Uganda** 7th Floor, Extelecoms House, Samora Av, Dar es Salaam; tel: 31004
**Zambia** 5/9 Sokoine Drive, Dar es Salaam; tel: 46389
**Zimbabwe** 6th Floor, NIC Building, Samora Av, Dar es Salaam; tel: 46259

## Climate
Hot and humid along the coast (particularly December to March); rains come from April to May and in November. On the central plateau it is warm and dry and gets a little cooler in the highlands.

## Highlights
Arusha, which is the gateway to the Serengeti National Park and Ngorongoro Crater. Zanzibar and its Stone Town with its beautiful winding roads and stunning beaches. Climbing Mount Kilimanjaro – Africa's highest mountain. In the south, Ruaha National Park and Selous Game Reserve.

## Where to stay
### Dar es Salaam
Accommodation options are limited and the best bet is to go 20km (12 miles) north along the Bagomoyo road to Kanducki Beach where there is a choice of two campsites – the *Rungwe Oceanic* and the *Silver Sands*. If you are intending to stay a night in the city, try the *Hotel Kilimanjaro* who charge hefty prices for parking the vehicle up for the night. Camping fees are US$2.50 to US$3 per person.

### Zanzibar
Various ferries and local *pirogues* leave daily and hourly from the main wharf in Dar es Salaam. Vaccination certificates are obligatory before a ticket is issued. You will need to leave your vehicle at a secure parking venue and head over to the island.

There is plenty of accommodation from hotels to pensions to campsites, and fees are standard. It's worth the effort as the island is really beautiful!

### Arusha
Stay at either the *Snake Park* (25km/15 miles outside town on the Crater road) or the *Masai Camp* (2.5km/1.5 miles outside on the old Moshi road). Both campsites have excellent facilities and offer similar services, and both are frequented by regular overland trucks, so don't expect a quiet night in the

bush. The Snake Park has a great bar and we particularly enjoyed the local Masai of the area. Camping fees are standard at both camps.

### The Serengeti and Ngorongoro Crater
As with Kenya, you'll pay exorbitant prices if you take your own vehicle. It is best to go with a tour company; both campsites mentioned under Arusha will refer you to the best tour operators. A five-day excursion costs US$500 per person, including all park fees, accommodation and meals.

### Kilimanjaro/Moshi
A good base for climbing Kilimanjaro is the Marangu Hotel in Moshi, 10km south of the main gate to the national park and near the start of the most popular route up the mountain. The safe and attractive campsite, with hot showers and pool, costs US$3 per person per night. Climbs can be organised here.

## Other
It has been said that UK citizens cannot get entry permits at the border and this is quite correct but also the luck of the draw. For most UK nationals it's best to get a visa before entering Tanzania. We managed to get one at the border, but you'll pay for it; part of the payment will be seen as *dash* towards rendering this service. It is also reputed that, although nationals of Commonwealth countries do not need visas, on arrival at the border, whatever your nationality, you should expect to pay a fee of between US$10 and US$25 for an entry permit.

## Further information
*Tanzania: The Bradt Travel Guide*, Philip Briggs
*Zanzibar: The Bradt Travel Guide*, David Else
www.tanzania-web.com

## TOGO

## Capital
Lomé

## Language
French is the official language.
International telephone code +228

## Currency and rate
West African CFA franc (CFA); US$1 = CFA760

## Red tape
At the border of Togo, officials will try to charge you for having your *carnet* stamped and the bureaucracy is very time-consuming. We left without the stamp, but it took time. It's up to you.

## Visas

Visas are required for all except nationals of the Economic Community of West African States (ECOWAS). Visas are available at Togo embassies, French consulates where Togo has no representation, and at the border (where they cost CFA10,000, do not require any photos but are valid only for a week). A yellow fever certificate is also required.

## Fuel costs

Diesel: US$0.37; petrol: US$0.42 per litre.

## Driving and roads

Drive on the right. The roads are in generally good condition, particularly along the coast.

## African embassies

**Democratic Republic of the Congo** 325 Bd du 13 Janvier (Bd Circulaire), Lomé; tel: 215155

**French Consulate** (issues visas for most French-speaking African countries) Rue Bissagne, Lomé; tel: 212576

**Ghana** 8 Rue Pauline Eklou, Tokoin, Lomé; tel: 213194

**Nigeria** 311 Bd du 13 Janvier (Bd Greulaire), Lomé; tel: 213455

## Climate

The rainy season is April to July, with shorter rains in October and November. The temperature is generally pleasant.

## Highlights

Lake Togo with its watersports and voodoo culture. Hiking in the beautiful hills of Kpalimé. The village compounds, markets and scenery of the Kandé area.

## Where to stay
### Lomé

Try camping at *Chez Alice*, 12km (7.5 miles) east of Lomé, on the beachfront. Camping costs US$3 per person.

### Lake Togo

This shallow lake, 30km (18 miles) east of Lomé, is popular for watersports. On the lake's northern shore lies Togoville, the centre of Togo's voodoo culture. There are no campsites in the immediate vicinity.

### Kpalimé

Try *Le Campement* where camping costs US$3 per person. It's a great base for hiking enthusiasts.

### Kandé

If at all possible, bush sleeping would be a better option than the rundown *Le Campement* in Kandé.

### Other

As discussed under the section on Ghana, touts at the border are frenetic and you will not be left alone. Just hang in there and ignore them.

### Further information

*West Africa*, Rough Guides or Lonely Planet
CIA website

## TUNISIA

### Capital

Tunis

### Language

Arabic is the official language.
International telephone code +216

### Currency and rate

Tunisian dinar (TD); US$1 = TD1.45

### Red tape

None of any significance.

### Visas

Nationals of most western European countries can stay in Tunisia for up to three months without a visa. Citizens of the USA, Canada, Germany and Japan can stay up to four months. Nationals of Australia, New Zealand and South Africa can opt for either a two- or four-week visa costing US$5–15.

Visas are not issued at the border and should be applied for at any Tunisian embassy or consulate beforehand. Israeli nationals are not allowed into the country. Visitor's entry permits are issued at the border.

### Fuel costs

Diesel: US$0.33; petrol: US$0.60 per litre.

### Driving and roads

Drive on the right. The roads are generally in good condition.

## African embassies

**Algeria** 136 Av de la Liberté, Tunis; tel: 28 3166
**Egypt** Av Mohammed V, Cité Montplaisir, Tunis; tel: 79 1181
**French Consulate** (issues visas for most French-speaking African countries) Place de l'Indépendance, Tunis; tel: 24 5700
**Libya** 35 Rue Alexander Dumas, Sfax; tel: 04 23332

## Climate

Mediterranean climate in the north and hot dry desert climate inland.

## Highlights

Tunisia has a number of ancient sites, including that of Carthage (near Tunis). Organised trips into the desert include camel-trekking and visits to Tuareg *campements*. Of the oasis towns in the south, Tozeur marks the limit of Roman Africa and is a fascinating blend of traditional architecture and present-day bustle. By contrast, the lunar landscape of Matmata conceals a busy community living underground, in caves chiselled out of the rock.

## Where to stay

Throughout Tunisia the best option is to bush sleep, but always ask the owners of the land for permission first. There are very few campsites.

## Other

Tunisia is easy-going by Muslim standards, particularly in areas frequented by tourists, but outside these areas life is still conservative and revolves around the mosque, *hammam* (local baths) and cafés. Act and dress accordingly.

## Further information

*Tunisia*, Barnaby Rogerson, Cadogan
www.tunisiaonline.com
www.arab.net/tunisia/tunisia_content.html

## UGANDA

### Capital

Kampala

### Language

English is the official language.
International telephone code +256

### Currency and rate

Ugandan shilling (USh); US$1 = USh1,822

### Red tape

The border was extremely efficient and quick. We didn't come across any road-blocks but this might have changed because of the civil war in the Democratic Republic of the Congo.

## Visas
Visas are not required for nationals of Canada, Denmark, Finland, France, Germany, Israel, Japan, Sweden and most Commonwealth countries – India, New Zealand and Nigeria are exceptions. Visas cost US$25–35.

## Fuel costs
Diesel: US$0.68; petrol: US$0.86 per litre.

## Driving and roads
Drive on the left. The roads are in generally good condition.

## African embassies
**Burundi** Plot 5, Nehru Av, Nakasero; tel: 231548
**Democratic Republic of the Congo** 20 Phillip Rd, Kololo, Kampala; tel: 233777
**French Consulate** (issues visas for most French-speaking African countries)
9 Parliament Av, Kampala tel: 242120
**Kenya** Nakasevo Rd, Kampala; tel: 258235
**Rwanda** Plot 60, Kera Rd, Kampala; tel: 231861
**South Africa** Plot 9, Malcolm X Av, Kololo, Kampala; tel: 259156
**Sudan** Plot 21, Nakasero Rd, Kampala; tel: 243518
**Tanzania** 6 Kagera Rd, Kampala; tel: 256272

## Climate
Uganda's position on the equator is tempered by its high altitude, giving it a very pleasant climate. The rainy seasons are March to June and October to December.

## Highlights
White-water rafting on the Nile while staying in Jinja. Gorilla trekking in the rainforests of Uganda. Murchison and Sipi Falls, Queen Elizabeth National Park, trekking in the Ruwenzori Mountains and relaxing for a few days on Ssese Island.

## Where to stay
### Kampala
Try the *Backpackers*, just off Naktete Road in Mengo suburb, west of town, which has a relaxed atmosphere. Camping costs US$3 per person.

### Jinja
Most people stop over in Jinja for the white-water rafting. There are two companies offering this service, including camping accommodation – Shearwater Rafting and Nile River Explorers.

## Fort Portal

It is best to head towards the Kibale Forest National Park, south of Fort Portal, and look out for the *Safari Hotel*, on your right at the Nkingo village. Charles runs this superb campsite, rustic but nice, and he is one of the best chefs in Africa – definitely worth a try!

## Ssese Islands

You'll have to leave your vehicle behind, but camping on Buggala Island is plentiful. One of the fisherman will take you over.

## Sipi Falls

To get to Sipi Falls you'll need to climb a steep and treacherous road up into the mountains, but it's worth the effort. Sipi Falls and the surrounding area are beautiful with green, hilly outcrops and villages dotted around the countryside. You can stay at the *Crows Nest Campsite* which is eco-friendly and has a superb view into Sipi Falls. Camping costs US$3 per person.

## Gorilla trekking

The two options are Bwindi National Park and Magahinga National Park. Most opt for Bwindi as they have three groups of gorillas that have been habituated, while Magahinga only has one. For either park you can get a permit in Kampala, costing US$250 per person, or you can get to either one of the parks and be put on standby, which costs US$150 per person. Both parks have similar accommodation facilities and charge US$6 for a site. It can get cold up in the mountains so come prepared.

## Other national parks

Murchison Falls National Park and Queen Elizabeth National Park are both worth a visit. The falls are particularly spectacular and there is abundant wildlife in the Queen Elizabeth National Park. You will need to be self-sufficient and carry all your supplies with you. During the rainy season the roads in either park can be treacherous. Camping with basic facilities costs US$5 per person; self-catering, where facilities include a basic hut and a staffed kitchen, is US$10–15 per person. Both charge a basic fee for entry of US$15 per person and $20 per vehicle.

## Further information

*Uganda: The Bradt Travel Guide*, Philip Briggs
www.uganda.co.ug
www.imul.com/uganda
www.nic.ug

## WESTERN SAHARA

Morocco virtually annexed the northern two-thirds of Western Sahara (formerly Spanish Sahara) in 1976, and the rest of the territory in 1979, following Mauritania's withdrawal. A guerrilla war with the Polisario Front contesting Rabat's sovereignty ended in a 1991 ceasefire; a referendum on final status has been repeatedly postponed and is not expected to occur until at least 2002. See *Morocco*, page 220.

### Further information

*Africa on a Shoestring*, Lonely Planet
www.arsa.org/index.html
http://sas.upenn.edu/African_
Studies/Country_Specific/
W_Sahara.html

## ZAMBIA

### Capital
Lusaka

### Language
English is the official language.
International telephone code +260

### Currency and rate
Zambian kwacha (ZK); US$1 = ZK2,500

### Red tape
None of any significance.

### Visas
All visitors except citizens of some Commonwealth countries need a visa. British and Irish citizens *do* need visas. A single-entry visa costs US$25–35. Visas are issued at the border.

## Fuel costs
Diesel: US$0.49; petrol: US$0.53 per litre.

## Driving and roads
Drive on the left. Roads have deteriorated, with the worst bitumen in the east and the south.

## African embassies
**Botswana** Haile Selassie Av, Lusaka; tel: 250555
**DRC** 1124 Parirenyetwa Rd, Lusaka; tel: 229044
**Malawi** Woodgate House, Cairo Rd, Lusaka; tel: 228296
**Mozambique** 46 Mulungushi Village in Kundadile Rd, Lusaka; tel: 290451
**Namibia** 6968 Kabanga Rd, Rhodes Park, Lusaka; tel: 252250
**Tanzania** Ujaama House, 5200 United National Av, Lusaka; tel: 227698
**Zimbabwe** 4th Floor, Memaco House, Cairo Rd, Lusaka; tel: 229382

## Climate
Sunny but cool from May to September; hot from October to November; rains from November to April (most parks and other resorts shut down during this time as the majority of roads are impassable).

## Highlights
White-water rafting and bungee jumping at Victoria Falls or an easy canoe trip down the Zambezi – to actually enjoy the surroundings! A trip to the South Luangwa National Park which has a vast array of wildlife.

## Where to stay
### Lusaka
There are two camping options a little out of town – *Pioneer Campsite* (signposted 5km south of the Great East Road, 18km east of the city centre, 3km east of the airport turn-off) or *Eureka Camping Park* (10km south of the city on Kafue Road). Both charge US$6 for the site and facilities are excellent. Both have nearby transport into Lusaka.

### Victoria Falls (Zambia side)
It seems that the only place to stay on Livingstonia Island is *Jungle Junction*. Reconfirm booking within 72 hours of arrival (tel: +260 3 324127; email: jungle@zamnet.zm). Most travellers that we met ended up staying here for several days. Camping costs US$3 per person.

### South Luangwa National Park
The park is not cheap, entry is US$15 per person, but worth every minute. There is masses of wildlife. There are also ample camping opportunities just outside the park and facilities are good at each of the camps. It costs US$5 per person to camp. Night drives are offered by most camps and cost US$25.

## Other

Crime is on the increase in Lusaka. Do not walk anywhere at night, take a taxi.

## Further information

*Zambia: The Bradt Travel Guide*, Chris McIntyre
www.zambia.co.zm
http://africa-insites.com/zambia/travel

## ZIMBABWE

**Warning** *At the time of writing there are violent disputes in Zimbabwe between President Mugabe's 'war veterans' and white farmers, and it is inadvisable to travel to the country. Most travellers have stated that tensions are running high. There is no fuel in most of Zimbabwe.*

## Capital

Harare

## Language

English, Shona and Sindebele are the official languages.
International telephone code +263

## Currency and rate

Zimbabwe dollar (ZD); US$1 = Z$38

## Red tape

With the current problems in Zimbabwe there are now major roadblocks and frequent police checks.

## Visas

Visas are not required for nationals of Commonwealth countries, members of the European Union, Japan, Norway, Switzerland or the USA. Citizens of the Republic of South Africa can pick up a visa at the border or port of entry. Vaccination certificates are obligatory. Visitor's entry pass is issued at the border.

## Fuel costs

Diesel: US$0.22; petrol: US$0.26 per litre.

## Driving and roads

Drive on the left. Roads are in relatively good condition.

## African embassies

**Angola** Doncaster House, 26 Speke Av, Harare; tel: 790075
**Botswana** 10 Bedford Rd, Belgravia, Harare; tel: 729553

**Democratic Republic of the Congo** Pevensey Av, Highlands, Harare; tel: 498594
**Kenya** 95 Park Lane, Harare; tel: 792901
**Malawi** Malawi House, 42/44 Harare St, Harare; tel: 705611
**Mozambique** 152 Herbert Chitepo Av, Harare; tel: 790837 (get there really early or you'll spend the whole day in a long queue)
**Namibia** 31A Lincoln Rd, Avondale, Harare; tel: 304855
**South Africa** Temple Bar House, 7 Elcombe Av/2nd St, Belgravia, Harare; tel: 753147
**Tanzania** 23 Baines Av, Harare; tel: 721870
**Zambia** 6th Floor, Zambia House, 48 Union Av, Harare; tel: 773777

## Climate
A temperate country due to its high altitude. Rainy season is December to March and cool season May to September.

## Highlights
The eastern highlands and exploring Chimanimani National Park. Visiting Great Zimbabwe near Masivingo.. The Lake Kariba district with its lake of dead trees. Victoria Falls which offers a variety of activities from white-water rafting to helicopter rides over the falls. Other national parks, including Hwange, Maria Pools and Matusadona.

## Where to stay
### Harare
Most travellers head for *The Rocks* on 18 Seke Road, but when we visited it was said that the campsite is closing. Another option is to head to *Coronation Park* where camping costs US$1 per person. Watch your stuff at night and pack everything away.

### Chimanimani National Park
*Heavens Lodge* is a great place to stay before trekking up the mountain. You can safely leave your vehicle at the park entrance and take all necessary goods with you while trekking the area for a few days. You'll need to be self-sufficient and camping is possible in the various caves and lodges dotted around the area. Park entry fees are US$5 per day.

### Lake Kariba
The options are limitless, but staying overnight in Matusadona National Park is worth the effort – the roads are not the best. Wildlife is abundant and often right in front of you. Remember to zip up as there was a recent report of a young man being dragged out of his tent and mauled by a lion at Matusadona. Camp entry fee is US$5 per day and the campsite costs US$6.

### Victoria Falls
Most travellers go to the *Town Council's Rest Camp and Caravan Park*. Facilities are a little rustic and the park can get very loud with all the travellers, but all

facilities are within walking distance from the campsite. Camping costs US$4 per person.

### Great Zimbabwe National Park

Park entry fees are US$5 and the campsite in the actual ruins is shady and comfortable, with excellent facilities. Camping costs US$6 for the site. Watch out for the vervet monkeys – they'll steal anything.

## Other

As you drive through Zimbabwe, particularly along Lake Kariba, you will see blue and silver screens dotted along the side of roads. The colours of the screens and pheromones placed under them attract the tsetse fly, which is a problem in certain areas of Zimbabwe. Tsetse flies give very vicious bites and people have broken windscreens in trying to get rid of one. You'll also come across tsetse fly control stations, where two people with a butterfly net in either hand search every part of your vehicle for the elusive fly that has actually by now probably crossed the border. This is a genuine search; not once were we asked for money or any other kind of bribe, but were sent on our way with a huge smile.

Zimbabwe is also known for its amusing signs – one that kept us smiling for days was on the major road to Harare where a sign stated 'Beware! Farm! Implements crossing!'

## Further information

*East and Southern Africa: The Backpacker's Manual*, Philip Briggs, Bradt Travel Guides
www.zimbabwe.net/tourism
www.tourismzimbabwe.co.zw
www.mother.com/~zimweb
www.escapeartist.com/zimbabwe.com/zimbabwe/zimbabwe.html

**ROY SAFARIS LIMITED**
P.O. BOX 50, ARUSHA, TANZANIA
TEL: 255-27-2508010/2115 Fax: 255-27-2548892
E-Mail: RoySafaris@intafrica.com   RoySafaris@haban.co.tz
Web: www.roysafaris.com

**MT. KILIMANJARO & MT. MERU TREKKING**
**CAMPING SAFARIS (BUDGET & SEMI-LUXURY)**
**LUXURY LODGE SAFARIS**
**TOURS TO ZANZIBAR & SELOUS**

We go thro' every measure
To give you wild pleasure

256

**For an extensive selection of off-roader manuals, books and videos, the easy way…**

# www.haynes.co.uk

or phone for our free 176 page, full colour Catalogue:
## 0800 9171898

**Haynes Publishing** Sparkford, Nr Yeovil, Somerset BA22 7JJ England
Telephone: +44 **(0)1963 442030** • Fax: +44 **(0)1963 440001**
E-mail: **sales@haynes-manuals.co.uk**

# Culture

Wherever you go, an understanding of local culture and history goes a long way towards enriching your experience. Making an attempt to learn about the countries you visit is one of the main elements that distinguishes travellers from tourists.

Africa has such a rich cultural heritage that you will probably only be able to scratch the surface. As you travel through Africa you will discover the diversity of this huge continent.

The visual arts are closely tied to the craft traditions of carving and weaving. These will best be appreciated as you travel. It is a good idea, however, to build up a knowledge and enjoyment of African music, literature and history before you leave.

## MUSIC

One of the easiest and most enjoyable ways to start learning about Africa is through its music. The growing interest over recent years in modern African music is a refreshing development and means a vast catalogue of material is now available.

Most good record shops stock a reasonable selection of African CDs. The variety and volume of African music means that any guide to the highlights will necessarily be a partial and personal selection. Below is a suggested list of musicians to look out for.

### Benin

One famed artist, Angélique Kidjo, who has successfully hit the European market, is worth a listen. Angélique Kidjo's albums include Ayé and Fifa, released in the late 1990s. For further information her website is www.imaginet.fr/~kidjo/

### Democratic Republic of the Congo (DRC)

The heart of African music. You will hear the sounds of *soukous* wherever you go in Africa, with its infectious jangling guitar lines and sweet vocals.

The king of *soukous*, Franco, sadly died in 1990. For a taste of him at his best listen to the 1985 release *Mario* and the compilation of his 1950s classics *Originalité*. Franco's band, OK Jazz, was for many years effectively a training school for all of the greats of DCR music. Thankfully, they continued after their leader's death, immediately recording the impeccable *Champions Du*

*Zaire* (they were rejoined for this album by former member Ndombe Opetum, whose solo albums are a delight).

One former member of OK Jazz who warrants special mention is Papa Noel – if only because he rarely receives the praise he so richly deserves. Two albums, *Nono* and *Ya Nono*, are among the most prized records in our collection. Pass them by at your peril.

Franco's great rival over many years was Tabu Ley, who has a similarly large catalogue of releases. Check also on his protégés Sam Mangwana and top female vocalist Mbilia Bel.

The 1980s saw a shift in the music of the Democratic Republic of the Congo (then known as Zaire), with the rise of a new generation of younger stars preferring to leap straight into the faster dance sections of the *soukous* style and dropping the traditional ballad sections. Top of this group of musicians is Kanda Bongo Man, possibly the most commonly played throughout Africa. Many of his albums are available, but try *Non Stop Non Stop*. Other bands at the forefront of this new wave are Pepe Kalle's Empire Bakuba, Zaiko Langa Langa and Papa Wemba.

## Gabon
An honourable mention should go to the Gabonese *soukous* band Les Diablotins. Their best-known albums are a whole series recorded in Paris in 1983 – the best is *Les Diablotins à Paris Volume 7*.

## Ghana
The greatest musical contribution from Ghana is 'highlife' – the danceband music that has developed throughout the 20th century with its synthesis of African and Western styles. The acknowledged king of highlife is E T Mensah. Look out for the excellent compilation of his 1950s hits, released under the title *All For You*. Also look out for Daddy Lumba, Highlife 2000, entitled *Aben Woaha*.

A superb compilation of 1950s and early 1960s highlife hits is *Akomko* – it features tracks from such greats as The Black Beats, Stargazers Dance Band and Red Spot. For a taste of more recent music from Ghana, the Guitar And The Gun compilations are also worth a listen.

## Guinea
Guinea shares the *griot* traditions of Mali and many musicians have moved between the two countries. Guinean *griot* Mory Kanté, for example, replaced Salif Keita in The Super Rail Band. He subsequently left and has released a number of excellent solo albums.

For many years, the national band of Guinea was the Beyla group Bembeya Jazz, who used modern electric instruments to interpret traditional themes. Although they have now disbanded, many of their recordings are available. Guinea's most popular performer of semi-acoustic Manding music is now former Bembeya Jazz singer Sekouba Bambina Diabaté. The all-woman equivalent band was Les Amazones (which was sponsored by the police). Two of its members, Sona Diabate and M'Mah Sylla, released an excellent album in 1988, called *Sahel*, featuring acoustic instruments.

The best-known musician from Guinea is now Mory Kanté, a wonderful singer whose breakthrough album was *Akwaba Beach*. He also appears with Kanté Manfila and Balla Kalla on the rootsy Kankan Blues – a much more raw sound recorded at the Rubis Nightclub in Kankan, Guinea.

## Kenya and Tanzania

East African music is dominated by three main styles – a local version of the *soukous* of the Democratic Republic of the Congo, the unique sound of Swahili Taarab music and the big band sound of Tanzania. For *soukous* try Orchestra Virunga or Orchestra Maquis Original. For the Swahili sound, try Black Lady and Lucky Star Musical Clubs' *Nyota: Classic Taraab from Tanga*. Of the Tanzanian big bands, the all time great was Mbaraka Mwinshehe. By the time of his death in 1979 he had recorded dozens of albums. Look out particularly for the Ukumbusho series.

## Mali

The traditional music of Mali is dominated by the *griots* – singers who have been charged through history with maintaining the oral literature of the area. Their pure voices typically combine with two beautiful instruments – the 21-stringed *kora* and the *balafon* (xylophone).

Since gaining independence, Mali has also produced a number of tremendous and quite distinctive large bands. Its contemporary music typically integrates traditional patterns and styles with modern instruments. Several former *griots* have made the transition.

One of the country's most successful musical exports has been Salif Keita, the singer with a voice of pure gold. If you are happy for the music to be filtered through modern Western pop, then solo albums like *Soro* and *Ko-Yan* are worth a listen. But if you want to hear Salif Keita at his best, look for the albums made between 1974 and 1984 with Les Ambassadeurs (the easiest to find is probably the 1984 release *Les Ambassadeurs Internationaux*).

One classic album from Mali that is reasonably easy to find is by Salif Keita's former group, The Super Rail Band. He left in 1973 but it was not until 1985 and the band's first UK release, *New Dimensions in Rail Culture*, that it achieved international success. This album features the voices of Sekou Kanté and Lanfia Diabate.

The Super Rail Band is based in Bamako, but the second largest town in Mali, Ségou, is home to the excellent Super Biton Band. Their best album is simply called *Super Biton de Ségou* (we bumped into the lead singer one day in a bar in town!).

Make sure you don't bypass the work of the magnificent Ali Farka Touré. His work is some of the most accessible to Western tastes, even though his music is based on traditional forms of Malian music. He reached an even wider audience with the 1994 release of *Talking Timbuktu*, recorded with American guitarist Ry Cooder.

## Nigeria

As well as having the largest population in Africa, Nigeria also has the most developed music industry. Its best-known musical style is *juju* – typically guitar-based bands, weaving melodies around a core of talking drums. Its best-known exponents are Ebenezer Obey, King Sunny Ade and Segun Adewale. A good introduction is Segun Adewale's *Ojo Je*.

No account of Nigerian music would be complete without reference to Fela Kuti, whose politically charged 'Afro-beat' music has ensured continual conflict with the authorities – he was even jailed from 1984 to 1986. A live concert is a real experience, with as many as 40 musicians on stage putting together complex patterns of cross-rhythms.

## Senegal

Another famed artist to hit the European market is Youssour N'Dour from Senegal. His latest album, featuring a few solo hits and some with his band, the Super Etoile, is called *The Guide*.

## South Africa

Paul Simon may have popularised the music of southern Africa with his *Graceland* album, but if you enjoyed the singing featured by Ladysmith Black Mambazo, far better to check out the records from their own large output.

The music of South Africa is incredibly varied, with everything from traditional music to township jive via some of the best jazz in the world. There are a number of very good compilation albums of various artists – in particular *Zulu Jive* and *The Indestructible Beat of Soweto*. Also, listen out for Johnny Clegg who has recorded various albums. More traditional and with a Mozambiquen influence is Steve Newman and Tananas. The ex-exiled Miriam Makeba and Dollar Band (Abdullah Ibrahim) are also worth a listen and traditionally South African.

## Zimbabwe

The modern music of Zimbabwe has been popularised in the West by The Bhundu Boys and The Four Brothers. Albums by both are readily available. But also try to listen to Oliver Mtukutzi and Thomas Mapfumo, Zimbabwe's number one singers and band leaders. A classic collection of Mapfumo's earlier work is *The Chimurenga Singles*. For Mtukutzi try *Shoko*. A great introduction to the dance music of Zimbabwe is provided in the compilation of various artists on *Viva Zimbabwe*.

The live music scene in Harare is one of the best in the world. All the top names play most nights of the week in the various hotels, beer gardens and clubs. Make sure you build in enough time for the music when you hit town.

## Record stores and websites

The best way to get any of the above mentioned is to buy them in Africa. If you would like to get a feel for African music beforehand, try the Africa Centre in London or www.africana.com.

# LITERATURE

The best of modern African literature has brought together the oral traditions of the past with alien Western traditions of the novel and theatre. A good starting point for anyone interested in the whole range of contemporary African writing is the anthology *Voices From Twentieth-Century Africa – Griots And Towncriers* (Faber and Faber). It is a collection that will lead you towards the strongest writers of the continent. *The Traveller's Literary Companion to Africa* by Oona Strathem (In Print Publishing) takes readers on a country-by-country literary tour.

The following is a guide to a handful of the most important writers to look out for.

**Chinua Achebe** Nigeria's great man of letters. The two novels that are most highly recommended were written some 30 years apart and reflect themes of very different periods in the country's history. The effect on African society of the arrival of Europeans is the subject of his first novel, *Things Fall Apart* (Heinemann), published in 1958. His subject matter moves on to the problems of corruption and governing modern Africa in his 1987 novel *Anthills of the Savannah*.

**Ayi Kwei Armah** Ghanaian novelist, much influenced by black American writers. Novels include *The Beautyful Ones Are Not Yet Born, Why Are We So Blest?* and *Two Thousand Seasons*.

**Sembene Ousmane** The Senegalese writer and film director is best known for his masterpiece novel *God's Bits of Wood* (Heinemann), which vividly tells the story of the great strike on the Bamako to Dakar railway. It is particularly recommended if you plan to take that route.

**Stanlake Samkane** Zimbabwe's best-known novelist and historian. His classic novel *On Trial for my Country* puts both Cecil Rhodes and the Matabele King Lobengula on trial to discover the truth behind the 1890 invasion of what became Rhodesia.

**Wole Soyinka** This prolific Nigerian playwright and poet was awarded the Nobel prize for literature in 1986. *The Man Died* (Arrow) is a vivid account of the two and a half years he spent in prison at the time of the Nigerian civil war in the late 1960s. *A Dance in the Forests* is one of his most ambitious and powerful plays, steeped in the beliefs and background of a Yoruba heritage.

**Ngugi Wa Thiong'o** Kenya's greatest writer has been highly critical of his homeland and has had many conflicts with the authorities as a result, including time in jail and in exile. Earlier books concentrated on the struggle against colonialism but he then moved on to criticise post-colonial Kenya as well, most forcefully in the classic *Devil on the Cross* (Heinemann).

## Literary criticism

The South African critic, novelist and short story writer **Es'kia Mphahlele** is reckoned to be the father of serious study of African literature. His book *The African Image* was the first comprehensive work of African literary criticism.

One other particularly interesting work we can recommend is *Land, Freedom and Fiction* by David Maughn-Brown (Zed). This successfully weaves together the history, literature and politics of Kenya by discussing the distortions and reworking of history by writers about the Mau Mau struggle that led to independence.

## Further information

www.heinemann.co.uk
www.africanwriters.com

## ART

Sculpture is one of Africa's greatest art forms. Wherever you travel, you are sure to come across wonderful carvings of one kind or another – each of them distinctive of their own particular region. Of course, the main tourist areas are swamped with souvenir reproductions of little merit, but take the trouble to visit the many national museums in Africa and you will discover a treasure trove of astounding proportions.

**Zimbabwe** has gained a particular reputation in the world of sculpture – with some experts claiming the country has no fewer than six of the world's top ten stone sculptors. A visit to the Chapungu Sculpture Park in Harare is an absolute must.

If you would like to get a flavour for African sculpture before you go, there is much on display in European museums. A comprehensive guide to African sculpture that can be seen in England and Scotland has been published as *African Assortment* by Michael Pennie (Artworth). It discusses and illustrates works on display in 34 separate museums.

# Appendix 1

## LANGUAGE
### French and Arabic translation list

Lacking in French and Arabic, we were often stuck in smaller towns, sometimes even in major cities, where we did not know the translation of a specific vehicle part, spare or tool. For the Arabic translation we have used more of a general dictionary, including some vehicle parts, spare and tools.

We have tried to list (in alphabetical order) all relevant vehicle parts in French and some of the parts in Arabic. The Arabic translation is phonetic, ie: the way one would say it rather than spell it.

### French

| | | | |
|---|---|---|---|
| accelerator jet | *gicleur de pompe* | clutch slave | *servodébrayage* |
| alternator | *alternateur* | cylinder | |
| anti-roll bar | *barre de stabilisateur* | coil | *bobine d'allumage* |
| armature | *induit de demarreur* | condenser | *condensateur* |
| axle casing | *corps de pont* | conrod | *bielle* |
| ball bearings | *roulement à billes* | contact points | *jeu de contacts,* |
| ball joint | *rotule* | | *rupteur* |
| battery | *batterie* | cotter pins | *bagues d'appui* |
| bearing | *coussinet* | crankshaft | *vilebrequin* |
| body | *carrosserie* | crescent spanner | *clé plate* |
| bolt | *boulon* | crown wheel and | *couple conique* |
| brake hose | *flexible de frein* | pinion | |
| brake lining | *garniture de frein* | CV joint | *joint homocinétique* |
| brake master | *maitre-cylindre* | cylinder block | *bloc-cylindres* |
| cylinder | | cylinder head | *culasse* |
| brake shoe | *machoires de frein* | differential | *diferential* |
| bumperbar | *pare chocs* | dipstick | *jauge d'huile* |
| camshaft | *arbre à cames* | disc brakes | *freins à disque* |
| carbon brush | *balai* | distance recorder | *compteur* |
| carburettor | *carburateur* | | *kilometrique* |
| chassis | *chassis* | distributor | *allumeur* |
| clutch | *embrayaga* | engine mounting | *tampon* |
| clutch master | *pompe d'embrayage* | exhaust valve | *soupape* |
| cylinder | | | *d'echappement* |
| clutch plate | *disque d'embrayage* | fan | *ventilateur* |

| fan belt | corroie de ventilateur |
| float | flotteur |
| float chamber | cuve à niveau constant |
| flywheel | volant |
| fracture in tyre | dechirure |
| fuel gauge | indicateur de niveau, jauge |
| fuel line | canalisation |
| fuel pump | pompe à essence |
| fuel tank | reservoir |
| fuse | fusible |
| gasket | joint |
| gear box | boite de vitesses |
| generator | dynamo |
| glow plug | bougie de prechauffage |
| gudgeon pin | axe de piston |
| hammer | marteau |
| handbrake cable | cable de frein à main |
| handbrake lever | levier de frein à main |
| hose | durite |
| ignition switch | contacteur d'allumage |
| inlet valve | soupape d'admission |
| jack | cric |
| leaf spring | lame de ressort |
| leakage | fuite |
| limited slip differentials | diferential autobloquant |
| lock nut | contre ecrou |
| locking washer | arretoir |
| main jet | gicleur d'alimentation |
| manifold | collecteur |
| needle valve | pointeau |
| nut | ecrou |
| oil cooler | radiateur d'huile |
| oil filter | filtre à huile |
| oil seal | bague d'étanchéité |
| patch | rustine |
| petrol cap | bouchon de reservoir |

| piston | piston |
| piston ring | segment |
| pitman arm | levier de direction |
| pliers | pince |
| pressure plates | plateau de pression |
| propeller shaft | arbre de transmission |
| pulley | poulie |
| puncture | crevaison |
| push rod (motor/engine) | tige de culbuteur |
| push rod (transmission) | tige de poussoir |
| push rod tube | couvercle de tige |
| radiator | radiateur |
| rear axle | pont arrière |
| regulator | regulateur |
| release bearing | butée d'embrayage |
| ring spanner | clé à oeillet |
| rocker | culbuteur |
| rockershaft | axe de culbuteur |
| rotor arm | rotor de distributeur |
| rubber bush | coussinet en caoutchouc |
| screwdriver | tournevis |
| set of pads | jeu de machoires |
| shock absorber | amortisseur |
| slow idle jet | gicleur de ralenti |
| socket | douille |
| socket spanner | clé à tube |
| solenoid | solenoid, bendix |
| spanner | clé |
| spare wheel | roue de secours |
| spark plug | bougie |
| speedo cable | flexible de tachymetre |
| speedometer | compteur |
| spring | ressort de suspension |
| starter motor | demarreur |
| steering column | colonne de direction |
| steering wheel | volant de direction |
| thermostat | thermostat |
| third gear | pignon de la troisième vitesse |
| throttle valve | papillon |

| | | | |
|---|---|---|---|
| tie road | *barre de connexion* | valve guide | *guide de soupape* |
| torque spanner | *clé dynamométrique* | valve spring | *ressort de soupape* |
| tube | *chambre à air* | water pump | *pompe à eau* |
| tyre | *pneu* | wheel | *roue* |
| tyre lever | *demonte pneu* | wheel hub | *moyeu de roue* |
| universal joint | *cardan de roue* | wheel rim | *jante* |
| valve cover | *couvercle de culasse* | windscreen | *pare-brise* |

## Arabic

When reading the imitated pronunciation, stress that part of the word which is underlined. Pronounce each word as if it were an English word and you should be understood sufficiently well.

### General

| | | | |
|---|---|---|---|
| accident | *haad<u>e</u>thah* | police station | *noqTat ash- sh<u>o</u>rTah* |
| accommodation | *m<u>a</u>skan* | policeman | *sh<u>o</u>rTee* |
| border | *hod<u>oo</u>d* | post office | *m<u>a</u>ktab bar<u>ee</u>d* |
| bread | *khobz* | reply to greeting | *al Laikoum* |
| camel | *j<u>a</u>mal* | | *salaam* |
| campsite | *mo<u>A</u>skar* | riverbed | *oued* |
| coffee | *qahwah* | road | *sh<u>aa</u>reA* |
| doctor | *tab<u>ee</u>bh* | road or piste | *tric* |
| drinking water | *maa' lesh-sh<u>o</u>rb* | sick | *mar<u>ee</u>D* |
| east | *sharq* | Sir | *Sidi* (only used for |
| encampment | *douar* | | a person of higher |
|   made up of tents | | | standing than |
| exchange rate | *s<u>e</u>Ar at-taHw<u>ee</u>l* | | oneself) |
| flat stony plain | *hammada* | small shops | *souks* |
| go away! | *<u>e</u>mshee!* | small rock | *gara* |
| greeting | *Salaam al Laikoum* |   standing in the | |
| How long will it | *Qad aysh waqt* |   plain | |
|   take? | *tast<u>a</u>ghreq be-taakhoz?* | south | *jan<u>oo</u>b* |
| How much? | *Kem?* | stop! | *g<u>e</u>ff!* |
| journey | *r<u>e</u>Hlah* | tea | *atai* |
| map | *khar<u>ee</u>Tah* | thank you | *sh<u>o</u>krahn* |
| married | *motaz<u>a</u>waj* | tip | *baqsh<u>ee</u>sh* |
| morning | *sabaah* | valley between dunes | *gassi* |
| mountain | *jebel* | water | *mey* |
| night | *layl* | west | *gharb* |
| no (response) | *laa* | Where can I park? | *Wayn <u>a</u>wqef as-* |
| north | *shem<u>aa</u>l* | | *say<u>aa</u>rah?* |
| office | *m<u>a</u>ktab* | yes | *n<u>o</u>Am* |
| passport | *jaw<u>aa</u>z s<u>a</u>far* | | |

## *Vehicle*

| | | | |
|---|---|---|---|
| accelerator | *dawaasat al-banzeen* | ignition | *jehaaz al-eshAal* |
| anti-freeze | *moDaad let-tajmeed* | inner tube | *anboob daakhelee* |
| | | long (as in How long?) | *taweel* |
| battery | *baTaareeyah* | mechanic | *meekaaneekee* |
| brake | *faraamel* | motorbike | *daraajah bokhaareeyah* |
| breakdown | *Ta Atal* | | |
| camshaft | *amood al-kaamah* | oil | *zayt* |
| car | *sayaarah* | park (as in park the vehicle) | *hadeeqah* |
| carburettor | *karboraateere* | | |
| clutch | *debreiyaaj* | piston | *makbas* |
| diesel | *deezel* | puncture | *thaqb* |
| distributor | *destrebyooter* | radiator | *raadiyateer* |
| drive | *yasooq* | screwdriver | *mafakk* |
| to drive | *yasooq* | seatbelt | *hezaam al-maqAd* |
| engine | *moHarrek* | spark plug | *belajaat* |
| exhaust | *shakmaan* | spanner | *meftaaH* |
| fanbelt | *sayr al-marwaHah* | | *sawaameel* |
| funnel | *qomA* | spares | *qeTaA ghiyaar* |
| garage (for fuel) | *maHaTTat banzeen* | speedometer | *adaad as-sorAh* |
| | | spring | *soostah* |
| garage (for repairs) | *garaaj meekaaneekee* | steering wheel | *ajalat al-qiyaadah* |
| | | to tow | *yasHab* |
| gears | *geer* | transmission | *naql al-Harakah* |
| handbrake | *faraamel* | tyre | *'eTaar or Taayer* |
| indicator | *mo'asher* | wheel | *ajalah* |

# Appendix

## DOCUMENTATION FOR CROSSING THE WESTERN SAHARA

When crossing the western Sahara from east to west, or vice versa, you will probably be required to answer several questions at the various roadblocks in Morocco and Western Sahara. In order to speed up the process, it's a good idea to draw up a completed version of the following sample document on A4 paper, then take copies of both this and your passport and driving licence for presentation as required. Of course, the information can be written out at each police post, but the officials don't mind the copied material, so why waste time?

Surname . . . . . . . . . . . . . . . . . . . . . . . . . . . . . . . . . . . . . . . . . . . . . . . . . . . . . . . .

Name . . . . . . . . . . . . . . . . . . . . . . . . . . . . . . . . . . . . . . . . . . . . . . . . . . . . . . . . . . . .

Date of birth . . . . . . . . . . . . . . . . . . . . . . . . . . . . . . . . . . . . . . . . . . . . . . . . . . . . . .

Place of birth . . . . . . . . . . . . . . . . . . . . . . . . . . . . . . . . . . . . . . . . . . . . . . . . . . . . .

Nationality . . . . . . . . . . . . . . . . . . . . . . . . . . . . . . . . . . . . . . . . . . . . . . . . . . . . . . . .

Passport number . . . . . . . . . . . . . . . . . . . . . . . . . . . . . . . . . . . . . . . . . . . . . . . . . . .

Date of issue . . . . . . . . . . . . . . . . . . . . . . . . . . . . . . . . . . . . . . . . . . . . . . . . . . . . . .

Date of expiry . . . . . . . . . . . . . . . . . . . . . . . . . . . . . . . . . . . . . . . . . . . . . . . . . . . . .

Place of issue . . . . . . . . . . . . . . . . . . . . . . . . . . . . . . . . . . . . . . . . . . . . . . . . . . . . . .

Profession . . . . . . . . . . . . . . . . . . . . . . . . . . . . . . . . . . . . . . . . . . . . . . . . . . . . . . . .

Marital status . . . . . . . . . . . . . . . . . . . . . . . . . . . . . . . . . . . . . . . . . . . . . . . . . . . . .

Permanent address . . . . . . . . . . . . . . . . . . . . . . . . . . . . . . . . . . . . . . . . . . . . . . . . .

Father's name . . . . . . . . . . . . . . . . . . . . . . . . . . . . . . . . . . . . . . . . . . . . . . . . . . . . .

Mother's name . . . . . . . . . . . . . . . . . . . . . . . . . . . . . . . . . . . . . . . . . . . . . . . . . . . .

Purpose of visit . . . . . . . . . . . . . . . . . . . . . . . . . . . . . . . . . . . . . . . . . . . . . . . . . . . .

Coming from . . . . . . . . . . . . . . . . . . . . . . . . . . . . . . . . . . . . . . . . . . . . . . . . . . . . . .

Going to . . . . . . . . . . . . . . . . . . . . . . . . . . . . . . . . . . . . . . . . . . . . . . . . . . . . . . . . . .

Driving licence number . . . . . . . . . . . . . . . . . . . . . . . . . . . . . . . . . . . . . . . . . . . . . .

# Appendix 3

## FURTHER INFORMATION
### Books
#### *History and politics*
Goldsworthy, David *Tom Mboya: The Man Kenya Wanted To Forget*
Heinemann. Fascinating book on the former Kenyan trade union leader
and politician who was murdered in 1969. Provides an insight to Kenya's
history in the 1950s and 1960s.
Macdonald Purnell *Nelson Mandela: A Long Walk to Freedom*. The
autobiography of Nelson Mandela and the ANC. Great insight into the
apartheid era of southern Africa.
Marable, Manning *African and Caribbean Politics* Verso. A good overview to
African history and politics, with particular reference to Ghana.
Odinga, Oginga *Not Yet Uhuru* Heinemann. Autobiography of the man who
went from being Kenya's vice-president under Jomo Kenyatta to a leading
opposition force in exile.
Panaf Books *Kwame Nkrumah*. An introduction to the man who led Ghana to
freedom in 1956 and also led the Pan-African liberation movement.
Panaf Books *Sékou Touré*. The story of Guinea's unique road to
independence and of its charismatic first leader.
Pathfinder *Thomas Sankara Speaks*. Key speeches by the inspiring and popular
former president of Burkina Faso.

#### *Travel guides*
*Africa On A Shoestring*, Lonely Planet. The classic budget travellers' guide to
Africa. A mine of information, although you do have to remember that
with a vast number of contributors its accuracy does vary considerably.
Not very helpful on places to stay if you have your own vehicle to worry
about.
*Africa & Madagascar: Total Eclipse 2001 & 2002* Bradt Travel Guides. How and
where to plan a trip to see the total eclipse.
Ash, Paul *South Africa: The Bradt Budget Guide*. South Africa for all visitors on
a tight budget, including hikes and South Africa for free.
Briggs, Philip *East and Southern Africa: The Backpacker's Manual*, Bradt Travel
Guides. A practical and comprehensive guide to 12 of Africa's most visited
countries, from Ethiopia to South Africa. 'A tightly written, non-nonsense
guide' *The Times*

Briggs, Philip *Ethiopia: The Bradt Travel Guide.* 'Thorough and reassuring' *The Daily Telegraph*

Briggs, Philip *Ghana: The Bradt Travel Guide.* From coastal forts to national parks, everything the visitor needs in Ghana.

Briggs, Philip *Malawi: The Bradt Travel Guide.* 'Excellent...up-to-date and reliable' *Times Literary Supplement*

Briggs, Philip *Mozambique: The Bradt Travel Guide.* 'Useful on-the-spot information' *Geographical Magazine*

Briggs, Philip *Tanzania: The Bradt Travel Guide.* 'The best for independent travellers' *The Daily Telegraph*

Briggs, Philip *Uganda: The Bradt Travel Guide.* 'The most comprehensive and best current guide' *Traveller*

de Villiers, Marq and Hirtle, Sheila *Into Africa* Weidenfeld & Nicolson in Great Britain, Jonathan Ball Publishers in South Africa, 1997.

*Egypt and the Sudan*, Lonely Planet. Out of print.

Glen, Simon *Sahara Handbook* Roger Lascelles. Now out of print. Although dated, a very comprehensive reference book.

McIntyre, Chris *Namibia: The Bradt Travel Guide.* Suggested itineraries for the driver, detailed accommodation listings and much more.

McIntyre, Chris *Zambia: The Bradt Travel Guide.* 'Definitely recommended' *Traveller's Times*

*Morocco, Algeria and Tunisia*, Lonely Planet. Out of print.

Oliver, Roland *The African Experience*, Pimlico, 1991.

Paice, Edward *Eritrea: The Bradt Travel Guide.* 'Comprehensive...a wealth of practical and background information' *Traveller*

Philips *Essential World Atlas,* in association with the Royal Geographical Society with the Institute of British Geographers, 1998.

Running Press *The Quotable Travellers*, 1994.

Scott, Chris *Desert Biking: A Guide to Independent Motorcycling in the Sahara,* The Travellers' Press. A mine of information for those planning a trip by motorbike – although specifically covering the requirements of desert biking rather than for a comprehensive African trip. Lots of advice on bikes and equipment as well as details of a number of North African routes. Available from the Travellers' Bookshop in London or from amazon.co.uk

Scott, Chris *Sahara Overland* Trailblazer, 1999.

St Pierre White, Andrew *The complete guide to a Four Wheel Drive in Southern Africa*, National Book Printers, 1998/1999.

*The Rough Guide to West Africa.* A substantial and excellent country-by-country guide to this extraordinary region.

Velton, Ross *Mali: The Bradt Travel Guide.* Excellent coverage of ecotourism and adventure travel as well as every aspect of Mali's attractions.

## Language

Eyewitness Travel Guides *Arabic Phrasebook*, Dorling Kindersley Ltd, 1998.

## Other useful reading

Barker, Hazel *Senile Safari: A Journey from Durban to Alexandria*. A retired couple's drive through Africa. Available from the author: 18 Louisa Road, Birchgrove, Sydney, Australia; tel/fax: (61 2) 810 5040.

Glen, Simon and Roger Lascelles *Sahara Handbook*. Now out of print. Although dated, a very comprehensive reference book.

Melville, K E M *Stay Alive In The Desert*, Roger Lascelles. All you need to know about desert survival – but in far more detail than most travellers will ever need.

Pandora *Half The Earth*. Excellent collection of guidance and personal encounters by women travellers, based on their experiences around the world.

Simon, Ted *Jupiter's Travels*, Penguin. The classic story of a round-the-world journey by motorbike – includes the trip from Tunis to Cape Town. As this was undertaken in 1974 to 1978, hard information is rather out of date (he rides through Libya). But it is the spirit of the book that makes it unmissable.

## Easy reads

Blixen, Karen *Out of Africa*, Putnam & Co. Ltd, 1937 (1st edition).

Foden, Giles *The Last King of Scotland* and *Ladysmith*. *The Last King of Scotland* revolves around Idi Amin through the eyes of his personal physician. *Ladysmith* is about the British occupation of this small town in southern Africa. Both are superb reads.

Galman, Kuki *I Dreamed of Africa*. This author has written several novels regarding her time with her family in Kenya.

Godwin, Peter *Mukiwa*. Rhodesia 1964 as seen through a young boy's eyes and his steady growth to the freedom of Rhodesia, now known as Zimbabwe.

*Mail and Guardian Bedside Book* (1999) is a selection of superb journalism from Africa's best read.

## Sourcing African literature and maps

All of the above-mentioned books can be ordered through Amazon on www.amazon.co.uk or www.amazon.com.

### United Kingdom

**Africa Book Centre Ltd** 38 King St, London WC2E 8JT; tel: 020 7836 1973; fax: 020 7836 1975; email: africacentre@gn.dpc.org

**Blackwells** 100 Charing Cross Rd, London WC2H 0JG; tel: 020 7292 5100; fax: 020 7240 9665; email: london@blackwellsbookshops.co.uk; web: www.blackwells.co.uk. For all literature and maps.

**Stanfords** 12–14 Long Acre, London WC2E 9LP; tel: 020 7836 1321; web: www.stanfords.co.uk

**Stanfords at British Airways Travel Shop** 156 Regent St, London SW1Y 4NX; tel: 020 7434 4444; web: www.stanfords.co.uk

**Travellers World Bookshop** Newmarket Court, Derby DE24 8NW; tel: 01332 573 7376; fax: 01332 573 399; email: service@map-guides.co.uk

## United States
**Book Passage** 15 Tamal Vista Boulevard, Court Madera, California; tel: 415 927 0960; fax: 415 924 7909; email: messages@bookpassage.com; web: www.bookpassage.com
**California Map and Travel Center** 3312 Pico Boulevard, Santa Monica, California; tel: 310 396 6277; fax: 310 392 8785; email: topo@mapper.com; web: www.mapper.com
**The Savvy Traveller** 310 South Michigan Av, Chicago, IL 60604; tel: 888 666 6200 (toll free); fax: 312 913 9866; email: mailbox@thesavvytraveller.com; web: www.thesavvytraveller.com
**Wide World Books and Maps** 4411A Wallingford Av North, Seattle, WA 98103; tel: 888 534 3453 (toll free) or 206 634 3453; fax: 206 634 0558; email: travel@speakeasy.com; web: www.travelbooksandmaps.com
**World Traveller** 400 South Elliot Rd, Chapel Hill, NC 21514; tel: 919 933 5111; fax: 919 933 7532; email: kathryn@travelbookshop.com; web: www.travelbookshop.com

For all other travel bookstores in your area get into the following website for listings: www.aaa-calif.com

## South Africa
**Exclusive Books** Shop U30, Hyde Park Corner, Jan Smuts Av, Craighall, Johannesburg/Gauteng; tel: 011 325 4298; fax: 011 325 5001; email: ebgthp@exclusivebooks.co.za; web: www.exclusivebooks.co.za
**Facts & Fiction** Shop 346–350, Rosebank Mall, Bath Av, Rosebank, Johannesburg/Gauteng; tel: 011 447 3039/3028; fax: 011 447 3062; email: ebgthp@exclusivebooks.co.za; web: www.exclusivebooks.co.za

# Useful websites
The authors on their Africa trip: www.users.globalnet.co.uk/~salka/index.htm
**Africanet** (general info on Africa including history and politics): www.africanet.com
**Africa Tour**: www.netsnake.com/africa-tour
**Bradt Travel Guides** www.bradt-travelguides.com
**The Columbus World Travel Guide:** www.wtgonline.com
**Independent Africa Overland Club** (a general overview on travelling overland in Africa): www.africa-overland.com
**Kingsmill** (a personal journey into Africa, including crossing the Sudan): www.sites.netscape.net/kingmill/africa
**Klaus Daerr Expedition** (in German only but excellent information on the Sahara): www.klaus.daerr.de/sahara
**Sahara Travel information**: www.sahara-overland.com
**Tips for driving in Africa**: www.geocities.com/MotorCity/1197/driving.html

Other useful sites include:
**http://i-cias.com**

www.africa.com
**www.africaguide.com** An excellent source of general information on individual African countries.
**www.africanconnections.com**
**www.africanet.com**
**www.africaonline.com**
**www.afrisearch.com**
**www.arab.net**
**www.ase.net** A useful source of information on accommodation.
**www.backpackafrica.com**
**www.countries.com**
**www.escapeartist.com**
**www.excite.com** (Excite Travel)
**www.infoplease.com**
**www.interknowledge.com**
**www.newafricaguide.com**
**www.odci.gov** (CIA webpage including details of every African country)
**www.safarinow.com**
**www.travelinafrica.co.za** Includes visa information in some detail.
**www.worldtravelguide.net**

# World Travel starts at Stanfords

**Maps and Guides for all corners of the world.**
Atlases. Travel Writing. Mountaineering. Maps and Books.
Globes. Instruments. Travel Accessories.

visit our Website:

# www.stanfords.co.uk

or one of our shops
**Stanfords Flagship Store: 12-14 Long Acre, London, WC2E 9LP**
**Telephone: 020 7836 1321 / Fax 020 7836 0189**
Stanfords at British Airways, 156 Regent Street, London, W1R 5TA
Stanfords at The Britain Visitor Centre, 1 Regent Street, London, SW1Y 4NX
Stanfords in Bristol, 29 Corn Street, Bristol, BS1 1HT

## The World's Finest Map and Travel Book Shops

# Appendix 4

## CHECKLIST

Below is an example of a useful checklist so that you can see at a glance whether you have everything you will need.

| ITEM | HAVE OR NOT | DETAILS | COST |
|---|---|---|---|
| **Finances** | | | |
| Travellers' cheques | | | |
| US dollars | | | |
| British pounds | | | |
| French francs | | | |
| Other denominations | | | |
| Credit cards | | | |
| **Route planning** | | | |
| Where, ie: planned route | | | |
| For how long | | | |
| Suggested itinerary | | | |
| *Guidebooks and maps* | | | |
| *Africa guidebooks* | | | |
| North Africa | | | |
| West Africa | | | |
| Central Africa | | | |
| East Africa | | | |
| South Africa | | | |
| *Africa maps* | | | |
| Bartholomew (Continental Travel Map) Africa | | | |
| Michelin 953 – North and West | | | |
| Michelin 954 – North East | | | |
| Michelin 958 – Algeria | | | |
| Michelin 959 – Morocco | | | |
| Michelin 957 – Côte d'Ivoire | | | |
| Michelin 955 – Central and South Africa | | | |

| ITEM | HAVE OR NOT | DETAILS | COST |
|---|---|---|---|
| **Bureaucracy** | | | |
| *Visas* | | | |
| For which countries | | | |
| Cost estimate | | | |
| Can get beforehand | | | |
| Other | | | |
| *Paperwork* | | | |
| *Passport* | | | |
| Validity | | | |
| Number of unused pages | | | |
| *Vaccination certificates* | | | |
| Cholera | | | |
| Diphtheria | | | |
| Hepatitis A and B | | | |
| Meningitis | | | |
| Polio | | | |
| Rabies (optional) | | | |
| Tetanus | | | |
| Tuberculosis | | | |
| Typhoid | | | |
| Yellow fever | | | |
| NB: Certificate signed by GP/clinic | | | |
| *Other* | | | |
| *Carnet de Passage (carnet)* | | | |
| Bond or insurance | | | |
| *Carnet* organised for every country mentioned that you will visit | | | |
| International certificate for motor vehicles, ie: *carte grise* (grey card) | | | |
| *Insurance* | | | |
| Medical insurance | | | |
| Vehicle insurance (optional) | | | |
| International driving licence | | | |
| References | | | |
| in English | | | |
| in French | | | |
| Passport photos | | | |
| | | | |
| **Vehicle selection** | | | |
| **4WD/2WD** | | | |
| Type | | | |
| Registration number | | | |
| Chassis number | | | |

| Item | Have or not | Details | Cost |
|---|---|---|---|
| Engine number | | | |
| Other | | | |
| **Motorbike** | | | |
| Type | | | |
| Registration number | | | |
| Chassis number | | | |
| Engine number | | | |
| Other | | | |
| **Bicycle** | | | |
| Type | | | |
| Other | | | |

## 4WD/2WD

### Preparation

| Item | Have or not | Details | Cost |
|---|---|---|---|
| Sleeping requirements | | | |
| Tent | | | |
| Rooftop tent | | | |
| Inside the vehicle | | | |
| Mattresses | | | |
| Pillows | | | |
| Sleeping bags | | | |
| Covers for pillows, etc | | | |
| Roof rack | | | |
| Security | | | |
| Padlocks and hasps | | | |
| Windows | | | |
| Curtains | | | |
| Safety box | | | |
| Alarm system (optional) | | | |
| Bull bar | | | |
| Baffle/bash plate | | | |
| Suspension | | | |
| Heavy-duty suspension fitted | | | |
| Spare battery and split charge system | | | |
| Oil cooler | | | |
| Raised air intake | | | |
| Tyres | | | |
| Spare tyres | | | |
| Inner tubes | | | |
| Valves | | | |
| Foot or electrical tyre pump | | | |
| Tyre repair kit | | | |
| Pressure gauge | | | |

| Item | Have or not | Details | Cost |
|---|---|---|---|
| Fuel and water tanks | | | |
|   Capacity | | | |
|     Fuel | | | |
|     Water | | | |
| Storage boxes | | | |
| Seat covers | | | |
| Steering-wheel cover | | | |
| Stereo | | | |
|   Type and make | | | |
|   Serial number | | | |
| Canopy | | | |

## Equipment

| Item | Have or not | Details | Cost |
|---|---|---|---|
| Recovery gear | | | |
| Electronic or manual winches | | | |
|   Type and make | | | |
|   Guarantees | | | |
| High-lift jack | | | |
| Hydraulic jack | | | |
| Two blocks of wood to place jack on | | | |
| Sand ladders | | | |
| Towing points | | | |
| Towing straps | | | |
| Shackles | | | |
| Compass and/or Global Positioning System (GPS) | | | |
|   Type and make | | | |
|   Mounting and storage system | | | |
|   Serial number | | | |
|   Guarantee | | | |
| Shovel or sand spades | | | |
| Axe or machete | | | |
| Warning triangles (2 or 3) | | | |
| Jerry cans | | | |
|   Carrying capacity for: | | | |
|     Fuel | | | |
|     Water | | | |
|     Oil | | | |
| Fire extinguisher | | | |
| Water | | | |
|   Water purification (eg: Chloromyn T, Puritabs) | | | |

| Item | Have or not | Details | Cost |
|---|---|---|---|
| Filter | | | |
| Type | | | |
| Capacity of filter before replacement | | | |
| Guarantee | | | |
| Table and chairs | | | |
| Mosquito net/s | | | |
| Refrigerator | | | |
| Type and make | | | |
| Runs on 12V DC or 240V AC or gas or all three | | | |
| Serial number | | | |
| Guarantee | | | |
| **Lighting** | | | |
| Car lights | | | |
| Fluorescent strip light | | | |
| Map light | | | |
| Torch and batteries | | | |
| **Cooking equipment** | | | |
| Petrol stoves | | | |
| Kerosene stoves | | | |
| Container for kerosene | | | |
| Meths burners | | | |
| Container for methylated spirits | | | |
| Gas stoves | | | |
| Gas bottle fitted | | | |
| Cooking utensils | | | |
| Saucepan | | | |
| Deep straight-edged frying pan | | | |
| Cooking pot or cast-iron pot | | | |
| Kettle | | | |
| Pressure cooker or wok (optional) | | | |
| Decent sharp knife | | | |
| Wooden spoon | | | |
| Strainer (optional) | | | |
| Tin opener | | | |
| Bottle opener | | | |
| Chopping board | | | |
| Plates and bowls (plastic or enamel) | | | |
| Mugs (plastic) | | | |
| Assortment of cutlery | | | |
| Matches and/or firelighters | | | |
| Fire grill (optional) | | | |

| ITEM | HAVE OR NOT | DETAILS | COST |
|---|---|---|---|
| **Cleaning up** | | | |
| Plastic bowl | | | |
| Washing-up liquid | | | |
| Washing-up cloth | | | |
| Scourer (optional) | | | |
| Drying up cloth | | | |
| **Spares and tools** | | | |
| Workshop manual | | | |
| 2 x oil filters | | | |
| 2 x fuel filters | | | |
| 2 x air filters | | | |
| Engine oil (enough for two changes) | | | |
| 5-litre of gear box and differential oil | | | |
| Grease | | | |
| 1 litre brake and clutch fluid oil | | | |
| 2 litres coolant | | | |
| Glow plugs/spark plugs | | | |
| Set of engine gaskets | | | |
| Set of all oil seals | | | |
| Set of wheel bearings | | | |
| Set of engine mounts | | | |
| Set of radiator hoses | | | |
| Accelerator cable | | | |
| 2 x fanbelts | | | |
| Set of brake pads | | | |
| Brake master cylinder rubbers | | | |
| Water pump | | | |
| Suspension rubbers and bushes | | | |
| Condenser | | | |
| Distributor cap | | | |
| Contact breaker points | | | |
| Lightbulbs | | | |
| U-bolts for leaf springs | | | |
| Clutch plate | | | |
| Fuses | | | |
| Funnel (make sure it fits the filler of your fuel tank) | | | |
| Jubilee clips | | | |
| Cable ties | | | |
| Electrical tapes | | | |
| Electrical wires | | | |
| Masking tape | | | |
| Assortment of wire | | | |

| Item | Have or not | Details | Cost |
|---|---|---|---|
| Assortment of nuts, bolts and washers | | | |
| Contact adhesive | | | |
| Prately putty | | | |
| 2m fuel hoses | | | |
| Flexible 'bathroom' sealant | | | |
| Instant gasket paste | | | |
| Exhaust repair putty | | | |
| Gasket paper | | | |
| Can of WD40 or Q20 | | | |
| *Tools* | | | |
| Good set of spanners (imperial or metric as required by your vehicle) | | | |
| Good set of sockets with power bar and ratchet | | | |
| Assortment of screwdrivers | | | |
| Adjustable spanner | | | |
| Mole wrench | | | |
| Pipe wrench | | | |
| Grease gun | | | |
| Metal and rubber hammers | | | |
| Torque wrench (essential for alloy engines) | | | |
| Pliers | | | |
| Circ clip removers | | | |
| Multi-size puller | | | |
| Jump leads | | | |
| Set of feeler gauges | | | |
| Hacksaw | | | |
| Multi-meter electrical tester | | | |
| Flat metal file | | | |
| Small round file | | | |
| Hand drill and kit (9V cordless drills can be connected directly to your battery) | | | |
| Tyre levers | | | |
| Tyre valve tool | | | |
| Wet and dry sandpaper | | | |
| Length of pipe (to extend your power bar for those stubborn nuts) | | | |

| Item | Have or not | Details | Cost |
|---|---|---|---|
| **Motorbike** | | | |
| **Spares and tools** | | | |
| Repair manual | | | |
| 1 x spare rear tyre | | | |
| 1 x front and rear heavy duty inner tubes | | | |
| 1 x good-quality puncture repair kit with lots of patches | | | |
| 1 x small mountain bike pump | | | |
| A few spare spokes | | | |
| Connecting links for chain | | | |
| 1 x clutch lever | | | |
| 1 x brake lever | | | |
| 1 x clutch cable | | | |
| 1 x throttle cable(s) | | | |
| 1 x air filter | | | |
| 3 x oil filters | | | |
| 1 x fuel filter | | | |
| 2 x spark plugs | | | |
| Fuel hose and jubilee clips | | | |
| Bulbs and fuses | | | |
| Electrical wire and connectors | | | |
| Assorted nuts, bolts and washers | | | |
| Main gaskets | | | |
| Duct tape | | | |
| Assorted cable ties (lots) | | | |
| Spare bungee rope/straps | | | |
| Instant gasket | | | |
| Silicon sealant | | | |
| Epoxy glue | | | |
| Liquid steel | | | |
| Loctite (for nut threads) | | | |
| Small tub of grease | | | |
| About 1 litre engine oil (for top up and oiling air filter) | | | |
| Standard small toolkit (combination spanners, 3/8" drive ratchet + relevant sockets, screwdrivers) | | | |
| Leatherman or Swiss army knife | | | |
| Feeler gauges | | | |
| File | | | |
| Spark plug spanner | | | |
| Tyre levers | | | |

| ITEM | HAVE OR NOT | DETAILS | COST |
|---|---|---|---|
| **Personal equipment** | | | |
| Jacket with built-in shoulder and elbow pads | | | |
| Spine protector with a waist band | | | |
| Full-length motorcross style boots (optional) | | | |
| Helmet and goggles | | | |
| Gloves | | | |
| | | | |
| **Bicycle** | | | |
| **Spares and tools** | | | |
| Panniers – Overlander by Carradice | | | |
| 2 x spare tyres | | | |
| 10 x inner tubes | | | |
| Puncture repair kit | | | |
| Cables | | | |
| Brakepads | | | |
| Grease and oil | | | |
| Bearings | | | |
| Wires and straps | | | |
| Pliers | | | |
| Set of Allen keys | | | |
| Cable cutter | | | |
| Spoke tensioner | | | |
| Set of spanners | | | |
| Screwdriver | | | |
| Bottom bracket tensioner | | | |
| Front bearing spanner | | | |
| Spokes | | | |
| Box of nuts and bolts, etc | | | |
| Chain link extractor | | | |
| Toothbrush | | | |
| **Personal equipment** | | | |
| Helmet | | | |
| Gloves | | | |
| Sunglasses | | | |
| 2 x whistles (as a warning and signal) | | | |
| Compass | | | |
| | | | |
| **Camping: Motorbike/bicycle** | | | |
| Tent | | | |
| Sleeping mat | | | |
| Sleeping bag | | | |

| Item | Have or not | Details | Cost |
|---|---|---|---|
| Nylon string | | | |
| Towel | | | |
| Torch | | | |
| Thermarest mattress | | | |
| *Cooking* | | | |
| Stove, eg: MSR high-quality petrol stove or Coleman's multifuel cooker | | | |
| 2 x spoons | | | |
| 2 x plastic bowls | | | |
| 2 x plastic cups | | | |
| Saucepan | | | |
| Penknife | | | |
| *Water* | | | |
| 2 x Travelwell military water purifiers | | | |
| 2 x 10-litre water bags | | | |
| Coloured water bottle (coloured is optional) | | | |
| Filter | | | |
| **Food** | | | |
| Salt | | | |
| Pepper | | | |
| Assortment of herbs and spices | | | |
| Tea and coffee | | | |
| Sugar | | | |
| Powdered milk | | | |
| Oats | | | |
| Jam | | | |
| Rice | | | |
| Pasta | | | |
| Tubes of tomato puree | | | |
| Stock cubes | | | |
| Tinned vegetables and fruit | | | |
| Packets of instant foods, ie: ready-made pasta, etc. | | | |
| Oil | | | |
| Vinegar | | | |
| Flour or cornflour | | | |
| Dried beans | | | |
| Mustard | | | |
| Lemon juice | | | |
| Dried mushrooms or other | | | |
| Dried fruit and nuts | | | |

| ITEM | HAVE OR NOT | DETAILS | COST |
|------|-------------|---------|------|
| Biscuits and crackers | | | |
| Boiled sweets | | | |
| Packets of dried food (specific for cyclists and bikers) | | | |
| Smaller tins of tuna or ham | | | |
| Instant mashed potato | | | |
| Small packets of parmesan cheese | | | |

## Medical kit
### *General*

| | | | |
|------|-------------|---------|------|
| Analgesics (painkillers) | | | |
| Aspirin for sore throat and mild pain | | | |
| Paracetamol for mild pain and temperature | | | |
| Ibuprofen for joint inflammation and pain | | | |
| Paracetamol/Codeine for moderate pain | | | |
| Buccastem for severe nausea, vomiting and vertigo | | | |
| Loperamide for acute diarrhoea | | | |
| Oral rehydration sachets for dehydration | | | |
| Senokot tabs for constipation | | | |
| Merocaine lozenges for sore throats | | | |
| Indigestion tabs for excessive acid and indigestion | | | |
| Loratidine for allergies | | | |
| Pseudoephedrine for nasal and sinus congestion | | | |
| Clove oil for toothache | | | |

### *Antibiotics*

| | | | |
|------|-------------|---------|------|
| Amoxycillin for chest, ear, cellulitis and urinary tract infection (general antibiotic) | | | |
| Ciprofloxacin for gut and urinary tract infections | | | |
| Tinidazole for amoebic dysentery and giardia | | | |
| Flucloxacillin for skin infections | | | |

| ITEM | HAVE OR NOT | DETAILS | COST |
|---|---|---|---|
| Erythromycin for skin and chest infections (if allergic to penicillin) | | | |
| Mebendazole for thread, round and hook worm infections | | | |
| **Malaria (prevention and treatment)** | | | |
| Anti-malaria tablets | | | |
| Quinine sulphate and Fansidar | | | |
| Quinine sulphate and doxycycline | | | |
| **Bilharzia** | | | |
| Biltracide | | | |
| **Eye, ear and nose** | | | |
| Chloramphenicol for eye infections | | | |
| Normal saline sachets for an eye wash | | | |
| Eye bath as a eye wash unit | | | |
| Ear drops | | | |
| Nose drops | | | |
| **Sterile surgical equipment (optional)** | | | |
| Sterile surgical gloves | | | |
| Scalpel (disposable) | | | |
| Mersilk suture of varying sizes | | | |
| Suturing forceps | | | |
| Stitch cutter | | | |
| Dental needles | | | |
| Syringes of varying sizes | | | |
| Variety of needles | | | |
| Pink and green Venflon for intravenous administration | | | |
| Sterile gauze to cleanse area of sterilisation | | | |
| Medical set for intravenous administration | | | |
| **Powder and creams for the skin** | | | |
| Hydrocortisone for skin allergies and insect bites | | | |
| Lactocalamine for sunburn, itching and rashes | | | |
| Daktarin cream for fungal infections | | | |
| Cicatrin powder for wound infections (antibiotic) | | | |
| Magnesium sulphate for treatment of boils | | | |

| Item | Have or not | Details | Cost |
|---|---|---|---|
| **Other items for the medical kit** | | | |
| Thermometer | | | |
| Permethrin mosi net treatment | | | |
| Repellent coils to burn at night | | | |
| Insect repellent | | | |
| Anti-itch cream | | | |
| Flu medication | | | |
| Medication for personal ailments | | | |
| Condoms, pill or other | | | |
| Tampons | | | |
| **Comprehensive first-aid kit (optional)** | | | |
| Granuflex dressing for tropical ulcers | | | |
| Gauze swabs for cleaning wounds | | | |
| Melolin of varying sizes for non-sticky wound dressing | | | |
| Micropore or zinc oxide tape used as surgical tape | | | |
| Assortment of plasters | | | |
| Crepe bandage for muscular injuries | | | |
| Steristrips for wound closures | | | |
| Wound dressing for heavily bleeding wounds | | | |
| Triangular bandage for securing broken limbs | | | |
| Safety pins | | | |
| Steripods (disposable antiseptic sachets) | | | |
| Water gel or Jelonet dressing for burns | | | |
| Scissors | | | |
| Tweezers | | | |
| Disposable gloves | | | |
| Lancets – sterile needles which can be used for popping blisters | | | |
| Betadine as antiseptic solution | | | |

## Personal kit
### Clothes

| Item | Have or not | Details | Cost |
|---|---|---|---|
| Jeans | | | |
| T-shirts | | | |
| Light cotton trousers | | | |
| Skirt | | | |

| Item | Have or not | Details | Cost |
|---|---|---|---|
| Sleeveless dress with light shirt to pull over | | | |
| Trousers and shirt | | | |
| Swimming costumes | | | |
| Wraparound skirts (also used as towels) | | | |
| Light scarf or shawl | | | |
| Sweatshirts | | | |
| Thick jerseys | | | |
| Woolly hats | | | |
| Hiking boots | | | |
| Sandals | | | |
| Raincoats | | | |
| Socks and underwear | | | |
| **Toiletries** | | | |
| Soap | | | |
| Shampoo | | | |
| Flannel | | | |
| Toothbrush & toothpaste | | | |
| Towels (or sarongs) | | | |
| Portable washing machine | | | |
|   Bucket with lid | | | |
|   Washing liquid/powder | | | |
|   Nylon or other string | | | |
|   Clothes pegs | | | |
| **Miscellaneous** | | | |
| Pens and pencils | | | |
| Writing paper | | | |
| Diary or other writing material | | | |
| Address book | | | |
| Games/playing cards | | | |
| Books and magazines | | | |
| Music on either tapes or CD | | | |
| Short-wave radio | | | |
| Pocket calculator | | | |
| Swiss army knife or Leatherman's | | | |
| Hammock | | | |
| Binoculars and various books on fauna, flora and wildlife | | | |
| Driver's logbook | | | |
| Gifts | | | |

| ITEM | HAVE OR NOT | DETAILS | COST |
|---|---|---|---|
| Photographic equipment | | | |
| Dust-proof storage system | | | |
| Camera | | | |
| Polaroid camera | | | |
| Lens/es | | | |
| Cleaning gear | | | |
| Film | | | |
| Other | | | |
| Serial number | | | |

# Travelling Light in Africa?

**Travelling Light makes an exclusive range of smart but practical cotton clothing for men and women travelling in hot countries.**

We also supply many high quality hard-to-find accessories.

Seven regional shops including 35 Dover Street, Piccadilly, London W1

Write or ring for free mail order catalogue to

# TRAVELLING LIGHT

(ABR), Morland, Penrith, Cumbria CA10 3AZ, UK. Telephone 01931 714488

## Safari Makers Ltd

Safaris & Car Hire Tours To All Tanzanian National Parks & Destinations Outside Parks

'Let Safari Makers Ltd **make** your safari'

Lodge Safaris
Camping Safaris
Walking/Cultural Tours
Mountain Climbing
Trekking
Beach Holidays

Fax: +255-27-7184
E-mail: safarimakers@habari.co.tz
Web: www.safarimakers.com

Member of Tanzania Association of Tour Operators

## Travelling?     Need Gear?

For everything you need consult our full colour catalogue.
Tried. Tested. Guaranteed. Shop or fast mail order. Get in touch NOW!

 SAFARIQUIP **The Stones, Castleton, Hope Valley, S33 8WX**
Tel: 01433 620320  Fax: 01433 620061
E-mail mail@safariquip.co.uk Website: www.safariquip.co.uk

# Index

In this index page references in **bold** type indicate main entries and those in *italic* type indicate maps.

# The Bradt Story

The first Bradt travel guide was written by Hilary and George Bradt in 1974 on a river barge floating down a tributary of the Amazon in Bolivia. From their base in Boston, Massachusetts, they went on to write and publish four other backpacking guides to the Americas and one to Africa.

In the 1980s Hilary continued to develop the Bradt list in England, and also established herself as a travel writer and tour leader. The company's publishing emphasis evolved towards broader-based guides to new destinations – usually the first to be published on those countries – complemented by hiking, rail and wildlife guides.

Since winning *The Sunday Times* Small Publisher of the Year Award in 1997, we have continued to fill the demand for detailed, well-written guides to unusual destinations, while maintaining the company's original ethos of low-impact travel.

Travel guides are by their nature continuously evolving. If you experience anything which you would like to share with us, or if you have any amendments to make to this guide, please write; all your letters are read and passed on to the author. Most importantly, do remember to travel with an open mind and to respect the customs of your hosts – it will add immeasurably to your enjoyment.

Happy travelling!

Hilary Bradt

19 High Street, Chalfont St Peter, Bucks SL9 9QE, England
Tel: 01753 893444  Fax: 01753 892333
Email: info@bradt-travelguides.com  Web: www.bradt-travelguides.com

# Need to know more?
# SAVE £2 OFF A BRADT GUIDE!

To order your copy of one or more of the Bradt guides listed in this book, post or fax us your order on the form below, together with the appropriate remittance, and we will despatch the book(s) within two working days.

Please send me a copy of each of the following Bradt guides at £2 off the retail price, post and packing *free* in the UK and Northern Ireland:

| No. | Title | Special price | Total |
|---|---|---|---|
| ☐ | Africa & Madagascar: Total Eclipse 2001 & 2002 | £8.95 | . . . . . |
| ☐ | Botswana: The Bradt Travel Guide (2001) | £10.95 | . . . . . |
| ☐ | East & Southern Africa: The Backpacker's Manual | £12.95 | . . . . . |
| ☐ | Eritrea: The Bradt Travel Guide | £8.95 | . . . . . |
| ☐ | Ethiopia: The Bradt Travel Guide | £9.95 | . . . . . |
| ☐ | Gambia: The Bradt Travel Guide (2001) | £10.95 | . . . . . |
| ☐ | Ghana: The Bradt Travel Guide | £9.95 | . . . . . |
| ☐ | Malawi: The Bradt Travel Guide | £9.95 | . . . . . |
| ☐ | Mali: The Bradt Travel Guide | £11.95 | . . . . . |
| ☐ | Namibia: The Bradt Travel Guide | £10.95 | . . . . . |
| ☐ | Rwanda: The Bradt Travel Guide (2001) | £10.95 | . . . . . |
| ☐ | South Africa: The Bradt Budget Guide | £9.95 | . . . . . |
| ☐ | Southern Africa by Rail | £10.95 | . . . . . |
| ☐ | Tanzania: The Bradt Travel Guide | £10.95 | . . . . . |
| ☐ | Uganda: The Bradt Travel Guide | £9.95 | . . . . . |
| ☐ | Zambia: The Bradt Travel Guide | £10.95 | . . . . . |

Sub-total      . . . . .
Post & packing outside UK
(£2 per book Europe; £3 per book rest of world)      . . . . .
TOTAL      . . . . .

Name . . . . . . . . . . . . . . . . . . . . . . . . . . . . . . . . . . . . . . . . . . . . . . . . . . . . . . . .

Address . . . . . . . . . . . . . . . . . . . . . . . . . . . . . . . . . . . . . . . . . . . . . . . . . . . . . .

Telephone . . . . . . . . . . . . . . . . . .      Email address . . . . . . . . . . . . . . . .

☐    I enclose a cheque for £. . . . . . made payable to Bradt Travel Guides
☐    I would like to pay by VISA or Mastercard
       Number . . . . . . . . . . . . . . . . . . . . . . . . . . .    Expiry date . . . . . . . . .
☐    Please add my name to your catalogue mailing list.

*Send your order on this form to:*
**Bradt Travel Guides/ABR**
19 High Street, Chalfont St Peter, Bucks SL9 9QE
tel: 01753 893444; fax: 01753 892333
email: info@bradt-travelguides.com
web: www.bradt-travelguides.com